Weight Watchers
PROGRAMME COOKBOOK

Weight Watchers* PROGRAMME COOKBOOK

By Jean Nidetch

NEW ENGLISH LIBRARY
TIMES MIRROR

Acknowledgements

The author wishes to thank all of the members and staff of Weight Watchers U.K. who contributed many of the creative recipes. A special thanks to Felice Lippert, Vice President—Food Research, and her staff at Weight Watchers International's headquarters for their guidance.

For more information about this cookbook, its recipes and the Weight Watchers Classroom Programme contact:
Weight Watchers U.K.
635/637 Ajax Avenue
Slough
Berkshire

Printed and bound in Great Britain by
Redwood Burn Limited
Trowbridge & Esher

ISBN: 0–450–04831–4

CONTENTS

 *

FOREWORD

*

Imagine eating delicious meals and snacks without paying for them in pounds.

These weight-conscious days, there is an increasing interest in losing weight—or maintaining it—while, at the same time, enjoying satisfying and nutritious foods. The Weight Watchers Organisation understands this and understands, also, that one of the most important ingredients in a successful eating plan is *variety*.

In 1977, the Weight Watchers Food Plan, which had already been so successful, was made even more rewarding. It became more flexible and easier to follow, with portion *ranges* and the interchanging of meals permitted. And with more 'do's' and fewer 'don'ts', a lot of the guilt has gone! As for variety . . . ! Imagine eating juicy cheeseburgers, cocoa milk shakes, smoked salmon and bagels, hot dogs on a roll, scones, yogurt and so many other favourites—in proper quantities, of course—while enjoying the 'dessert' of weight loss! It is a Food Plan that allows 'legal' to fit into any lifestyle. ('Legal' means foods that are acceptable for use on the Weight Watchers Food Plan.)

Of course, the aim is not only to reach goal weight but to *stay* there! So our Programme also includes a revised Maintenance Plan, which brings back forbidden foods within expert, easy-to-follow, portion-controlled guidelines.

You will find both the weight reduction Food Plan and the Maintenance Plan—for men, women and teenagers—in this book. It is a Programme that combines food expertise with the on-the-spot knowledge gained from our millions of hours of worldwide classroom experience.

'Millions of hours . . .' That is an awe-inspiring statistic, isn't it? I would like to share with you what it reflects, for those 'millions' began with one.

1

Yes, we began with one Weight Watchers class, in 1963. It met each week in a small loft in Little Neck, New York. By unbelievable contrast, *hundreds of thousands* of men, women, and teenagers now attend weekly classes, not just in a corner of one city but in thousands of cities—and villages—in all fifty of the States and throughout most of western Europe, as well as Canada, Mexico, Brazil, the Caribbean, South Africa, Israel, Japan, Australia, New Zealand and Hong Kong. And the list is constantly growing. Truly, the 'sun never sets' on Weight Watchers classes!

Perhaps the major reason we have grown into the largest and—I am proud to say—most respected weight control organisation in the world is that we are not content to stand still. Under the leadership of our dedicated Chairman of the Board and Chief Executive Officer, Albert Lippert, we have unceasingly searched for ever-better ways to help overweight individuals.

This means helping people not only to lose weight but also to learn to eat properly. A professional Food Research Department, headed by Felice Lippert, includes a medical director and a staff of nutritionists who supervise the Food Plan, making certain it is well-balanced and geared to optimum nutrition. It was this department that researched and created the new Programme.

Our concern, however, extends beyond teaching people what to eat, to include *how*—and *why*—we turn to food. One of our most exciting developments has been a behaviour modification programme, aimed at helping Weight Watchers members learn to cope with problem times in non-food ways, and to suppress self-destructive eating habits. For only by developing new eating patterns can weight loss be *maintained*.

Our world-wide classes provide invaluable empathy and support, and they are staffed with lecturers who have travelled that same route from FAT to SLIM. To me, these classes are the roots of our organisation, but our *branches* now reach in a multitude of other directions as well. Walk into almost any supermarket and you will find us, for we have Weight Watchers pre-portioned frozen lunches and dinners, as well as a wide range of foods and beverages.

We also have Weight Watchers camps in the U.S.A., together with magazines and books which are published throughout the world.

To produce this book, the talented chefs and home economists who also staff our Food Research Department busied themselves in our test kitchen for many months. The result? They have 'celebrated' the revised Programme by creating some of the newest, most delectable dishes we have ever tasted! You will find the recipes in this book.

We have also selected our members' favourite recipes and gathered them together in one appetising chapter. As an additional guide, we have included sample menus.

What this all adds up to is a book for every weight-conscious person who wants to enjoy tasty, tempting meals and, at the same time, learn about portion control. So whether or not you are on our Programme, the *Weight Watchers Programme Cookbook* provides you and your family with a nutritious pattern for streamlined eating.

I am confident you will enjoy the delicious results.

FOUNDER
WEIGHT WATCHERS INTERNATIONAL

WEIGHT WATCHERS
FOOD PROGRAMME,
INCLUDING MENU PLANS

This chapter has been designed to help you understand the Food Plan. Please read it carefully before you proceed.

Remember to eat only the foods listed on your Menu Plan—in the quantities and weights specified. Never, never skip a meal. As you will learn from these pages, there is a wide range of approved foods. They may be combined in various ways, as described in our recipes, but remember to count all ingredients. Keeping a daily food diary, as outlined on page 14, will help you do this.

The word 'serving' appears throughout the Food Plan. A serving may be defined as *a portion of food which equates to the amount of food allowed on Programme.*

1. FRUITS
A list of fruits and serving sizes is given on page 20. You may use fresh, canned or frozen fruit, with no sugar added. This is true of approved fruit juices as well. Fruits rich in Vitamin C are marked with an asterisk, and one of these fruits must be taken daily.

2. EGGS AND CHEESE
Select 4 standard (size 4/5) eggs a week, cooked in the shell, poached, scrambled without fat, made into omelettes or soufflés or used in other ways in other dishes. See page 36 for further details.

CHEESE: Cottage cheese (curd type preferred) and skim milk ricotta cheese are approved soft cheeses. Use in the amounts indicated on your Menu Plan.

SEMISOFT AND HARD CHEESES are limited to 4 oz weekly. Examples of semisoft cheeses are Brie, Camembert, Danish Blue. Examples of hard cheeses are Caerphilly, Cheddar, Cheshire, Edam, Gruyere, Leicester.

3. BREAD, CEREAL, CHOICE GROUP

Use whole grain bread, rolls or baps. Use packaged, presliced bread or packaged rolls; approximately 1 oz per serving. See page 76 for further details.

CEREAL may be selected up to 3 times weekly, if desired. When cereal is taken, bread may be taken at the Morning Meal or another meal. You may have 1 oz of ready-to-eat (not presweetened) or uncooked cereal, with at least ½ serving of milk. See page 92 for further details.

You may substitute a Choice Group item up to 3 times a week by omitting 1 serving of bread each time you make this selection. See page 95 for additional information.

4. MILK

Select servings from this group daily, at any time, in the amount allowed on your Menu Plan.

A serving of SKIM MILK is 10 fl oz. The skim milk may be made from nonfat dry milk, or it may be commercially prepared liquid skim milk.

A serving of BUTTERMILK is 10 fl oz.

A serving of NATURAL UNSWEETENED YOGURT is 5 fl oz.

5. POULTRY, MEAT, FISH AND DRIED PEAS/BEANS

Your Menu Plan gives net cooked weight (fat, skin and bones trimmed away from fish, meat and poultry; cooking liquid drained from dried peas/beans). See individual sections for further explanations. A ½ serving of poultry, meat or fish may be combined with cheese, egg or dried peas/beans.

POULTRY, VEAL, GAME: Select chicken, turkey or other poultry (not duck or goose), veal or wild game. Serve poultry with skin removed.

'BEEF' GROUP: This includes beef, ham, lamb, pork and tongue. Select up to 3 times a week, if desired. Use lean meats and remove all visible fat before eating. Once a week, if desired, in place of 1 'Beef' Group selection, you may use bologna, frankfurters, knackwurst, beef sausages or offal (such as hearts, kidneys and sweetbreads).

LIVER: Select once a week, in the amounts specified on your Menu Plan. All liver is legal. See section beginning on page 180 for details.

FISH: Select any fish in the marketplace at least 3 to 5 times weekly. Vary selections. Use fresh, frozen, canned or smoked fish. All canned fish must be well drained. It is strongly recommended that 5 fish meals be eaten weekly. However, if fish is selected 3 or 4 times per week, chicken must be substituted for the 1 or 2 omitted fish meals. See page 193 for more details.

DRIED PEAS/BEANS: They are available canned or packaged. Select up to 3 times weekly, if desired. For further details, see page 221.

6. VEGETABLES

Select reasonable amounts of all but the 'limited vegetables'. You must select at least 2 servings daily. Vegetables must be eaten at both the midday and evening Meals. They may also be eaten at any other time. Vary your selections, using both raw and cooked vegetables throughout the week. Each serving is 3 oz. See page 238 for more details.

LIMITED VEGETABLES: These are optional and must be weighed. Do not exceed a combined total of 4 oz, drained weight, daily, of the vegetables listed on pages 238–9.

7. FATS

Select 3 servings daily, at mealtime only, of the fats listed on page 276. The fat may be used in a spread, salad dressing or sauce, or it may be used in cooking, if you follow the methods on page 276.

8. OPTIONAL

Many juices, beverages, condiments, seasonings and other foods are permitted on the Weight Watchers Food Plan. They are not required. Use them only if you wish, but do not exceed the prescribed amounts. The section beginning on page 293 has full details.

Menu Plan for Women

Morning Meal:
Fruit, 1 serving
Choice of:
    Egg, 1
        or
    Cheese, soft 2½ oz
        or
    Cheese, semisoft
        or hard, 1 oz
        or
    Cereal, 1 oz with
        ½ serving Milk
        or
    Fish, cooked, 2 oz
        or
    Poultry or Meat,
        cooked, 1 oz
Bread, 1 serving
Beverage, if desired

Midday Meal:
Choice of:
    Poultry, Meat or Fish
        cooked, 3 to 4 oz
        or
    Eggs, 2
        or
    Cheese, soft, 5 oz

        or
    Cheese, semisoft or
        hard, 2 oz
        or
    Dried   Peas/Beans,   6 oz,
        cooked
Vegetables
Bread, 1 serving, if desired
Beverage, if desired

Evening Meal:
Choice of:
    Poultry, Meat or Fish,
        cooked, 4 to 6 oz
        or
    Dried   Peas/Beans,   8 oz,
        cooked
Vegetables
Bread, 1 serving (if not eaten
    at Midday Meal)
Beverage, if desired

Daily:
Milk, 2 servings at any time
Fats, 3 servings, at mealtime
Fruits, 3 servings (1 at
    Morning Meal, 2 at any
    time)

Note: The Midday Meal may be interchanged with the Evening Meal.

Menu Plan for Men

Morning Meal
Fruit, 1 serving
Choice of:
  Egg, 1
  or
  Cheese, soft, 2½ oz
  or
  Cheese, semisoft or
    hard, 1 oz
  or
  Cereal, 1 oz with ½
    serving Milk
  or
  Fish, cooked, 2 oz
  or
  Poultry or Meat,
    cooked, 1 oz
Bread, 1 serving
Beverage, if desired

Midday Meal
Choice of:
  Poultry, Meat or Fish,
    cooked, 3 to 4 oz
  or
  Eggs, 2
  or

Cheese, soft 5 oz
  or
Cheese, semisoft or
  hard, 2 oz
  or
Dried Peas/Beans, 6 oz,
  cooked
Vegetables
Bread, 2 servings
Beverage, if desired

Evening Meal:
Choice of:
  Poultry, Meat or Fish,
    cooked, 6 to 8 oz
Dried Peas/Beans, 12 oz,
  cooked
Vegetables
Bread, 1 serving
Beverage, if desired

Daily:
  Milk, 2 servings at any time
  Fats, 3 servings at mealtime
  Fruits, 3 to 5 servings (1 at
    Morning Meal, 2 to 4 at any
    time)

Note: The Midday Meal may be interchanged with the Evening Meal.

Menu Plan for Teenagers

Morning Meal:
Fruit, 1 serving
Choice of:
Egg, 1
or
Cheese, soft, 2½ oz
or
Cheese, semisoft or
hard, 1 oz
or
Cereal, 1 oz with ½
serving Milk
or
Fish, cooked, 2 oz
or
Poultry or Meat,
cooked, 1 oz
Bread, 1 serving
Beverage, if desired

Midday Meal:
Choice of:
Poultry, Meat or Fish,
cooked, 3 to 4 oz
or
Eggs, 2
or
Cheese, soft, 5 oz

or
Cheese, semisoft or
hard, 2 oz
or
Dried   Peas/Beans,   6 oz,
cooked
Vegetables
Bread, 2 servings
Beverage, if desired

Evening Meal:
Choice of:
Poultry, Meat or Fish,
cooked, 4 to 6 oz
or
Dried   Peas/Beans,   8 oz,
cooked
Vegetables
Bread, 1 serving
Beverage, if desired

Daily:
Milk, 3 to 4 servings at any
time
Fats, 3 servings, at mealtime
Fruits, 3 to 5 servings (1 at
Morning Meal, 2 to 4 at any
time)

Note: The Midday Meal may be interchanged with the Evening Meal.

Menu Suggestions for One Week

Follow your Menu Plan as to amount permitted; complete Programme requirements where necessary (see page 13).

Morning Meal

Monday Vegetable juice, ½ serving; Blackberry Muffins (see page 84), beverage

Tuesday Orange, 1 serving; Cooked Cereal with Fruit (see page 92); beverage

Wednesday Ginger Figs (see page 26); Not-So-Danish Pastry (see page 301); beverage

Thursday Grapefruit juice, 1 serving; Currant French Toast (see page 47); beverage

Friday Fruit 'Cream' (see page 26); 1 oz Cheddar Cheese on 1 serving rye bread; beverage

Saturday Prune Bread Custard (see page 85); beverage

Sunday Honeydew, 1 serving; 1 oz ready-to-eat cereal with ½ serving skim milk; currant bread, 1 serving; beverage

Midday Meal

Monday California Orange Chicken Salad (see page 137); Carrot and Pineapple Mould (see page 248); Brandylike Alexander (see page 181)

Tuesday Instant 'Pizza' (see page 83); Tossed Salad with Lemony Mayonnaise (see page 281); strawberries, ¾ serving; Hot Chocolate (see page 118)

Wednesday Split Pea Soup (see page 235); Oriental Vegetable Mix (see page 271); canteloupe, 1 serving; beverage

Thursday Seafood Salad (see page 214); granary bread, 1 serving; Apple-Strawberry Whisk (see page 121); Cappuccino Chiller (see page 118).

Friday	Sweet-and-Sour Tongue with Water Chestnuts (see page 179); Sliced Tomatoes with Rémoulade Sauce (see page 282); rye bread, ½ serving; Pineapple Water Ice (see page 33); beverage
Saturday	Courgette Soup (see page 126): Cornish Crab Cakes (see page 206); Hearts of Lettuce with Pimiento Dressing (see page 313); Mint Sorbet (see page 319); beverage
Sunday	Cheese Soufflé (see page 65); Cooked Mushrooms (see page 257); Baked Apple (see page 23); Lemonade (see page 322)

Evening Meal

Monday	Grapefruit, 1 serving: Lemon-Grilled Trout (see page 204); Baked Aubergine Casserole (see page 251); Whole Kernel Corn, 3 oz; beverage
Tuesday	Sauerbraten (see page 160); Sauerkraut with Prunes (see page 266); green beans, 1 serving; Coffee 'Brandy' (see page 318)
Wednesday	Veal-Stuffed Cannelloni (see page 151); Green Salad with Basic French or Vinaigrette Dressing (see page 283); Cinnamon Peach Dessert (see page 122); beverage
Thursday	Clear Tomato Bouillon (see page 299); Chicken Livers in Orange Sauce (see page 189); cauliflower, 1 serving; Tossed Salad with Tangy French Dressing (see page 314); Hot Mint Tea (see page 319)
Friday	Spiked Tomato juice on the rocks, 1 serving: Baked Fish Creole (see page 200); Currants, 1 serving with Easy Whipped Topping (see page 317); Chocolate Milk Shake (see page 119)
Saturday	Tomato juice, 1 serving; Quick-and-Easy Lamb Dinner (see page 170); Minty Hot Cucumber (see page 251); Cooked Celery (see page 249); orange and grapefruit sections, 1 serving; beverage
Sunday	Steamed Fish Chinese Style (see page 205); cooked rice, 3 oz; Mexican Cauliflower and Pepper Salad (see page 270); Rhubarb-Strawberry Dessert (see page 34); beverage

Additional Programme Requirements to Complete Menu Plan on Pages 11– 12*

Monday
Add: ¼ serving Fat
        ½ serving Milk (5 fl oz skim milk)

Tuesday
Add: ½ serving Milk (5 fl oz skim milk)

Wednesday
Add: 1 serving Milk (10 fl oz skim milk)

Thursday
Add: $^7/_{10}$ serving Milk (7 fl oz skim milk)

Friday
Add: ¼ serving Milk (2½ fl oz skim milk)

Saturday
Add: ½ serving Milk (5 fl oz skim milk)

Sunday
Add: 1 serving Milk (10 fl oz skim milk)

> *Note: *Men and Teenagers*—Add additional foods—bread, fruit, milk and additional amount of meat, fish, poultry and dried peas/beans as allowed on the Programme daily (see pages 9–10)

GENERAL INFORMATION

1. Wherever specific amounts are given, they relate to the Women's Menu Plan. Adapt for Men and Teenagers.
2. The herbs used in these recipes are dried unless otherwise indicated.
3. When combining two recipes (e.g. pie crust and pie filling), be sure to include *both* equivalencies in your day's food allotment.
4. Nonstick pans make it possible for you to cook without fat. Use pans manufactured with a nonstick surface.
5. Recipe directions may sometimes look as if they're taking the long way around, but remember, they're all shortcuts to your goal weight! Never try to 'get away with' using one pan when we call for two. Always take the trouble to measure and weigh—don't think you can judge portions by eye.

WEIGHT WATCHERS STRONGLY ADVISE YOU TO CONSULT YOUR DOCTOR WHILE PARTICIPATING IN THE PROGRAMME.

Daily Food Record

To help you keep track of your daily and weekly use of foods, rule a notebook page into eight columns. List the following headings across the page:

Food   Mon.   Tues.   Wed.   Thurs.   Fri.   Sat.   Sun.

14

List the following headings down the page, in the Food column:

Fruit*
Fruit
Eggs
Soft Cheese
Hard Cheese
Bread
Bread (once-a-week selection)
Cereal
Choice Group
Milk
Poultry, Veal and Game
'Beef' Group

'Beef' Group (once-a-week
   selection)
Liver
Fish
Dried Peas/Beans
Vegetables
Limited Vegetables
Fats
Bonus
Something Extra
Speciality Foods (15 calories)

Oven Heats

If your oven does not have a thermostat or regulator, the following chart will give you an idea of the equivalent amount of heat required for each temperature range.

225°F	Gas Mark ¼	Very cool oven
250°F	Gas Mark ½	Very cool oven
275°F	Gas Mark 1	Cool oven
300°F	Gas Mark 2	Cool oven
325°F	Gas Mark 3	Moderate oven
350°F	Gas Mark 4	Moderate oven
375°F	Gas Mark 5	Moderately hot oven
400°F	Gas Mark 6	Moderately hot oven
425°F	Gas Mark 7	Hot oven
450°F	Gas Mark 8	Hot oven
475°F	Gas Mark 9	Very hot oven

Oven thermostats should be checked at least once a year. If your oven does not have a thermostat, an oven thermometer can be purchased and placed in the oven to help determine the degree of heat.

* Rich in Vitamin C.

Since foods bake faster in heat-resistant glass than in shiny metal pans, lowering the temperature 25°F is generally recommended when baking in glass.

Your Microwave Oven

Many of our recipes can be done in your microwave oven. You will have to experiment with your unit and follow manufacturer's advice for timing, since there is no one standard that applies to all, but generally, you should allow about ¼ of the cooking time. That is, if our recipe suggests 16 minutes, allow 4 minutes in your microwave oven (or slightly less, since it's wiser to undercook than overcook). Please also note that our roasting procedures for beef, ham, lamb and pork require the use of a rack, so that during cooking the fat drains off into the pan. A plastic griddle is available for use in a microwave oven.

Our kitchens tested a number of basic foods and have the following timing tips for you:

Baked Apple (1 medium): Put in ovenproof glass dish, cook 3 minutes; let stand for several minutes. Makes 1 serving.
Each serving is equivalent to: 1 serving Fruit

Baked Fish Fillets (1 lb): Cook for 7 minutes; let stand for several minutes. Divide evenly. Makes 2 evening meal servings.
Each serving is equivalent to: 6 oz Fish

Baked Potato (1 × 3 oz): Make crosswise cut, cook for 4 minutes; let stand for 2 to 3 minutes. Makes 1 serving. Serve at mealtime only.
Each serving is equivalent to: 1 serving Choice Group

Roast Beef (1 lb boneless): On plastic griddle set in baking dish, cook for 4 minutes; turn, cook for 4 minutes more; let stand for 10 to 15 minutes. Divide evenly. Makes 2 evening meal servings.
Each serving is equivalent to: 6 oz 'Beef' Group

Hamburger Patty (6 oz, 4" diameter): Coat with browning sauce. Place on plastic griddle, set in baking dish. Cover with greaseproof paper. Cook for 2 minutes; turn patty, cook for 1 minute. Makes 1 midday meal serving.
Each serving is equivalent to: 4 oz 'Beef' Group

Roast Chicken (4 to 4½ lbs): Place breast-side down on plastic griddle set in baking dish. Cook for 7 minutes; turn breast side up cook for 7 minutes turn dish, cook for another 7 minutes. Let stand for 10 to 15 minutes. Remove skin. Weigh portions. Makes about 6 evening meal servings.
Each serving is equivalent to: 6 oz Poultry

Roast Pork (1 lb boned and rolled): Place on plastic griddle set in baking dish, cook for 6 minutes. Turn roast, cook for 6 minutes more. Turn roast, cook for 4 minutes. Let stand for 10 to 15 minutes. Divide evenly. Makes 2 evening meal servings.
Each serving is equivalent to: 6 oz 'Beef' Group

Slow Cookers

If you enjoy using this appliance, there's no reason why you can't adapt many of our recipes. We're giving you a head start on your own experiments with the following guidelines from our kitchen. (See index for the recipes.)

Portuguese-Style Bean Soup: Combine all ingredients except salt and pepper in slow cooker; cook, covered, on low for 6 to 8 hours. Season.

Poached Liver: Combine all ingredients in slow cooker. Add water to cover. Cook, covered, on low for 6 to 8 hours.

'Old-Fashioned' Pot Roast: Combine beef and remaining ingredients in slow cooker; cook, covered, on high for 6 to 9 hours.

Chicken Stock: Combine all ingredients in slow cooker; cover and cook on low for 12 hours. Strain.

Chicken Italian Style: After browning the chicken in nonstick pan, combine in slow cooker with remaining ingredients. Cook, covered, on low for 6 to 8 hours.

Minestrone (Vegetable Soup Italian Style): Combine all ingredients except macaroni in slow cooker; cook, covered, on low for 6 to 8 hours. Add macaroni; cook for 15 to 20 minutes longer.

Artificial Sweeteners

The use of artificial sweeteners on the Weight Watchers Food Programme has always been optional. Natural sweetness is available in the form of fruits, which we do permit on our eating plan. Your use of artificial sweeteners is completely optional; and we believe that the decision about using them should be made by you. If you decide against these products, you will find many recipes in this book which are artificial sweetener-free.

FRUITS

*

Apples, peaches, plums, berries, and dozens of other fruits are listed in the first category in the Programme. You may enjoy them fresh, canned, or in prepared desserts, such as Apple Crumble, Apricot Almond Mousse, Banana Pudding, Pineapple Sherbet, and Orange Gelatine Cream. However you use your allotted fruits, they are a satisfying and nutritious component of our Food Programme.

Rules For Using Fruits

1. Amounts:
   Women: 3 servings daily
   Men: 3 to 5 servings daily
   Teenagers: 3 to 5 servings daily
2. One serving must be taken at the morning meal.
3. Use fresh, frozen or canned fruit or fruit juices, with no sugar added.
4. Fruits must be measured frozen, not thawed.
5. Each day, select at least one fruit marked with an asterisk(*).
6. Fruits marked with an asterisk (*) are rich sources of Vitamin C. If these fruits are heated, the Vitamin C is affected. Therefore, an additional fruit marked with an asterisk (*) must be consumed that day.
7. Dried prunes are the only dried fruits permitted.

Fruit Servings

Juices

*grapefruit, 4 fl oz
*orange, 4 fl oz
*orange and grapefruit, 4 fl oz
 prune, 2½ fl oz
*tomato or mixed vegetable juice, 8 fl oz

Fruits

 apple, 1 medium;
  canned, 4 oz
 apricots, fresh, 2 medium;
  canned, 4 halves with 2 tablespoons juice
 banana, ½ medium
 berries
  blackberries, 5 oz
  blueberries, 5 oz
  boysenberries, 5 oz
  cranberries, 5 oz
  gooseberries, 5 oz
  loganberries, 5 oz
  raspberries, 5 oz
* strawberries, 5 oz
*cantaloupe, ½ medium or 5 oz cup chunks or balls
 cherries, fresh, 10 large or 15 small; canned, 4 oz
*currants, 3 oz black, red or white
 damsons, 3 medium or 4 small
 figs, fresh, 2 small
 fruit cocktail or salad, 4 oz
*grapefruit, ½ medium
*grapefruit sections, 4 oz
 grapes, 12 medium or 20 small
*honeydew or similar melon, 2-inch wedge or
  5 oz chunks or balls

*kiwi fruit, (Chinese gooseberry) 1 medium
mandarin orange, 1 large or 2 small
mandarin orange sections, canned 4 oz
mango, ½ small
nectarine, 1 medium
*orange, 1 medium
*orange sections, 4 oz
*papaya, ½ medium
peach, fresh, 1 medium; canned, 2 halves with 2 tablespoons juice,
  or 4 oz sliced
pear, fresh, 1 small;
  canned, 2 halves with 2 tablespoons juice
persimmon, 1 medium
pineapple, fresh, ¼ medium;
  canned, chunks, crushed, tidbits,
  4 oz, or sliced, 2 slices with 2 tablespoons juice
plums, fresh, 2 medium;
  canned, whole, 2 with 2 tablespoons juice
prunes, dried, 4 medium or 3 large
rhubarb, 9 oz
tangerine, 1 large or 2 small
*ugli fruit, 1 medium
watermelon, 5 oz cubed, or triangle 3 inches × 1½ inches

Apple and Pear Pie

3 medium Golden Delicious apples,
  peeled, cored and sliced
3 small pears, peeled, cored and
  sliced
½ teaspoon cinnamon

1 tablespoon cornflour, dissolved in
  1 tablespoon water
2 tablespoons margarine, melted
  (optional)
9-inch Pie Crust (see page 81)

In medium saucepan combine fruit, cinnamon and enough water to
cover. Cook over medium heat for 7 minutes. Add cornflour, stirring constantly. Cook until thickened. Remove from heat. Stir in
margarine if desired. Pour fruit mixture into crust. Bake at 350°F,
Gas Mark 4, for 40 minutes or until fruit is tender. Serve warm or
chilled. Divide evenly. Makes 6 servings. Serve at mealtime only.

Each serving is equivalent to: 1 serving Fruit; ½ serving Something Extra (½ teaspoon cornflour); 1 serving Fat (optional); 9-inch Pie Crust (see page 81)

Apple Crumble

4 medium Golden Delicious apples,
  peeled, cored and sliced
4 fl oz water
1 tablespoon cornflour

½ teaspoon cinnamon
2 slices currant bread, made into
  crumbs
1 tablespoon margarine

Layer apples in 8 × 8 × 2-inch nonstick baking tin. Combine water, cornflour and cinnamon in measuring jug; stir to dissolve cornflour; pour over apples. In bowl combine breadcrumbs and margarine, mixing with hands until particles are the size of peas. Sprinkle over apples. Bake at 350°F, Gas Mark 4, for 40 to 45 minutes. Divide evenly. Serve warm or cool. Makes 4 servings. Serve at mealtime only.

Each serving is equivalent to: 1 serving Fruit; ¾ serving Something Extra (¾ teaspoon cornflour); ½ serving Bread; ¾ serving Fat

Apple Sauce

6 medium Golden Delicious apples,
  peeled, cored and sliced
3 fl oz water

small piece lemon rind
cinnamon and nutmeg to taste
  (optional)

Combine apples, water and lemon rind in saucepan. Cover; simmer for 10 minutes, or until apples are very soft. Stir in spices, if desired, and serve as is; or put through food mill. The puréed sauce may be cooked in saucepan until thickened, if desired. Serve hot or cold. Divide evenly. Makes 6 servings.

Each serving is equivalent to: 1 serving Fruit

Note: Golden Delicious apples are naturally sweet enough to be cooked without artificial sweeteners. If other varieties are used, you may wish to add artificial sweetener to taste.

Baked Apples

Bake apples at the same time you are cooking an oven meal.

4 medium Golden Delicious apples,
  cored
4 fl oz water

1 teaspoon lemon juice
½ teaspoon vanilla flavouring
½ teaspoon cinnamon

Peel apples halfway down. Place in shallow casserole. Add water, lemon juice and vanilla. Sprinkle apple with cinnamon. Cover; bake at 400°F, Gas Mark 6, for 20 minutes or until apples are tender. Divide evenly. Makes 4 servings.

Each serving is equivalent to: 1 serving Fruit

Apricot Almond Mousse

With fast-setting recipes like this one, it's a good procedure to set out all the measured ingredients beforehand.

8 canned apricot halves with 4
  tablespoons juice, no sugar
  added
1 tablespoon unflavoured gelatine
2 fl oz boiling water
2 oz nonfat dry milk

artificial sweetener to equal 1
  teaspoon sugar, or to taste
  (optional)
1 teaspoon lemon juice
¼ teaspoon almond flavouring
3 to 4 ice cubes

Pour apricot juice into blender container. Sprinkle gelatine over juice and let stand a few minutes to soften. Add boiling water and blend until gelatine is dissolved. Add 6 apricot halves, milk, sweetener if desired, lemon juice and flavouring. Blend until combined. Add ice cubes, one at a time, blending after each addition, until smooth. Pour mousse immediately into 2 large dessert dishes, dividing evenly. Garnish each serving with 1 apricot half, diced or sliced. Makes 2 servings.

Each serving is equivalent to: 1 serving Fruit; 1 serving Something Extra (1½ teaspoon gelatine); 1 serving Milk (10 fl oz skim milk)

Note: The season for apricots is short—from late May to early August—so eat them fresh while you can, or buy them frozen or canned, no sugar added.

Apricot Tarts

12 canned apricot halves with 6
    tablespoons juice, no sugar
    added
3 tablespoons frozen orange juice
    concentrate

1 tablespoon lemon juice
2 teaspoons cornflour, dissolved in
    2 teaspoons water
6 Toast Cups II (see page 81)

In medium saucepan combine first 4 ingredients. Cook, stirring often until thickened. Divide evenly into 6 toast cups. Chill until firm. Makes 3 servings, 2 tarts each. Serve at mealtime only.

Each serving is equivalent to: 1½ servings Fruit; ²/₃ serving Something Extra (²/₃ teaspoon cornflour); Toast Cups II (see page 81)

Banana Mousse

1 tablespoon unflavoured gelatine
2 fl oz cold water
4 fl oz boiling water
1 ripe medium banana, diced
2 oz nonfat dry milk
artificial sweetener to equal 1

teaspoon sugar, or to taste
    (optional)
1 teaspoon lemon juice
6 to 7 drops yellow food colouring
4 to 6 ice cubes

In blender container sprinkle gelatine over cold water to soften; add boiling water. Blend to dissolve. Add ¾ of diced banana, milk, sweetener if desired, lemon juice and food colouring. Blend until smooth. Add ice cubes, one at a time, blending after each addition. Pour into bowl. Fold in remaining banana. Divide mousse evenly into 2 dessert glasses. Makes 2 servings.

Each serving is equivalent to: 1 serving Something Extra (1½ teaspoons gelatine); 1 serving Fruit; 1 serving Milk (10 fl oz skim milk)

Banana Pudding

4 standard eggs, separated
4 ripe medium bananas
5 fl oz skim milk

3 teaspoons vanilla flavouring
¼ teaspoon cream of tartar
pinch salt

Preheat oven to 350°F, Gas Mark 4. In medium bowl beat egg yolks until lemon-coloured. Slice and add 3 bananas, milk and 2 teaspoons vanilla. Pour into 8-inch round baking tin or pie dish. In large bowl, combine egg whites, cream of tartar and salt, beat until stiff but not dry. Mash remaining banana. Fold banana and 1 teaspoon vanilla into beaten whites. Pile on top of banana-yolk mixture. Bake for 30 minutes or until pudding is set and meringue is golden brown. Divide evenly. Makes 4 morning or midday meal servings. Supplement as required.

Each serving is equivalent to: 1 Egg; 2 servings Fruit; ⅛ serving Milk (1¼ fl oz skim milk)

Old-Fashioned Blackberry Dessert

20 oz blackberries or blueberries
1 tablespoon cornflour
pinch salt
2 fl oz water
artificial sweetener to equal 3
   teaspoons sugar, or to taste
pinch ground cloves

2 tablespoons plus 2 teaspoons
   margarine
8 slices currant bread
2 recipes Best Whipped Topping (8
   servings, see page 317), or
10 fl oz natural unsweetened
   yogurt

In medium saucepan, toss berries with the cornflour and salt. Add water and sweetener; simmer, stirring constantly, until berries are cooked but still whole, about 5 minutes. Add cloves. Remove from heat, cool slightly. Spread 1 teaspoon of margarine on each slice of bread. Arrange 4 slices, margarine side up, in 10 × 8 × 2-inch serving dish. Spread half the berry mixture over bread. Top with remaining 4 slices of bread, margarine side up. Spread with remaining berry mixture. Cover and refrigerate several hours or overnight. Serve with Whipped Topping or yogurt. Divide evenly. Makes 8 servings. Serve at mealtime only.

Each serving is equivalent to: ½ serving Fruit; ³/₈ serving Something Extra (³/₈ teaspoon cornflour); 1 serving Fat; 1 serving Bread; Best Whipped Topping (see page 317) or ¼ serving Milk (1¼ fl oz yogurt)

Fruit 'Cream'

Good way to serve blackberries, loganberries, or raspberries.
For each serving put 5 oz ripe, fresh berries in stemmed dessert glass. Spoon 2½ fl oz natural unsweetened yogurt over the fruit. Makes 1 serving.
Each serving is equivalent to: 1 serving Fruit; ½ serving Milk (2½ fl oz yogurt)

Cherry Torte

7½ fl oz prune juice
2 tablespoons cornflour, dissolved
  in 2 tablespoons water
½ teaspoon almond flavouring

¼ teaspoon grated lemon rind
pinch salt
60 large fresh cherries
9-inch Pie Crust (see page 81)

In medium saucepan combine first 5 ingredients. Cook over medium heat, stirring, until thickened. Add cherries. Pour into pie crust. Bake at 400°F, Gas Mark 6, for 15 minutes. Cool and serve. Divide evenly. Makes 6 servings. Serve at mealtime only.
Each serving is equivalent to: 1½ servings Fruit; 1 serving Something Extra (1 teaspoon cornflour); 9-inch Pie Crust (see page 81)

Ginger Figs

4 small fresh figs
4 fl oz water

1 teaspoon lemon juice
1 slice fresh ginger root

Combine all ingredients in saucepan; cover. Cook over low heat for 15 minutes or until figs are tender. Remove ginger and discard. Serve with juice, warm or chilled. Divide evenly. Makes 2 servings.
Each serving is equivalent to: 1 serving Fruit

Kiwi Fruit

This fruit with the light brown skin is the size of a hen's egg, comes from New Zealand and has bright green flesh that tastes something like watermelon with a hint of strawberry. It is soft when ripe. Cut it in half, sprinkle with lemon juice and eat it out of the shell with a teaspoon. Or peel, slice thin and serve it with cheese and natural unsweetened yogurt at your morning or midday meal. One medium kiwi fruit is equivalent to 1 serving Fruit.

Lemon Tricks

1. You get more juice from a lemon if it's at room temperature. Roll it on the bench before squeezing.
2. For a small amount of juice, poke a hole in the lemon with a toothpick. Remove the toothpick and squeeze out juice. Replace the toothpick in the hole; refrigerate the lemon for future use.
3. Freeze lemon shells to use as decorative containers for salad dressing, parsley sprigs, or other foods.
4. *Basket*—Freeze a serving of ripe cherries or seedless green grapes. Serve frozen in lemon or orange shells.

Orange Jelly Cream

Two tablespoons unflavoured
   gelatine
16 fl oz water
4 fl oz frozen orange juice
concentrate, thawed
1 teaspoon lemon juice
2 oz nonfat dry milk
pinch nutmeg (optional)

In saucepan soften gelatine in 8 fl oz water. Heat, stirring until gelatine is dissolved. Stir in orange juice concentrate and lemon juice. Chill until syrupy, but do not allow to set. Meanwhile, mix nonfat dry milk with 8 fl oz water in measuring jug. Turn gelatine mixture into large bowl and whisk, preferably with electric mixer, until light and frothy. Still whisking, gradually add milk. Continue whisking for a few minutes longer. Pour into wetted mould or divide between 4 individual moulds. Chill until set, turn out and sprinkle with nutmeg if desired. Makes 4 servings.

Each serving is equivalent to: 1 serving Something Extra (1½ teaspoons gelatine); 1 serving Fruit; ½ serving Milk (5 fl oz skim milk)

Variation: For a tart flavour, fold 10 fl oz natural unsweetened yogurt into the gelatine mixture instead of the nonfat dry milk and add 4 drops artificial sweetener (optional).

Orange Sauce

Delicious with poultry or veal.

2 fl oz cider vinegar
2 tablespoons frozen orange juice
  concentrate
1 tablespoon soy sauce
1½ teaspoons cornflour, dissolved

in 2 teaspoons water
½ teaspoon cherry flavouring
2 slices fresh ginger root
8 oz orange sections, no sugar
  added

In small saucepan combine all ingredients except orange sections. Cook, stirring often, until thickened. Remove ginger root. Add orange sections. Divide evenly. Makes 3 servings.

Each serving is equivalent to: 1 serving Fruit; ½ serving Something Extra (½ teaspoon cornflour)

Grilled Spiced Peaches

A quickie . . . delicious too. Serve with grilled chicken or liver, as garnish for ham after it is baked or as a dessert.

8 canned peach halves with 8
  tablespoons juice, no sugar
  added
1 teaspoon lemon juice
½ cinnamon stick

1 clove
2 teaspoons cornflour, dissolved in
  2 teaspoons water
2 teaspoons low-fat spread

In shallow grill pan, grill peach halves cut side up, about 4 inches from source of heat, for 5 minutes or until peaches begin to brown.

While peaches are grilling, combine peach juice, lemon juice, cinnamon stick and clove in a small saucepan. Bring to boil. Reduce heat, simmer for 2 to 3 minutes. Discard cinnamon stick and clove. Add cornflour and cook, stirring until thickened. Remove from heat, stir in low-fat spread. Divide juice mixture evenly into peach cavities; grill 1 minute longer. Makes 4 servings, 2 peach halves each. Serve at mealtime only.

Each serving is equivalent to: 1 serving Fruit; ½ serving Something Extra (½ teaspoon cornflour); ¼ serving Fat

Peach Custard

1 slice currant bread, torn into
  small pieces
1 medium peach, peeled and sliced
10 fl oz skim milk

1 standard egg
½ teaspoon vanilla flavouring
pinch cinnamon

Make a layer of bread in 1-pint baking dish. Arrange peach slices over bread. Combine remaining ingredients in blender container and blend; pour over peach slices and bread. Bake at 325°F, Gas Mark 3, for 30 minutes or until custard is set. Makes 1 morning or midday meal serving. Supplement as required.

Each serving is equivalent to: 1 serving Bread; 1 serving Fruit; 1 serving Milk (10 fl oz skim milk); 1 Egg

Compôte of Pears and Prunes

16 dried medium prunes
8 fl oz hot tea
2 ripe small pears, peeled, cored
  and quartered

1 lemon, sliced
½ teaspoon vanilla flavouring
2½ fl oz natural unsweetened
  yogurt

In medium bowl combine prunes and tea. Let stand 8 hours or overnight. Remove prunes from liquid, stone and set aside. In medium saucepan combine prune liquid, pears and lemon slices. Bring to a boil. Reduce heat. Simmer, basting pears often, until fruit is tender. Stir in vanilla, add prunes and chill. Divide prunes, pears and liquid evenly into 4 dessert dishes. Top each serving with an equal amount of yogurt. Makes 4 servings.

Each serving is equivalent to: 1½ servings Fruit; ⅛ serving Milk (⅝ fl oz yogurt)

Spiced Pear Salad

6 canned pear halves with 6
tablespoons juice, no sugar
added
2 fl oz red wine vinegar

¼ cinnamon stick
1 clove
4½ oz lettuce, shredded
3 tablespoons mayonnaise

Combine pear juice with vinegar, cinnamon stick and clove in medium saucepan. Bring to the boil; cook until mixture is reduced to about 2 fl oz. Place pear halves in medium bowl. Pour hot juice over pears and chill for several hours, turning fruit occasionally. Drain pears, strain and reserve liquid. Arrange pear halves on shredded lettuce. Combine liquid with mayonnaise and serve over pears as salad dressing. Divide evenly. Makes 6 servings. Serve at mealtime only.

Each serving is equivalent to: ½ serving Fruit; ¼ serving Vegetables; 1½ servings Fat

Preparing Pineapple

Select a ripe medium pineapple with a showy crown of leaves and prepare it in one of the following ways:
1. *Pineapple Quarters:* Cut pineapple from crown through the bottom, first in half, then in quarters. Using a small, sharp knife, cut away the hard, fibrous core, leaving the crown attached. Loosen fruit by cutting close to the rind with a sharp straight or curved serrated knife. Cut crosswise through the loosened fruit, then cut lengthwise once or twice to make bite-size pieces. Serve each quarter garnished with mint. Makes 4 servings.
2. *Sliced Fresh Pineapple:* Cut off the crown. Hold fruit upright on cutting board and, with long, sharp knife, cut away rind in strips,

working from top to bottom. With small, pointed knife, remove the 'eyes'. Cut out centre core. Cut fruit in slices about ½ inch thick. Place in bowl and cover with foil or plastic wrap. Chill for several hours or until ready to serve. Divide evenly. Makes 4 servings.

3. *Pineapple Container:* Cut off crown about 2 inches from the top and set aside. Hold the fruit upright and with a long, sharp knife remove the pineapple pulp, cutting close to the rind. Don't pierce through the rind, or it will leak. Refrigerate the rind and crown to use as container. Dice pulp and serve in pineapple rind. Divide evenly. Makes 4 servings. Pulp may also be used for Pineapple Water Ice (see page 33), fruit cup, or other desserts.

Each serving is equivalent to: 1 serving Fruit

Pickled Pineapple-Pepper Relish

Delicious with curries and colourful too.

16 oz canned crushed pineapple, no sugar added
6 oz green pepper, seeded and minced
6 oz red pepper, seeded and minced
2 oz celery, minced
2 fl oz cider vinegar
1 tablespoon unflavoured gelatine

Combine all ingredients, except gelatine, in large bowl. Marinate for 2 hours. Drain liquid into small saucepan. Sprinkle gelatine over liquid to soften. Heat, stirring to dissolve. Combine with pineapple mixture. Spoon into 2-pint mould. Chill until set. Turn out. Divide evenly. Makes 8 servings.

Each serving is equivalent to: ½ serving Fruit; ½ serving Vegetables; ¼ serving Something Extra (³/₈ teaspoon gelatine)

Pineapple-Cherry Dessert with Whipped Topping

16 oz canned crushed pineapple, no sugar added
8 oz frozen, stoned, sweet cherries, no sugar added, partially thawed
½ teaspoon cherry flavouring

½ teaspoon pineapple flavouring
artificial sweetener to equal 2 teaspoons sugar, or to taste
Whipped Topping (see following recipe)

Place 12 oz pineapple in blender container; blend until smooth. Pour into 3-pint bowl. Cut all but 6 cherries into quarters over bowl to catch juice. Combine cut cherries and remaining pineapple with puréed pineapple. Stir in flavourings and sweetener. Divide evenly into 6 dessert glasses. Top each with 1 serving of Whipped Topping and 1 cherry. Refrigerate or serve immediately. Makes 6 servings.

Whipped Topping

1 tablespoon unflavoured gelatine
2 fl oz cold water
4 fl oz boiling water
2 oz nonfat dry milk

artificial sweetener to equal 2 teaspoons sugar, or to taste
1 teaspoon vanilla flavouring
6 to 8 ice cubes

Sprinkle gelatine over cold water in blender container, to soften. Add boiling water. Blend until dissolved. Add remaining ingredients except ice cubes. Blend until smooth. Add ice cubes, one at a time, blending after each addition, until topping sets. Divide evenly. Makes 6 servings.

Each serving is equivalent to: 1 serving Fruit; ⅓ serving Something Extra (½ teaspoon gelatine); ⅓ serving Milk ($3\frac{1}{3}$ fl oz skim milk)

Pineapple Peach Sorbet

You can create dozens of different water ices and sorbets by varying the basic ingredients. Use fruit, water, fruit juice, skim milk, buttermilk, yogurt, artificial sweetener and flavourings. This one is sure to be a favourite.

1 medium peach, peeled and quartered
2 slices canned pineapple with 2 tablespoons juice, no sugar

added
5 fl oz natural unsweetened yogurt
½ teaspoon raspberry flavouring

Combine all ingredients in blender container. Blend until smooth. Place in freezer container and freeze until firm, about 20 minutes. Remove from freezer and beat with a rotary beater. Refreeze until icy. Divide evenly into 2 dessert glasses. Makes 2 servings.

Each serving is equivalent to: 1 serving Fruit; ½ serving Milk (2½ fl oz yogurt)

Variation: A very small amount of unflavoured gelatine is often added to sorbet to keep its texture smooth. In small saucepan soften ½ teaspoon of unflavoured gelatine in 2 fl oz water. Heat, stirring to dissolve. Add to ingredients in blender container and follow above recipe. Add ⅙ serving Something Extra (¼ teaspoon gelatine) to equivalent listing.

Pineapple Water Ice

This is brought to the table in a pineapple shell for an attractive presentation.

1 ripe medium pineapple
8 fl oz water
1 tablespoon lemon juice

Prepare pineapple container according to directions on page 31 and set aside. In medium saucepan combine diced pineapple, water, and lemon juice. Cook about 5 minutes. Place in blender container and blend, in 2 batches if necessary, until smooth. Place in freezer container. Freeze until firm. Remove from freezer and beat until fluffy. Spoon into pineapple shell and freeze until ready to serve. Divide evenly. Makes 4 servings.

Each serving is equivalent to: 1 serving Fruit

Oven-Stewed Prunes

To save fuel put this dish in the oven when baking a casserole or other food.

16 dried medium prunes	½ lemon, thinly sliced
8 fl oz water	small piece cinnamon stick

Place all ingredients in 1-pint ovenproof dish; cover. Bake at 350°F, Gas Mark 4, for 1 hour or until prunes are very tender. Remove cinnamon stick. Divide evenly. Makes 4 servings.

Each serving is equivalent to: 1 serving Fruit

Rhubarb-Strawberry Dessert

1 lb 2 oz rhubarb	artificial sweetener to equal 6
10 oz strawberries	teaspoons sugar, or to taste

Combine rhubarb and strawberries in 3-pint casserole. Cover and bake at 300°F, Gas Mark 2, for 1 hour or until rhubarb is tender. Remove from oven; cool. Add sweetener, mix well; chill, if desired. Divide evenly. Makes 4 servings.

Each serving is equivalent to: 1 serving Fruit

Watermelon Froth

5 oz seeded and cubed watermelon,	pineapple, no sugar added
¼ medium pineapple, peeled and	3 ice cubes (optional)
diced, or 4 oz canned crushed	2 mint sprigs

Blend fruit in blender container until puréed. If desired, add ice cubes, one at a time, blending after each addition until all ice is crushed. Divide evenly into 2 glasses. Garnish with mint sprigs. Makes 2 servings.

Each serving is equivalent to: 1 serving Fruit

Minted Summer Delight

1 medium cantaloupe melon
5 oz watermelon, seeded and cubed
bunch of fresh mint

5 oz strawberries
5 oz honeydew melon balls
5 oz blackberries

Cut cantaloupe in half. Remove seeds. Cut skin from fruit, keeping pulp intact. Cut each cantaloupe half lengthwise into about 6 crescent-shaped slices. Arrange sprigs of mint on serving dish, reserving 6 sprigs for garnish. Arrange cantaloupe slices over mint, with the points of the melon slices meeting in the centre of the dish, like spokes of a wheel. Arrange remaining fruit between cantaloupe slices. Chop remaining mint and sprinkle over fruit. Divide evenly. Makes 6 servings.

Each serving is equivalent to: 1 serving Fruit

EGGS

The egg is nature's marvel, and our test kitchen staff have hatched some marvellous ideas for using it. Make our famous French Toast . . . our fluffy soufflés and filling Italian Omelette. We show you how to fill an omelette with everything from spinach or mushrooms to prunes or cheese. Best of all, we show you how to make a two-part meal, or desserts like custard and meringues, from one egg!

Rules for Using Eggs

1. Amounts:
   Women, Men and Teenagers: 1 egg at the morning meal
   2 eggs at the midday meal
2. Select 4 standard eggs a week. They may be cooked over direct heat, without fat; or in the shell. Raw eggs are 'legal'.'
3. Egg whites and egg yolks may be prepared in separate recipes, provided that both whites and yolks are consumed as part of the same meal.

Hard-Boiled Eggs

If possible, bring eggs to room temperature before cooking. Put standard eggs in saucepan and add enough water to cover eggs by at least 1 inch. Cover; bring rapidly just to boiling. Turn off heat; if necessary, remove pan from burner to prevent further boiling. Let stand in the hot water 12 to 15 minutes. Cool immediately and thoroughly in cold water—shells are easier to remove and it is less likely you will have a dark surface on yolks. To remove shell: crackle it by tapping gently all over. Roll egg between hands to loosen shell; then peel, starting at large end. Hold egg under running cold water or dip in bowl of water to help ease off shell.

Poached Eggs

Pour about 1 inch of water in a shallow pan or frying pan. Add 1 to 2 teaspoons white vinegar if desired and ½ to 1 teaspoon salt, depending on the size of the pan. Bring water to boil. Break 1 standard egg into small cup. Reduce heat to simmer; gently slide egg into water. Repeat with remaining eggs, but be sure not to crowd them. Cook for 2 to 3 minutes or until done to taste. Remove eggs from water with slotted spoon. If eggs are to be served cold, gently place them in cold water. If they are to be served hot, serve them at once or slightly undercook them and reheat in simmering water for about 30 seconds. For a more decorative effect, the edges of the egg whites can be trimmed and combined with minced herbs and served over the eggs.

Variation: Reheat 1 poached egg in 4 fl oz simmering tomato juice or chicken bouillon seasoned to taste. Serve egg and liquid in soup bowl. Makes 1 morning or midday meal serving. Supplement as required.

Each serving is equivalent to: 1 Egg; ½ serving Bonus (4 fl oz tomato juice) or ⅔ serving Something Extra (4 fl oz bouillon)

Scrambled Eggs

Beat 1 standard egg in bowl. For a lighter product, add up to 1 tablespoon water before beating. Pour into preheated nonstick frying pan. When the egg begins to firm, stir, scraping mixture from bottom and sides of pan, until done to taste. Season as desired. Makes 1 morning meal serving.

Coddled Eggs

Follow procedure for hard-boiled eggs but let eggs stand in hot water only 1 to 4 minutes, according to taste. Cool for a few seconds in cold water.

Sunnyside Up

Use heated nonstick or heavy iron pan. Break 1 standard egg into cup, slide it into pan, and cook until done to taste. To firm the top without burning egg, cover pan. Makes 1 morning meal serving.

Poached Eggs in Rice

3 oz cooked rice   1 teaspoon margarine (optional)
1 standard egg, poached

If rice is cold, heat by placing in strainer and steaming over boiling water. Transfer to breakfast bowl and top with egg. Dot with margarine if desired and allow to melt. Makes 1 morning meal serving.

Each serving is equivalent to: 1 serving Choice Group; 1 Egg; 1 serving Fat (optional)

Double Boiler Scrambled Egg and Potato

This method enables you to scramble eggs with fat and to reheat cold fillings without using a second pan. Also, eggs stay moist and creamy.

2 tablespoons margarine   1 teaspoon chopped fresh parsley
6 oz peeled cooked potato, diced   or chives
4 standard eggs, beaten   ½ teaspoon salt
3 tablespoons liquid (water or   pepper to taste
   potato liquid)

Melt margarine in top of double boiler over boiling water. Add potato and heat. Combine eggs with liquid, parsley or chives, salt and pepper. Add to margarine-potato mixture. Cook, stirring frequently, until done to taste. Divide evenly. Makes 2 midday meal servings.

Each serving is equivalent to: 3 servings Fat; 1 serving Choice Group; 2 Eggs

Variations:

Rice Scramble—Use 6 oz cooked rice instead of potato in basic recipe and season with hot sauce to taste before adding eggs.

Mexican Scramble—Following preceding method, cook 3 oz green pepper, seeded and diced, in the melted margarine until tender. Add dash hot sauce and a pinch of cumin. Replace potato with 6 oz canned, whole kernel corn. Add ½ serving Vegetables to equivalent listing.

Smoked Salmon Scramble

2 tablespoons margarine   **6 oz smoked salmon, diced**
4 oz onion or spring onions, diced   **4 standard eggs, beaten**
6 oz green pepper, seeded and diced

Melt margarine in top of double boiler over boiling water. Add green pepper and onion. Cover and cook until soft. Add smoked salmon and mix well. Pour in eggs; cook, stirring occasionally, until eggs are done to taste. Divide evenly. Makes 4 midday meal servings.

Each serving is equivalent to: 1½ servings Fat; ½ serving Vegetables; 1 oz Limited Vegetable; 1½ oz Smoked Fish; 1 Egg

Variation: Omit smoked salmon. Sprinkle lemon juice over 8 oz drained canned tuna or other flaked, cooked fish and use in preceding recipe. In equivalent listing, substitute 2 oz Fish for the 1 oz Smoked Fish.

Scrambled Eggs with Potato

6 oz peeled cooked potato, diced
4 standard eggs, beaten
3 tablespoons liquid (water or
  potato liquid)

1 teaspoon chopped fresh parsley
½ teaspoon salt
pepper to taste

Brown potato in preheated nonstick frying pan. Turn to brown all sides. Combine remaining ingredients and add to pan. Scramble with a fork until done to taste. Divide evenly. Makes 2 midday meal servings.

Each serving is equivalent to: 1 serving Choice Group; 2 Eggs

Baked Herb Omelette

4 standard eggs, separated
2 fl oz water
1 teaspoon chopped fresh parsley
¼ teaspoon chives
¼ teaspoon marjoram

¼ teaspoon chervil
¼ teaspoon tarragon
¼ teaspoon thyme
¼ teaspoon salt
⅛ teaspoon pepper

Preheat oven to 350°F, Gas Mark 4. In large bowl, beat egg whites until stiff, but not dry. In another large bowl, beat egg yolks with remaining ingredients until thick. Fold whites into yolk mixture. Transfer to preheated nonstick omelette pan with ovenproof handle. Cook until brown on bottom. Transfer pan to oven and bake for 15 minutes or until brown on top. Serve at once on hot dish. Divide evenly into 4 wedges. Makes 4 morning or midday meal servings. Supplement as required.

Each serving is equivalent to: 1 Egg

Bread Omelette

1 slice white bread, cubed
2 fl oz skim milk
2 standard eggs, separated

pinch each salt and pepper
watercress or parsley sprigs
  to garnish

Combine bread and milk in medium bowl. Add beaten egg yolks, salt and pepper; stir to combine. In separate bowl beat egg whites until stiff but not dry; fold into yolk mixture. Transfer to preheated 8-inch nonstick pan with flameproof handle, and cook until bottom is brown. Place under preheated grill, as close to heat source as possible, until lightly brown and puffy. Remove from grill, fold omelette in half, and garnish with watercress or parsley. Serve immediately. Makes 1 midday meal serving.

Each serving is equivalent to: 1 serving Bread; $^1/_5$ serving Milk (2 fl oz skim milk); 2 Eggs

Creamy Omelette

1 standard egg   pinch celery salt
½ fl oz natural unsweetened
   yogurt

In small bowl beat egg, yogurt and celery salt until blended. Pour into preheated nonstick frying pan and cook over medium heat. As edges and bottom begin to set, lift edges of egg mixture so that the uncooked portion flows underneath. When dry on top, fold in half and serve on warm plate. Makes 1 morning or midday meal serving. Supplement as required.

Each serving is equivalent to: 1 Egg; $^1/_{10}$ serving Milk (½ fl oz yogurt)

Creole Omelette

1½ oz green pepper, seeded and   1 oz onion, diced
   diced   salt and pepper to taste
½ oz tomato, diced   curry powder to taste (optional)
1 oz pimiento, diced   1 standard egg, beaten

In nonstick frying pan combine green pepper, pimiento, tomato and onion. Season with salt and pepper. Add curry powder, if desired. Cook, stirring occasionally, until vegetables are tender and mixture is almost dry. Add egg; stir quickly to combine. Cook until egg is brown on bottom. Turn with spatula to brown other side. Makes 1 morning or midday meal serving. Supplement as required.

Each serving is equivalent to: 1 serving Vegetables; 1 oz Limited Vegetable; 1 Egg

Variation:

Ratatouille Omelette—Serve omelette with 1 serving hot Ratatouille (see page 272). Add equivalents to preceding equivalent listing.

Italian Omelette

2 standard eggs, separated
6 oz cooked courgettes, diced
1½ oz Mozzarella cheese, grated
½ oz Parmesan cheese, grated

salt and pepper to taste
4 teaspoons tomato ketchup
   (optional)

In bowl beat egg whites until stiff but not dry. In separate bowl beat yolks until frothy. Add courgettes, cheeses, salt and pepper. Fold in whites. Pour into nonstick frying pan with flameproof handle. Cook until bottom is brown; then place pan under grill as close to heat source as possible. Cook until omelette is browned and puffy. Serve with tomato ketchup if desired. Divide evenly. Makes 2 midday meal servings.

Each serving is equivalent to: 1 Egg; 1 serving Vegetables; 1 oz Hard Cheese; 1 serving Something Extra (2 teaspoons tomato ketchup) (optional)

Variations:

1. Add 2 teaspoons chopped fresh mint leaves and 1 teaspoon basil to beaten eggs and courgettes before folding in whites.

2. Omit cheese. Makes 2 morning meal servings. Eliminate cheese from equivalent listing.

Luncheon Cheese Omelette

1 standard egg, beaten

1 oz Cheddar or other hard cheese, grated

In small bowl combine egg with ½ oz cheese. Pour into preheated nonstick frying pan or omelette pan with flameproof handle. Cook until almost solid on top; sprinkle with remaining cheese. Place under grill as close to heat source as possible. Grill until cheese is melted. Makes 1 midday meal serving.

Each serving is equivalent to: 1 Egg; 1 oz Hard Cheese

Variation:
Luncheon Fish Omelette—Omit cheese. Combine 2 oz drained canned tuna, flaked, or 2 oz cooked mussels with egg. Add a dash of lemon juice. Cook in nonstick frying pan until done to taste. Brown under grill if desired.

Substitute 2 oz Fish for 1 oz Hard Cheese in equivalent listing.

Prune Omelette

4 dried medium prunes   ½ **teaspoon vanilla flavouring**
1 standard egg, beaten

Place prunes in small saucepan and add enough water to cover. Bring to boil, reduce heat, and cook until prunes are soft. Drain and reserve liquid. Stone prunes; purée in blender container and set aside. Combine egg, 1 tablespoon reserved liquid and vanilla. Pour mixture into preheated nonstick frying pan or omelette pan. Cook until bottom is brown. Top with prune purée and fold in half. Serve at once on heated serving plate. Makes 1 morning or midday meal serving. Supplement as required.

Each serving is equivalent to: 1 serving Fruit; 1 Egg

Variation: Prepare omelette as in preceding recipe, using frying pan with flameproof handle. If desired, other fruits may be substituted for prunes in the preceding recipe. See page 20 for 'Fruit Servings'. After omelette is folded, top with 2½ oz strawberries, sliced. Dot with 1 teaspoon margarine. Grill for 1 minute, close to heat source, to melt margarine. Remove from grill and serve at once. Add ½ serving Fruit and 1 serving Fat to equivalent listing.

Puffy Omelette

4 standard eggs, separated	¼ teaspoon salt
2 fl oz water	¼ teaspoon cream of tartar

Preheat oven to 350°F, Gas Mark 4. In bowl beat egg yolks until thick and lemon-coloured, about 5 minutes. In separate bowl combine egg whites with water, salt and cream of tartar. Beat until stiff but not dry. Fold whites into yolks. Heat 10-inch nonstick frying pan with ovenproof handle. Pour in omelette mixture, smooth surface with spatula. Reduce heat to medium; cook until lightly browned on bottom. Transfer to oven and bake for 12 to 15 minutes or until top is firm and dry. Fold and turn onto warm dish. Divide evenly. Makes 2 midday meal servings.

Each serving is equivalent to: 2 Eggs

Vegetable Omelettes

Omelettes bursting with savoury fillings are yours for the making. For a morning or midday meal, allow about 1½ oz vegetable filling for a one-egg omelette. The filling may be mixed into the batter, added to the partly cooked egg, added just before the omelette is folded, or spooned on top of the folded omelette as a hot sauce. Vary flavours by adding small amounts of flavourings to taste. Use heavy iron omelette pan or frying pan or nonstick pan. Keep in mind that omelettes continue to cook by retained heat after they are removed from the cooker.

1 standard egg	salt, pepper and seasonings to taste
1 tablespoon water or vegetable liquid	batter filling from following list

In bowl combine egg, water and seasonings, and beat. Add batter filling from following list. Mix well and pour into preheated pan. Cook at moderate heat. When edges are firm, lift so uncooked portion flows underneath. Repeat as necessary. When bottom is set and inside almost done to your taste, fold in half. Serve on heated plate. Makes 1 morning or midday meal serving. Supplement as required.

Mushrooms-Peas Omelette—Combine ½ oz cooked, diced mushrooms, 1 oz cooked peas and 1 teaspoon chives. Mix into batter. Serve omelette with watercress garnish.

Each serving is equivalent to: 1 Egg; ⅙ serving Vegetables; 1 oz Limited Vegetable

Herb-Asparagus Omelette—Add 2 teaspoons chopped fresh herbs such as parsley or marjoram and ¼ teaspoon dried herbs such as tarragon or chervil to batter. Layer 1½ oz hot, cooked asparagus spears lengthwise on cooked omelette before folding it over to serve; 1½ oz cooked courgettes slices may be substituted for the asparagus.

Each serving is equivalent to: 1 Egg; ½ serving Vegetables

Artichoke Omelette—Combine 2 oz cooked, diced artichoke hearts and 1 teaspoon (¼ oz) tomato purée. Season with ⅛ teaspoon instant chicken stock powder. Mix well and add to batter.

Each serving is equivalent to: 1 Egg; 2 oz Limited Vegetable; ⅛ serving Bonus (1 teaspoon tomato purée); ⅛ serving Something Extra (⅛ teaspoon chicken powder)

Variation: Prepare any of the preceding omelettes. After they are cooked, cool, dice, and serve over mixed green salad.

Savoury Ham Omelette

2 standard eggs, separated
salt and pepper to taste
3 oz cooked ham, diced
1 oz onion, diced
1½ oz green pepper, seeded and
  diced

½ oz celery, diced
1 fl oz skim milk
4 teaspoons tomato ketchup
  (optional)

In bow beat egg whites until stiff but not dry. Set aside. In separate bowl beat egg yolks until frothy. Season with salt and pepper. Add ham, onion, green pepper, celery and skim milk to egg yolks. Fold in whites. Pour into nonstick frying pan with flameproof handle. Cook until bottom is brown; then place pan under grill, as close to heat source as possible. Cook until omelette is browned and puffy.

Serve with tomato ketchup if desired. Divide evenly. Makes 2 midday meal servings.

Each serving is equivalent to: 1 Egg; 1½ oz 'Beef' Group (smoked); ½ oz Limited Vegetable; $^1/_3$ serving Vegetables; $^1/_{20}$ serving Milk (½ fl oz skim milk); 1 serving Something Extra (2 teaspoons tomato ketchup) (optional)

Baked French Toast with Fruit

For a treat, when you have guests you can make two elegant dishes from your morning egg. Serve the French Toast with either of the two meringue-topped fruits. Toast and fruit can be baked at the same time. If you are making more than 3 servings, the baking time may need to be increased. Watch closely to avoid underbaking or overbaking.

Baked French Toast

1 standard egg yolk*	dash vanilla flavouring
1 teaspoon water	1 slice currant bread
pinch salt	

In a shallow bowl, combine egg yolk, water, salt and vanilla. Soak bread in mixture, turning at least once. Let stand until all liquid is absorbed. Place bread on baking sheet; bake at 350°F, Gas Mark 4, for 10 to 12 minutes or until lightly browned. Makes 1 morning meal serving. Supplement as required.*

Each serving is equivalent to: 1 Egg Yolk*; 1 serving Bread

*Baked French Toast must be consumed at the same meal as either Grapefruit with Meringue Topping or Pineapple with Meringue Topping, which contains remaining egg white.

Grapefruit with Meringue Topping

½ medium grapefruit	⅛ teaspoon cream of tartar
1 standard egg white*	pinch salt

With knife, loosen the pulp from grapefruit; discard seeds and tough centre membrane. In medium bowl beat egg white with cream of tartar and salt until it stands in peaks. Pile mixture on top of grapefruit. Place in small foil pan. Bake at 350°F, Gas Mark 4, for 10 to 12 minutes or until topping begins to brown. Makes 1 morning meal serving. Supplement as required.*

Each serving is equivalent to: 1 serving Fruit; 1 Egg White*

Pineapple with Meringue Topping

4 oz canned pineapple chunks, no
  sugar added
few drops each, orange and
  coconut flavourings
1 standard egg white*

artificial sweetener to equal 1
  teaspoon sugar, or to taste
⅛ teaspoon cream of tartar
pinch salt

Arrange pineapple chunks in small oven-to-table casserole. Sprinkle with flavourings. In medium bowl, beat egg white with sweetener, cream of tartar and salt until it stands in peaks. Pile mixture on top of pineapple. Bake at 350°F, Gas Mark 4, for 10 to 12 minutes or until topping begins to brown. Makes 1 morning meal serving. Supplement as required.*

Each serving is equivalent to: 1 serving Fruit; 1 Egg White*

*Grapefruit with Meringue Topping or Pineapple with Meringue Topping must be consumed at the same meal as Baked French Toast which contains remaining egg yolk.

Currant French Toast

Wholemeal or white bread may replace currant bread.

1 standard egg, beaten
1 tablespoon skim milk
¼ teaspoon vanilla flavouring

pinch salt
1 slice currant bread

In shallow bowl, combine egg, milk, vanilla and salt. Soak bread in mixture, turning at least once. Let stand until as much liquid as possible is absorbed. Place in preheated nonstick frying pan. Pour any remaining egg mixture over bread. Cook until brown on one side; turn to brown other side. Serve hot. Makes 1 morning or midday meal serving. Supplement as required.

Each serving is equivalent to: 1 Egg; $\frac{1}{20}$ serving Milk ($\frac{1}{2}$ fl oz skim milk); 1 serving Bread

Variations:

1. Follow preceding directions but let bread stand in batter overnight in refrigerator. In the morning, slip the bread onto non-stick baking sheet. Pour any remaining egg mixture over bread; bake at 400°F, Gas Mark 6, for 12 minutes or until top is puffy and brown. This is an easy way to get a lot of puffy toast for a big family or guests without last-minute fuss.

2. For the midday meal, top French toast with a 1 oz slice of hard cheese and grill until cheese is bubbly hot and melted. Makes 1 midday meal serving. Add 1 oz Hard Cheese to equivalent listing.

Baked Pancake

2 standard eggs, beaten	1 tablespoon flour
$\frac{1}{2}$ oz nonfat dry milk	$\frac{1}{4}$ teaspoon vanilla flavouring
2 tablespoons water	1 tablespoon lemon juice (optional)
2 tablespoons margarine, melted	4 teaspoons low-calorie jam

Combine all ingredients except lemon juice and low-calorie jam in small bowl. Beat until smooth. Pour into a preheated nonstick frying pan with ovenproof handle. Bake at 425°F, Gas Mark 7, for 15 minutes or until browned on top. Sprinkle with lemon juice, if desired. Serve with low-calorie jam. Divide evenly. Makes 2 morning or midday meal servings. Supplement as required.

Each serving is equivalent to: 1 Egg; $\frac{1}{4}$ serving Milk ($2\frac{1}{2}$ fl oz skim milk); 3 servings Fat; $1\frac{1}{2}$ servings Something Extra ($1\frac{1}{2}$ teaspoons flour); Speciality Foods (2 teaspoons low-calorie jam, 15 calories)

Cottage Cheese Pancakes

2 standard eggs, separated
5 oz cottage cheese
2 tablespoons flour
1 teaspoon baking powder

¼ teaspoon salt
5 fl oz natural unsweetened yogurt
   (optional)

In medium bowl, combine egg yolks, cottage cheese, flour, baking powder and salt. Beat egg whites in small bowl until stiff but not dry. Fold into yolk mixture. Drop batter from mixing spoon onto preheated nonstick griddle. Brown pancakes on both sides, turning once with spatula. Divide evenly. Serve 2½ fl oz yogurt as topping on each portion if desired. Makes 2 midday meal servings.

Each serving is equivalent to: 1 Egg; 2½ oz Soft Cheese; 3 servings Something Extra (1 tablespoon flour); ½ serving Milk (2½ fl oz yogurt) (optional)

Variation:
Banana Cheese Pancakes—Do not separate eggs. Combine all ingredients except yogurt in blender container. Add 1 medium banana, sliced. Blend until smooth. Proceed as in basic recipe. Add 1 serving Fruit to equivalent listing.

Yogurt Pancakes

1 standard egg, beaten
1 teaspoon flour

½ fl oz natural unsweetened
   yogurt
pinch salt

In bowl combine egg and flour. Add yogurt and salt; beat again. Drop by spoonfuls onto preheated nonstick griddle or nonstick frying pan. Cook, turning once to brown both sides. Makes 2 large or 4 small pancakes; 1 morning or midday meal serving. Supplement as required.

Each serving is equivalent to: 1 Egg; 1 serving Something Extra (1 teaspoon flour); $1/_{10}$ serving Milk (½ fl oz yogurt)

Russian Egg Salad

1½ oz carrots, finely diced
1½ oz celery, finely diced
2 oz cooked peas

4 standard eggs, hard-boiled and
   diced
lettuce leaves
Russian Mayonnaise (see page 282)

In bowl combine first 4 ingredients. Chill. Serve on lettuce leaves with Russian Mayonnaise. Divide evenly. Makes 2 midday meal servings.

Each serving is equivalent to: ½ serving Vegetables; 1 oz Limited Vegetable; 2 Eggs; Russian Mayonnaise (see page 282)

Tuna-Stuffed Egg Platter

4 standard eggs, hard-boiled
8 oz drained canned tuna, flaked
2 tablespoons plus 2 teaspoons
   vegetable oil
14 capers
¼ teaspoon dry mustard

pinch allspice
freshly ground pepper to taste
1 lb tomatoes, sliced
10 oz chilled cooked green beans
2 tablespoons red wine vinegar

Cut eggs in half lengthwise. Remove yolks; place in medium bowl; mash. Add 1 oz tuna, 2 teaspoons oil, 6 chopped capers, mustard, allspice and pepper. Mix well. Divide evenly and fill egg whites, mounding mixture in the centre. Top each with 1 caper. On each of 4 salad plates arrange 4 oz sliced tomato, 2½ oz green beans and 2 filled egg halves. Divide remaining tuna evenly and arrange 1 portion on each plate. Combine remaining oil with vinegar and sprinkle equal amounts over the green beans and tomato on each plate. Makes 4 midday meal servings.

Each serving is equivalent to: 1 Egg; 2 oz Fish; 2 servings Fat; 2⅙ servings Vegetables

Custard

1 standard egg, beaten	½ teaspoon vanilla flavouring
10 fl oz skim milk	pinch salt
artificial sweetener to equal 2 teaspoons sugar, or to taste	pinch cinnamon

Combine all ingredients in blender container. Blend. Pour into small ovenproof bowl. Set bowl in baking tin and pour in ½ inch hot water. Bake at 325°F, Gas Mark 3, for 1 hour or until knife inserted in centre comes out clean. Serve warm or chilled. Makes 1 morning or midday meal serving. Supplement as required.

Each serving is equivalent to: 1 Egg; 1 serving Milk (10 fl oz skim milk)

Variations:
Mocha Custard—Substitute 5 fl oz hot coffee for 5 fl oz skim milk, and add 1 teaspoon unsweetened cocoa. Prepare as in basic recipe. Sprinkle instant coffee lightly over chilled custard before serving. Makes 1 morning or midday meal serving. Supplement as required.

Each serving is equivalent to: 1 Egg; ½ serving Milk (5 fl oz skim milk); 1 serving Something Extra (1 teaspoon cocoa)

Cheese Custard—Omit vanilla flavouring and add ¼ teaspoon dried onion flakes, reconstituted in water, and 1 oz grated Cheddar or other hard cheese. Makes 1 midday meal serving. Add 1 oz Hard Cheese to equivalent listing.

Apricot Custard—Put 2 canned apricot halves, no sugar added, in bottom of the bowl before adding custard mixture. Serve 1 tablespoon apricot juice over custard. Garnish with grated orange rind. Add ½ serving Fruit to equivalent listing.

SOUFFLÉS

Soufflés made with vegetables and a creamy sauce are pretty and scrumptious-tasting midday meal dishes. They are easy to manage if you handle the whites properly.

1. For best results start with eggs at room temperature, about 70°F. The whites will then beat to a maximum volume.
2. Separate eggs carefully so no yolk mixes with the whites.
3. Beat egg yolks, with or without other ingredients according to recipe directions.
4. Beat whites in clean dry bowl. For stability, add pinch of cream of tartar to egg whites after they have been whipped until they are foamy. Beat until they stand in stiff peaks and are glossy, not dry.
5. Fold in egg whites gently so they don't lose volume.
6. Be sure to preheat the oven when making soufflés.
7. To make a soufflé with a crown, use a rubber spatula and make a groove 1 inch from the edge of the dish and 1½ inches deep.

Basic Vegetable Soufflé

3 tablespoons margarine
3 tablespoons flour
1 oz nonfat dry milk
4 fl oz water
4 fl oz vegetable liquid or tomato
  juice

cooked finely diced vegetables (see
  following list)
seasonings (see following list)
4 standard eggs, separated
¼ teaspoon cream of tartar
  (optional)

Preheat oven to 350°F, Gas Mark 4. Melt margarine in top of double boiler, over boiling water. Stir in flour until mixture is smooth. Cook for 2 to 3 minutes. Add liquids, a little at a time, continuing to stir until mixture is thickened and smooth. Add vegetables and seasonings. Beat egg yolks. Stir a spoonful of the sauce into yolks, then add yolks to sauce. Stir to combine. Cook for 1 minute; remove from heat. Cool slightly. Beat egg whites until frothy; add cream of tartar, if desired, and continue beating until stiff but not dry. Fold whites into the vegetable-yolk mixture. Trans-

fer to 7-inch soufflé dish. Bake uncovered for 35 to 45 minutes or
until puffy and browned. For a soft crust, stand soufflé dish in pan
of hot water to bake. For a crisp crust, bake it on baking sheet.
Divide evenly. Makes 4 midday meal servings. Supplement as
required.

Amounts & Seasonings for Vegetables
10 oz Asparagus: ¼ teaspoon tarragon.
9 oz Broccoli or Cauliflower: ½ teaspoon dill weed, minced
chives or celery seed.
10 oz Carrots: 1 teaspoon dried onion flakes, 1 tablespoon
chopped fresh parsley and pinch marjoram or thyme.
10 oz Mushrooms: 1 tablespoon chopped fresh parsley and pinch
chervil or dill weed.
12 oz Spinach: ¼ teaspoon basil, mace, marjoram or nutmeg.
15 oz Courgettes: pinch cinnamon, cloves, fennel, ginger or
rosemary.
Each serving is equivalent to: 2¼ servings Fat; 2¼ servings
Something Extra (2¼ teaspoons flour); ¼ serving Milk (2½ fl oz
skim milk); ⅛ serving Bonus (1 fl oz tomato juice) (optional);
Vegetables (see Vegetable list above); 1 Egg

Variations:
Tomatoes and Onion—In place of cooked diced vegetables use
6 oz canned, medium tomatoes, finely chopped, and 8 oz steamed
chopped onion. Season to taste with thyme, salt and pepper, or 1
garlic clove, well crushed. Add 2 oz Limited Vegetables to equivalent listing.
Corn—In place of vegetables use 12 oz drained canned whole
kernel corn and in place of 4 fl oz vegetable liquid or tomato juice
and 1 oz nonfat dry milk with 4 fl oz water, use 1 oz nonfat dry
milk with 8 fl oz water.
Each serving is equivalent to: 2¼ servings Fat; 2¼ servings
Something Extra (2¼ teaspoons flour); ¼ serving Milk (2½ fl oz
skim milk); 1 serving Choice Group; 1 Egg

'Creamed' Eggs and Mushrooms

9 oz mushrooms, sliced
14 fl oz water
1 teaspoon lemon juice
1 tablespoon flour, mixed with 2
  tablespoons water
¼ teaspoon paprika
pinch cayenne pepper

1 oz nonfat dry milk
3 standard eggs, hard-boiled and
  separated
3 slices white bread, toasted and
  cut diagonally
salt and freshly ground pepper to
  taste

In saucepan combine mushrooms, 10 fl oz water and lemon juice. Simmer for 10 minutes or until mushrooms are tender. Remove mushrooms with slotted spoon and set aside. Reduce mushroom liquid to about 2 fl oz and stir in flour, paprika and cayenne pepper. Add milk and remaining water and cook, stirring constantly, until mixture is smooth and thickened. Chop egg whites. Add egg whites and mushrooms to sauce. Put yolks through a sieve. Serve mushroom sauce on toast, topped with yolks. Season with salt and pepper. Divide evenly. Makes 3 morning or midday meal servings. Supplement as required.

Each serving is equivalent to: 1 serving Vegetables; 1 serving Something Extra (1 teaspoon flour); ⅓ serving Milk (3⅓ fl oz skim milk); 1 Egg; 1 serving Bread

Eggs 'Benedict'

1 English muffin, split and toasted
1½ oz cooked ham
1 standard egg, poached
2 teaspoons mayonnaise

1 caper or ½ teaspoon chopped
  fresh parsley
1 teaspoon low-fat spread
  (optional)

Cover one muffin half with ham. Top with poached egg. Spread with mayonnaise. Place under preheated grill for 1 minute to heat. Garnish with caper or parsley. Serve with remaining muffin half, spread with low-fat spread, if desired. Makes 1 midday meal serving.

Each serving is equivalent to: 2 servings Bread (once-a-week-selection); 1½ oz 'Beef' Group (smoked); 1 Egg; 2 servings Fat; ½ serving Fat (optional)

Eggs Mimosa

3 tablespoons margarine
2 tablespoons flour
1 teaspoon dried onion flakes
¼ teaspoon salt
⅛ teaspoon Worcester sauce

pepper and paprika to taste
10 fl oz skim milk
4 standard eggs, hard-boiled
4 slices white bread, toasted

Melt margarine in top of double boiler over boiling water. Add flour and seasonings. Stir until smooth. Gradually stir in milk. Separate egg whites from yolks. Chop whites and add to sauce. Divide sauce evenly over hot toast on serving plate. Force egg yolk through a sieve over each serving. Makes 4 morning or midday meal servings. Supplement as required.

Each serving is equivalent to: 2¼ servings Fat; 1½ servings Something Extra (1½ teaspoons flour); ¼ serving milk (2½ fl oz skim milk); 1 Egg; 1 serving Bread

Prune Pudding

12 fl oz hot water or tea
8 dried medium prunes
2 slices white bread, cubed

2 standard eggs
½ teaspoon grated lemon rind
½ teaspoon lemon juice

Combine water or tea and prunes in a small saucepan. Cook prunes, uncovered, until fruit is very soft. Remove and discard stones. Place fruit and liquid in blender container with bread, eggs, lemon rind and juice. Blend until smooth. Divide evenly into 2 individual ovenproof serving dishes and bake for 30 minutes at 350°F, Gas Mark 4. Serve warm. Makes 2 morning or midday meal servings. Supplement as required.

Each serving is equivalent to: 1 serving Fruit; 1 serving Bread; 1 Egg

CHEESE

 *

You can do so much with an ounce or two of cheese! On our list are some that are mild and mellow, nippy and salty, sweet and nutlike, or sharp and pungent. Use your favourite in dips, open-faced sandwiches, au gratin, in salads, quiches and soufflés. Yes, even in our own special version of cheesecake. You can discover how to make our version of that most luscious of all French cheese dishes, Coeur à la Creme.

Keep a variety on hand for convenience. Storage of cheese is not difficult when you know how. The enemies are evaporation and mould that wasn't planned at the cheesemakers. To keep hard or semisoft cheeses from drying out, always cover the cut side tightly; it will retain freshness for several weeks. You cannot expect such longevity for soft cheeses. Use them within a few days.

Hard cheeses can be kept even longer by freezing. Divide into serving amounts because, once unfrozen, the cheese should be used promptly. Wrap in small, airtight packages, or grate and store in convenient sizes in the freezer. Use for cooking, following your Menu Plan.

Rules for Using Cheese

1. Amounts:
   Morning meal: 2½ oz soft cheese, or 1 oz semisoft or hard cheese.
   Midday meal: 5 oz soft cheese, or 2 oz semisoft or hard cheese.
2. Do not use more than 4 oz of semisoft or hard cheese weekly.

3. *Examples of Soft Cheeses*

Cottage   skim milk Ricotta
Curd

4. *Examples of Semisoft and Hard Cheeses*

Bel Paese	Gouda
Brie	Gruyere
Camembert	Mozzarella
Cheddar	Parmesan
Cheshire	Port de Salut
Danish Blue	Romano
Edam	Roquefort
Emmenthaler	Stilton
Feta	Tilsit
Gorgonzola	

Bean and Cheese Salad

2 teaspoons vegetable oil
2 teaspoons lemon juice
hot sauce to taste
salt to taste
3 oz fresh bean sprouts, blanched,
   if desired

3 oz cooked dried white beans or
   chick peas
1 oz feta cheese, crumbled
½ teaspoon poppy seeds (optional)

In serving bowl combine first 4 ingredients. Add remaining ingredients, toss. Makes 1 midday meal serving.

Each serving is equivalent to: 2 servings Fat; 1 serving Vegetables; 3 oz Dried Beans; 1 oz Hard Cheese; ½ serving Something Extra (½ teaspoon poppy seeds) (optional)

Caesar Salad

1 garlic clove, crushed
1 small lettuce, torn into bite-size
   pieces
1 oz Parmesan cheese, grated
1 standard egg, coddled (see page
   38)
2 teaspoons vegetable oil

2 teaspoons lemon juice
dash Worcester sauce
salt and freshly ground pepper to
   taste
1 slice white bread, toasted and
   diced

Rub salad bowl with garlic. Place lettuce in bowl, sprinkle with cheese and top with egg. In small bowl combine oil, lemon juice, Worcester sauce, salt and pepper; pour over salad. Add diced toast. Toss and serve immediately. Makes 1 midday meal serving.

Each serving is equivalent to: 1 serving Vegetables; 1 oz Hard Cheese; 1 Egg; 2 servings Fat; 1 serving Bread

Chef's Salad

6 oz salad greens (e.g. iceberg and cabbage lettuce and endive)
3 oz green pepper, sliced and seeded
2 oz tomato, cut into 4 wedges
1½ oz cooked ham or cooked smoked tongue, or 2 oz skinned and boned, cooked chicken, cut into thin strips
1 oz hard cheese, cut into thin strips
¼ recipe Basic French Dressing (1 serving, see page 283)

Place salad greens in serving bowl. Arrange vegetables, meat and cheese over greens. Serve with French Dressing. Makes 1 midday meal serving.

Each serving is equivalent to: $3^2/_3$ servings Vegetables; 1½ oz 'Beef' Group (smoked) or 2 oz Poultry; 1 oz Hard Cheese; Basic French Dressing (see page 283)

Harvest Salad with Fruit French Dressing

4 × 1½ oz heads of chicory, cut into ½-inch slices
20 oz cottage cheese
*2 medium apples, cored and sliced
4 oz grapefruit sections, no sugar added
4 oz orange sections, no sugar added
Fruit French Dressing (see following recipe)

Arrange chicory, evenly divided, on each of 4 salad plates. Top each with 5 oz cottage cheese. Arrange fruit, evenly divided, around cottage cheese. Serve each salad chilled with 1 serving Fruit French Dressing. Makes 4 midday meal servings.

*Apple slices may be dipped in lemon juice to prevent discolouring.

Fruit French Dressing

4 fl oz orange juice
2 tablespoons vegetable oil
1 tablespoon lemon juice or cider
vinegar

1 teaspoon chopped fresh mint
(optional)
salt and pepper to taste

Combine all ingredients in small jar with tight-fitting lid. Shake well. Divide evenly. Serve with Harvest Salad. Makes 4 servings. Serve at mealtime only.

Each serving is equivalent to: ½ serving Vegetables; 5 oz Soft Cheese; 1¼ servings Fruit; 1½ servings Fat

Tomato Salad with Creamy Cheese Dressing

4 × 4½ oz tomatoes
4 lettuce leaves
20 oz cottage cheese or 10 oz
cottage cheese and 4 oz Danish
Blue cheese, crumbled

1 garlic clove, crushed
salt and pepper to taste
1 teaspoon chives
Creamy Cheese Dressing (see
following recipe)

Remove core from stem end of tomatoes. Make 2 criss-cross cuts through each tomato almost to the bottom, so that tomato opens. Set each tomato on a lettuce leaf. Blend cottage cheese in blender container until smooth. Set aside 2 tablespoons for Creamy Cheese Dressing. Add Danish Blue cheese if used, garlic, salt and pepper, and blend until smooth. Stir in chives. Stuff each tomato with ¼ of the cheese mixture. Refrigerate. Serve with Creamy Cheese Dressing, evenly divided. Makes 4 midday meal servings.

Creamy Cheese Dressing

1 tablespoon mayonnaise
2 tablespoons blended cottage
cheese (see preceding recipe)
½ teaspoon salt

½ teaspoon paprika
2 tablespoons vegetable oil
1 tablespoon plus 1½ teaspoons
cider vinegar

In small bowl combine mayonnaise, cheese, salt and paprika. Slowly add oil, beating constantly, until thick. Add vinegar and continue to beat until well blended. Keep refrigerated until ready to serve. Serve with Tomato Salad.

Each serving is equivalent to: 1 serving Vegetables; 5 oz Soft Cheese or 2½ oz Soft Cheese and 1 oz Hard Cheese; 2¼ servings Fat

Blue Cheese Salad Ring

Serve with Tangy French Dressing (see page 314)

2 tablespoons unflavoured gelatine
7 fl oz water
10 oz cottage cheese
4 oz Danish Blue cheese, crumbled
1 oz nonfat dry milk

4 tablespoons mayonnaise
1 teaspoon Worcester sauce
dash hot sauce
salt to taste

In small saucepan, sprinkle gelatine over 2 fl oz water to soften. Heat, stirring to dissolve. In bowl, combine remaining ingredients. Stir in gelatine mixture. Pour into 2-pint mould and chill until firm. Turn out on a serving dish. Divide evenly. Makes 4 midday meal servings.

Each serving is equivalent to: 1 serving Something Extra (1½ teaspoons gelatine); 2½ oz Soft Cheese; 1 oz Hard Cheese; ¼ serving Milk (2½ fl oz skim milk); 3 servings Fat

Fruit Cocktail Cottage Cheese Ring with Tangy Dressing

2 lbs canned fruit cocktail, no
  sugar added
1 tablespoon unflavoured gelatine
7½ oz cottage cheese
artificial sweetener to equal 1
  teaspoon sugar, or to taste
  (optional)

2 oz spring onions
celery, radish roses and parsley
  sprigs to garnish
Tangy Dressing (see following
  recipe)

Drain juice from fruit cocktail into measuring jug, set fruit aside. Combine juice with enough water to make 8 fl oz. Pour into a small saucepan; sprinkle gelatine over liquid to soften. Stir over low heat until gelatine dissolves. Chill until syrupy. Blend cottage cheese in blender container until smooth. Stir into gelatine mixture. Fold in 16 oz fruit cocktail and sweetener, if desired. Pour mixture into ring mould. Chill until firm. Turn out onto serving platter and fill centre of ring with remaining fruit cocktail. Garnish with onion, celery, radishes and parsley. Serve with Tangy Dressing. Divide evenly. Makes 4 midday meal servings. Supplement as required.

Tangy Dressing

2½ oz cottage cheese
10 fl oz natural unsweetened
   yogurt
1½ oz green pepper, seeded and
   chopped
½ oz carrot, grated

1 tablespoon water
1 teaspoon chopped chives
1 teaspoon lemon juice
salt, pepper, and garlic powder to
   taste.

Blend cottage cheese in blender container until smooth. Combine with remaining ingredients. Serve with Fruit Cocktail Cottage Cheese Ring.

Each serving is equivalent to: 2 servings Fruit; ½ serving Something Extra (¾ teaspoon gelatine); 2½ oz Soft Cheese; ½ oz Limited Vegetable; ½ serving Milk (2½ fl oz yogurt); $\frac{1}{6}$ serving Vegetables

Hard-and-Soft-Cheese Mould

2 tablespoons unflavoured gelatine
24 fl oz Beef Stock (see page 157)
10 oz cottage cheese
2 fl oz skim milk
4 oz Danish Blue cheese, crumbled
8 oz drained canned water
   chestnuts, sliced

4 slices white bread, toasted and
   quartered
20 small tomatoes, about ½ oz
   each, halved
parsley sprigs to garnish

In saucepan sprinkle gelatine over stock to soften. Heat, stirring to dissolve. Pour a 1-inch layer of gelatine mixture into round 2-pint mould and chill until firm. Reserve remaining gelatine. In blender container combine cottage cheese and milk. Blend until smooth. Transfer to small bowl and combine with Danish Blue cheese. Spread over gelatine in mould. Pour a ¼-inch layer of reserved gelatine mixture over cheese. Chill until firm. Pour remaining gelatine mixture into mould. Refrigerate for several hours until firm. Turn out and transfer to serving dish; surround with water chestnuts, toast quarters, tomatoes and parsley. Divide evenly. Makes 4 midday meal servings.

Each serving is equivalent to: 2 servings Something Extra (1½ teaspoons gelatine, 6 fl oz stock); 2½ oz Soft Cheese; $^1/_{10}$ serving Milk (½ fl oz skim milk); 1 oz Hard Cheese; 2 oz Limited Vegetable; 1 serving Bread; $^1/_6$ serving Vegetables

Two-Tone Salad

Tomato Aspic Layer

1 tablespoon unflavoured gelatine
12 fl oz mixed vegetable juice
2 teaspoons lemon juice

¼ teaspoon celery seed
¼ teaspoon seasoned salt

Cottage Cheese Layer

2 tablespoons unflavoured gelatine
8 fl oz water
1½ oz nonfat dry milk
15 oz cottage cheese
6 oz cucumber, peeled, seeded and
    chopped

¾ teaspoon salt
¼ teaspoon paprika
lettuce leaves
lemon wedges to garnish

Tomato Aspic Layer: In medium saucepan sprinkle gelatine over vegetable juice to soften. Heat slowly, stirring until gelatine is dissolved. Add remaining ingredients; mix well. Pour into large mould and chill until almost firm.

Cottage Cheese Layer: In saucepan sprinkle gelatine over 3 fl oz water to soften. Heat to dissolve; cool slightly. Mix dry milk with remaining water. In bowl combine gelatine mixture with cottage cheese, cucumber, milk, salt and paprika. Spoon evenly over tomato layer. Chill until firm. Turn out on lettuce leaves and garnish with lemon wedges. Divide evenly. Makes 6 midday meal servings. Supplement as required.

Each serving is equivalent to: 1 serving Something Extra (1½ teaspoons gelatine); ¼ serving Bonus (2 fl oz mixed vegetable juice); 2½ oz Soft Cheese; ⅓ serving Vegetables; ¼ serving Milk (2½ fl oz skim milk)

Cheese Spread

Serve with a dish of crisp fresh vegetables.

10 oz cottage cheese	**2 tablespoons water**
4 oz very sharp Cheddar cheese, grated	**few drops hot sauce**

Combine all ingredients in blender container; blend until smooth. Add more water, a few drops at a time, if necessary. Spoon into small bowl, cover and chill for several hours. Divide evenly. Makes 4 midday meal servings.

Each serving is equivalent to: 2½ oz Soft Cheese; 1 oz Hard Cheese

Variation: Substitute Danish Blue or Gorgonzola, or other semisoft or hard cheese for the Cheddar.

Chive Creamy Cheese

1½ teaspoons unflavoured gelatine	**5 oz cottage cheese**
½ oz nonfat dry milk mixed with	**2 teaspoons chives**
2 fl oz water	**1 teaspoon chopped fresh parsley**
2 teaspoons margarine	

In small saucepan, sprinkle gelatine over milk and let stand to soften. Place over low heat, stirring until gelatine dissolves. Remove from heat and stir in margarine. Blend cottage cheese in blender container until smooth. Stir in chives and parsley. Add to gelatine mixture. Mix well. Spoon into small mould and chill until firm. Divide evenly. Makes 2 morning or midday meal servings. Supplement as required.

Each serving is equivalent to: ½ serving Something Extra (¾ teaspoon gelatine); ¼ serving Milk (2½ fl oz skim milk); 1 serving Fat; 2½ oz Soft Cheese

Variation: For a morning meal treat, divide Chive Creamy Cheese evenly into 4 portions and serve each portion with 1 oz smoked salmon. Serve each on a bagel with 1½ oz sliced tomato and capers. Garnish with lemon wedges.

Each serving is equivalent to: ¼ serving Something Extra (³/₈ teaspoon gelatine); ⅛ serving Milk (1¼ fl oz skim milk); ½ serving Fat; 1¼ oz Soft Cheese; 1 oz Smoked Fish; 2 servings Bread (once-a-week selection); ½ serving Vegetables

Creamy Cheese Sauce

2 tablespoons margarine	2 oz Cheddar cheese, grated
2 tablespoons flour	dash Worcester sauce, hot sauce or
10 fl oz skim milk	pinch nutmeg (optional)

Melt margarine in top of double boiler over boiling water. Blend in flour. Add milk; cook, stirring constantly, until thickened. Stir in cheese. Season with Worcester sauce, hot sauce, or nutmeg if desired. Divide evenly. Makes 2 morning or midday meal servings. Supplement as required.

Each serving is equivalent to: 3 servings Fat; 3 servings Something Extra (1 tablespoon flour); ½ serving Milk (5 fl oz skim milk); 1 oz Hard Cheese

Creamy Blue Cheese Dressing

1 oz Danish Blue cheese	salt and pepper to taste
1 tablespoon water	pinch dry mustard
1 tablespoon mayonnaise	pinch celery seed
1 tablespoon lemon juice	

In small bowl mash cheese with fork; stir in water, mayonnaise, lemon juice and seasonings. Serve on green salad. Makes 1 midday meal serving. Supplement as required.

Each serving is equivalent to: 1 oz Hard Cheese; 3 servings Fat

Variation: Replace water and mayonnaise with 1 fl oz natural unsweetened yogurt and add 1 small crushed garlic clove.

Each serving is equivalent to: 1 oz Hard Cheese; $\frac{1}{5}$ serving Milk (1 fl oz yogurt)

Quick-and-Easy Cheese Sauce

Serve over hot vegetables.

4 oz Cheddar cheese, diced
2 fl oz skim milk
dash Worcester sauce

pinch cayenne pepper
salt and pepper to taste

Combine all ingredients in top of double boiler over boiling water. Cook, stirring occasionally, until cheese is melted. Divide evenly. Makes 4 morning or midday meal servings. Supplement as required.

Each serving is equivalent to: 1 oz Hard Cheese; $\frac{1}{20}$ serving Milk ($\frac{1}{2}$ fl oz skim milk)

Variation: *Mushroom-Cheese Sauce*—Before serving, blend 10 oz sliced, cooked mushrooms and 1 teaspoon dried onion flakes into Cheese Sauce in preceding recipe. Serve at midday meal over 20 oz hot, cooked courgettes, broccoli or asparagus. Divide evenly. Makes 4 midday meal servings. Supplement as required. Add 2½ servings Vegetables to equivalent listing.

Cheese Soufflé

2 tablespoons margarine
2 tablespoons flour
2 oz nonfat dry milk
10 fl oz water
4 oz Cheddar cheese, grated

¼ teaspoon salt
⅛ teaspoon dry mustard
dash hot sauce
4 standard eggs, separated

Preheat oven to 350°F, Gas Mark 4. Melt margarine in top of double boiler over boiling water; stir in flour. Mix dry milk and water. Gradually add milk and cook over low heat, stirring constantly, until sauce is thick and smooth. Add cheese; stir until cheese melts. Add seasonings. Beat egg yolks in medium bowl. Stir a few tablespoons of hot cheese sauce into yolks, then stir egg yolks into sauce in pan and heat for one minute. Remove from heat. In separate bowl beat egg whites until stiff. Stir ⅓ of egg whites into sauce. Gently fold in remaining egg whites. Pour into nonstick 2-pint soufflé dish. Bake for 45 minutes or until the soufflé is set. Serve at once. Divide evenly. Makes 4 midday meal servings.

Each serving is equivalent to: 1½ servings Fat; 1½ servings Something Extra (1½ teaspoons flour); ½ serving Milk (5 fl oz skim milk); 1 oz Hard Cheese; 1 Egg

Variations:
Two-Cheese Soufflé—For extra flavour, use half Cheddar cheese and half Parmesan. Add 1 tablespoon chopped fresh parsley or 1 teaspoon basil, sage, thyme or other favourite herb.
Devilled Cheese Soufflé—Add 1 tablespoon plus 1 teaspoon tomato ketchup, 1 teaspoon Worcester sauce and dash hot sauce to the cheese-yolk mixture with other seasonings. Add ½ serving Something Extra (1 teaspoon tomato ketchup) to equivalent listing.

Quick-and-Easy Cheese Soufflé

This is delicious served with Tomato Sauce (see page 288)

3 slices white bread, made into
  crumbs
6 fl oz skim milk
3 oz Cheddar cheese, grated
¼ teaspoon salt

dash hot sauce
pinch dry mustard
3 standard eggs, separated
3 tablespoons margarine

Preheat oven to 375°F, Gas Mark 5. In saucepan combine breadcrumbs and milk; simmer over very low heat for 3 minutes. Stir in cheese and seasonings. Heat, stirring often, until cheese is melted. In small bowl beat egg yolks and add to cheese mixture; heat gently for 4 minutes longer. Remove from heat; stir in margarine until melted. Beat egg whites until stiff but not dry. Fold into cheese-yolk mixture. Transfer to 2-pint nonstick soufflé dish. Set in pan holding 1 inch of water and bake for 30 minutes or until set. Serve at once. Divide evenly. Makes 3 midday meal servings.

Each serving is equivalent to: 1 serving Bread; $^{1}/_{5}$ serving Milk (2 fl oz skim milk); 1 oz Hard Cheese; 1 Egg; 3 servings Fat

Cheese Kebab

Cut 2 oz of Cheddar, Edam or other hard cheese into cubes. Spear on toothpicks alternating with pineapple chunks made from ¼ medium fresh pineapple or 20 small grapes. Makes 1 midday meal serving.

Each serving is equivalent to: 2 oz Hard Cheese; 1 serving Fruit

Welsh Rarebit for One

You may omit the English muffin and serve rarebit on 3 oz of sliced tomato.

1½ oz (about 2 tablespoons) tomato purée	pinch salt
2 tablespoons water	pinch dry mustard
2 oz Cheddar cheese, grated	dash hot sauce
	1 English muffin, split and toasted

Combine all ingredients, except muffin, Cook in top of double boiler, over boiling water, stirring constantly, until cheese melts. Serve over warm muffin halves. Makes 1 midday meal serving.

Each serving is equivalent to: ¾ serving Bonus (1½ oz tomato purée); 2 oz Hard Cheese; 2 servings Bread (once-a-week selection)

Cheddar Macaroni

5 fl oz skim milk	cooked Brussels sprouts
2 oz Cheddar cheese, grated	3 oz tomato, sliced
3 oz cooked elbow macaroni, cauliflower, or broccoli, or 4 oz	chopped fresh parsley or chives to garnish

Heat milk in small saucepan. Add cheese; stir until cheese melts. Pour over macaroni or vegetables in bowl. Serve with tomato slices and garnish with parsley or chives. Makes 1 midday meal serving.

Each serving is equivalent to: ½ serving Milk (5 fl oz skim milk); 2 oz Hard Cheese; 1 serving Choice Group or 1 serving Vegetables or 4 oz Limited Vegetable; 1 serving Vegetables

Cottage Cheese with Poppy Seed Noodles—Hungarian Style

12 oz cooked broad noodles
10 oz cottage cheese
5 fl oz natural unsweetened yogurt
2 teaspoons poppy seeds

½ teaspoon paprika
½ teaspoon Worcester sauce
salt and pepper to taste

Combine all ingredients in medium saucepan. Heat slowly, stirring often, until cheese begins to melt. Divide evenly. Makes 4 midday meal servings. Supplement as required.

Each serving is equivalent to: 1 serving Choice Group; 2½ oz Soft Cheese; ¼ serving Milk (1¼ fl oz yogurt); ½ serving Something Extra (½ teaspoon poppy seeds)

Mexican Cheese, Corn and Courgettes

4 oz onion, finely chopped
1 tablespoon plus 1 teaspoon
  margarine
20 oz courgettes, sliced
12 oz drained canned whole kernel
  corn

1 pint skim milk
4 oz Cheddar cheese, grated
dash hot sauce
salt and pepper to taste

In top of double boiler, over boiling water, combine onion and margarine. Cook for 10 minutes or until onion is tender. Stir in remaining ingredients. Transfer vegetable-cheese mixture to a large casserole. Cover and bake at 375°F, Gas Mark 5, for 30 minutes. Divide evenly. Makes 4 midday meal servings. Supplement as required.

Each serving is equivalent to: 1 oz Limited Vegetable; 1 serving Fat; 1²/₃ servings Vegetables; 1 serving Choice Group; ½ serving Milk (5 fl oz skim milk); 1 oz Hard Cheese

Spinach Quiche on Rice Crust

9 oz cooked brown rice
3 standard eggs
3 oz sharp Cheddar cheese, grated
salt to taste
6 oz cooked spinach, chopped

7½ fl oz skim milk
3 oz onion, finely diced
pinch freshly ground pepper
pinch nutmeg

In bowl combine rice, 1 egg, 1½ oz cheese, and salt. Press an even layer of mixture on the bottom and sides of a 9-inch pie dish. Bake at 425°F, Gas Mark 7, for 25 minutes. Squeeze all liquid out of spinach. In bowl combine spinach with remaining ingredients. Pour into crust. Bake at 375°F, Gas Mark 5, for 35 minutes. Divide evenly. Makes 3 midday meal servings.

Each serving is equivalent to: 1 serving Choice Group; 1 Egg; 1 oz Hard Cheese; ¼ serving Milk (2½ fl oz skim milk); 1 oz Limited Vegetable

Vegetable Cheese Loaf for One

If lighting the oven for one seems a bit selfish, you can bake this with the family dinner and have it cold the following day. Any kind of vegetable can be used, either raw or cooked. You can change the texture completely by adding 5 fl oz skim milk and puréeing everything in the blender. There is no end to the seasonings that can be included. This loaf is nice with a topping of Tomato Sauce (see page 288) sliced tomato, or Ratatouille (see page 272).

1½ oz peeled cooked potato, coarsely chopped
1½ oz drained canned beetroot, coarsely chopped
1½ oz carrots, coarsely chopped
1 oz spinach leaves, coarsely chopped
1 oz celery, coarsely chopped
1 oz onion, coarsely chopped
1 standard egg
1 slice white bread, made into crumbs
1½ oz drained canned whole kernel corn
1 oz Cheddar cheese, diced
1 tablespoon margarine, melted
salt, pepper and cinnamon to taste

Combine first 6 ingredients in bowl and stir in egg, breadcrumbs, corn, cheese, margarine, salt, pepper and cinnamon. Mix well and transfer to nonstick loaf tin or casserole. Bake at 350°F, Gas Mark 4, for 45 minutes. Makes 1 midday meal serving.

Each serving is equivalent to: 1 serving Choice Group; 2½ oz Limited Vegetable; 1$^1/_6$ servings Vegetables; 1 Egg; 1 serving Bread; 1 oz Hard Cheese; 3 servings Fat

Cheese Bologna Tidbits

2 oz grated Cheddar or crumbled Danish Blue cheese
3 oz bologna, sliced
1½ oz drained canned pimiento, sliced

Layer cheese evenly between the slices of bologna, beginning and ending with a bologna slice. Wrap in greaseproof paper. Press firmly; chill. Cut into 4 wedges. Secure with toothpicks. Garnish with pimiento. Divide evenly. Makes 2 midday meal servings.

Each serving is equivalent to: 1 oz Hard Cheese; 1½ oz Bologna; ¼ serving Vegetables

Baked Cheesy Sandwich

2 thin slices white bread (see page 77)
1½ oz cooked ham
1 oz hard cheese

Place ham and cheese between bread slices. Place in nonstick baking tin. Bake at 400°F, Gas Mark 6, for 10 minutes. Serve at once.

Makes 1 midday meal serving.

Each serving is equivalent to: 1 serving Bread; 1½ oz 'Beef' Group (smoked); 1 oz Hard Cheese

Variation: Substitute 2 oz sliced cooked turkey for ham. Substitute 2 oz Poultry for 1½ oz 'Beef' Group in equivalent listing.

Ham and Cheese Canapés

Chill hard cheese before grating to make the job easier.

6 oz cooked ham
1 oz onion
2 teaspoons prepared mustard
dash hot sauce

4 slices white bread, toasted
4 oz Cheddar cheese, grated
½ teaspoon chopped fresh parsley

Put ham and onion through the mincer. Stir in mustard and hot sauce. Divide evenly into 4 portions and spread 1 portion on each slice of toast. Top each with 1 oz cheese and sprinkle with parsley. Place on griller pan and grill until cheese melts. Cut in quarters and serve. Makes 4 midday meal servings.

Each serving is equivalent to: 1½ oz 'Beef' Group (smoked); ¼ oz Limited Vegetable; 1 serving Bread; 1 oz Hard Cheese.

Fun Fondue

1 oz nonfat dry milk mixed with
 4 fl oz water
2 oz hard cheese, grated
pinch each dry mustard and
 cayenne pepper, dash sherry
 flavouring

4½ oz crisp raw vegetables
(carrot, cucumber, celery, or
fennel sticks)

Heat milk in small saucepan. Add cheese and seasonings; stir until cheese melts. Serve warm and use as a dip with vegetables. Makes 1 midday meal serving.

Each serving is equivalent to: 1 serving Milk (10 fl oz skim milk); 2 oz Hard Cheese; 1½ servings Vegetables

Green Beans au Gratin

Any vegetable may be done this way. Be sure to weigh or measure in accordance with the Weight Watchers Programme.

6 oz cooked green beans
3 oz mushrooms, sliced
2 oz hard cheese, grated
½ teaspoon dried herbs
salt and pepper to taste

1½ oz (about 2 tablespoons)
    tomato purée
1 tablespoon water
1 slice white bread, made into
    crumbs

In small ovenproof casserole, layer cooked green beans, mushrooms, 1½ oz cheese and herbs. Sprinkle with salt and pepper. Top with tomato purée mixed with water. Combine remaining cheese and crumbs; sprinkle over casserole. Bake at 350°F, Gas Mark 4, for 25 minutes or until hot and bubbly. Makes 1 midday meal serving.

Each serving is equivalent to: 3 servings Vegetables; 2 oz Hard Cheese; ¾ serving Bonus (1½ oz tomato purée); 1 serving Bread

Mexican Pepper and Cheese

6 oz onion, chopped
1½ lbs green peppers
1 lb tomatoes, chopped
2 fl oz water

½ teaspoon salt
10 oz curd or cottage cheese
8 tortillas, 6 inches each

Brown onion in nonstick saucepan. Halve peppers, remove seeds and membranes and grill until skin can be rubbed off easily. Chop. Add peppers, tomatoes, water and salt to onion. Bring to boil, reduce heat and simmer for 15 minutes. Stir in cheese and heat. Divide evenly and spoon over tortillas. Makes 4 midday meal servings, 2 tortillas each. Supplement as required.

Each serving is equivalent to: 1½ oz Limited Vegetable; 2¹⁄₃ servings Vegetables; 2 oz Soft Cheese; 2 servings Bread (once-a-week selection)

Portuguese Tower

4 oz tomato
1 standard egg, lightly scrambled

1 oz Cheddar cheese
salt and pepper to taste

Cut a thin slice off the top of the tomato. Scoop out pulp, leaving at least ¼ inch thickness on all sides. Fill cavity with egg and top with cheese. Bake at 350°F, Gas Mark 4, until cheese melts. Chop tomato pulp; season with salt and pepper. Spoon over melted cheese. Makes 1 midday meal serving.

Each serving is equivalent to: 1⅓ serving Vegetables; 1 Egg; 1 oz Hard Cheese

Cheesecake Pudding

4 oz canned pineapple chunks, no
    sugar added
1 standard egg
1 teaspoon lemon juice

⅛ teaspoon vanilla flavouring
2½ oz skim milk ricotta cheese
1 teaspoon margarine
cinnamon to taste

Combine pineapple chunks, egg, lemon juice, and vanilla in blender container. Blend until smooth. Add cheese and blend. Pour into a 1-pint ovenproof casserole. Dot with margarine; sprinkle with cinnamon and bake at 350°F, Gas Mark 4, for 40 minutes. Serve chilled. Makes 1 midday meal serving.

Each serving is equivalent to: 1 serving Fruit; 1 Egg; 2½ oz Soft Cheese; 1 serving Fat

Fruity Cottage Cheese

You can create many different flavours using any of the fruits on the Food Programme (see 'Fruit Servings' on page 00).

5 oz cottage cheese
5 oz blueberries or blackberries

artificial sweetener to equal 2
    teaspoons sugar, or to taste
    (optional)

Blend cottage cheese in blender container until smooth. Transfer to small serving dish. Mash berries in small bowl or blend until puréed. Add sweetener to berries, if desired. Gently fold into cheese to give a marble effect. Chill. Makes 1 midday meal serving.

Each serving is equivalent to: 5 oz Soft Cheese; 1 serving Fruit

Orange 'Coeur à la Creme'

1 tablespoon unflavoured gelatine	½ teaspoon orange flavouring
4 fl oz cold water	½ teaspoon vanilla flavouring
4 fl oz boiling water	½ teaspoon coconut flavouring
10 oz cottage cheese	1 medium orange, peeled and
artificial sweetener to equal 2	sectioned
teaspoons sugar, or to taste	

Sprinkle gelatine over cold water in blender container to soften. Add boiling water; blend until gelatine is dissolved. Add remaining ingredients except orange; blend until smooth. Pour into small bowl; chill until consistency of unbeaten egg whites. Dice all but two orange sections; fold diced sections into gelatine mixture. Divide evenly into 2 small moulds; chill until set. Turn out and garnish each serving with one reserved orange section. Makes 2 midday meal servings.

Each serving is equivalent to: 1 serving Something Extra (1½ teaspoons gelatine); 5 oz Soft Cheese; ½ serving Fruit

Strawberry-Cheese Yogurt Pie

5 oz ripe strawberries	10 fl oz natural unsweetened
8-inch Pie Crust (see page 81)	yogurt
1½ teaspoons unflavoured gelatine	2 fl oz frozen orange juice
4 fl oz water	concentrate, thawed
10 oz cottage cheese	1 teaspoon vanilla flavouring

Set aside 4 small strawberries for garnish; slice remaining berries and arrange in bottom of baked pie crust. In small saucepan soften gelatine in water. Heat, stirring until dissolved. Combine with remaining ingredients in blender container. Blend until smooth. Pour into pie crust. Chill for several hours, until firm. Garnish with reserved berries. Divide evenly. Makes 4 midday meal servings. Supplement as required.

Each serving is equivalent to: ¾ serving Fruit; 8-inch Pie Crust (see page 81); ¼ serving Something Extra (⅜ teaspoon gelatine); 2½ oz Soft Cheese; ½ serving Milk (2½ fl oz yogurt)

BREAD AND CEREAL

 *

You can't live by bread alone, but it's the basic ingredient for our Croutons, Crumb Pie Crusts, Fruit Cake and Bread Stuffing. Gingerbread and Blueberry Muffins, Chocolate Currant Cake with Apricot Sauce, and three different pie crusts are included. So, too, are matzo recipes for the Passover Holiday only, and a crunchy granola made with wheat germ and sesame seeds. You can even use your allotted bread to make seasoned crumbs for 'oven-fried' fish and chicken. This chapter shows you how.

Rules for Using Bread, Rolls and Baps

1. Amounts:
   Women: 2 servings daily
   Men: 4 servings daily
   Teenagers: 4 servings daily
2. One serving must be taken at the morning meal unless Cereal or Choice Group is selected.
3. Use packaged, presliced white or whole grain bread or packaged rolls or baps weighing approximately 1 oz per serving; up to 75 calories per oz.
4. The bread must be eaten at mealtimes only; never between meals.
5. Approved breads include cracked wheat, pumpernickel, rye and currant.
6. Thin-sliced bread is 'legal' if 2 slices weigh approximately 1 oz and do not exceed 75 calories.

7. Once a week you may omit 2 servings of bread and select one of the following. These items should weigh approximately 2 oz each and contain about 150 calories.

   bagel or pita
   English muffin
   hamburger roll
   hard roll
   2 tortillas (6-inch diameter)
      or similar type bread

8. If the once-a-week bread item is selected at the midday or evening meal, women must have cereal for breakfast.

9. For the week of Passover only, ½ board of matzo—regular, egg, or wholemeal—may be used in place of one serving of bread.

Thin-Sliced Bread

Use the following for making Melba Toast (see page 80) and Toast Cups (see page 80–81)

1. Packaged, presliced, thin-sliced bread. (see rule 6).
2. A standard 1 oz slice of bread, cut horizontally in half. A very sharp knife will make it easier to slice bread in this fashion.

Breadcrumbs

The following is the procedure for making breadcrumbs. Cover blender container. Turn blender on high speed. Remove the clear plastic handle in the blender container cover. Tear each slice of bread into about 4 or 5 pieces. Drop each piece, one at a time, through the opening in the cover; place your hand over the opening to prevent crumbs from scattering. Continue until all bread is crumbled. If crumbs stop moving in blender container, empty container into a bowl and continue with remaining bread. Do not over-process. For large crumbs, leave blender on for a few seconds; for fine crumbs, process longer.

Breadcrumbs au Gratin

Use as a topping for vegetables before baking.

**1 slice white bread, made into   1 oz hard cheese, grated
  crumbs   1 teaspoon margarine**

In small bowl combine all ingredients. Makes 1 midday meal serving. Supplement as required.

Each serving is equivalent to: 1 serving Bread; 1 oz Hard Cheese; 1 serving Fat

'Buttery' Oven Toast

You get fine toast this way. Spread 1 slice white bread with 1 teaspoon margarine. Place on baking sheet, margarine side up. Bake at 400°F, Gas Mark 6, until browned. Makes 1 serving. Serve at mealtime only.

Each serving is equivalent to: 1 serving Bread; 1 serving Fat

Cheese Toast

Serve with tossed salad.

**1 slice white bread   ½ teaspoon sesame, poppy, or
1 teaspoon margarine   caraway seeds, or curry powder
1 oz hard cheese   to taste
prepared mustard to taste   salt and pepper to taste**

Spread bread with ½ teaspoon margarine. Top with cheese. Spread cheese with remaining margarine and mustard. Sprinkle with seeds or curry powder and salt and pepper. Bake at 375°F, Gas Mark 5, until cheese melts. Cut into 8 pieces. Makes 1 midday meal serving. Supplement as required.

Each serving is equivalent to: 1 serving Bread; 1 serving Fat; 1 oz Hard Cheese; ½ serving Something Extra (½ teaspoon seeds) (optional)

Croutons for Soup

1 slice white bread   garlic salt to taste

Cut bread into 8 pieces. Place on baking sheet. Bake at 300°F, Gas Mark 2, to 350°F, Gas Mark 4, until brown, turning several times, or grill 5 inches from source of heat. Check frequently to avoid burning and turn as necessary to brown all sides. When done, combine with garlic salt in plastic bag and shake. Divide evenly. Makes 2 servings. Serve at mealtime only.
  Each serving is equivalent to: ½ serving Bread

Italian Breadcrumbs

1 teaspoon salt   ¼ teaspoon rosemary
¼ teaspoon paprika   pinch garlic powder (optional)
¼ teaspoon basil   2 slices white bread, made into
¼ teaspoon oregano   crumbs

Combine seasonings in plastic bag. Add breadcrumbs and shake to mix. Divide evenly. Makes 4 servings. Serve at mealtime only.
  Each serving is equivalent to: ½ serving Bread

Seasoned Crumbs

2 slices white bread, made into   1 small garlic clove, mashed with 1
  crumbs   teaspoon salt
1 to 2 teaspoons fresh herbs   2 teaspoons margarine, melted

In a bowl combine first 3 ingredients. Add margarine and mix well. Divide evenly. Makes 4 servings. Serve at mealtime only.
  Each serving is equivalent to: ½ serving Bread; ½ serving Fat

Melba Toast

Use 2 thin slices white bread (see page 77 for explanation). Cut bread into halves or quarters and place on baking sheet. Bake at 250°F, Gas Mark 1, until crisp, turning as necessary. Makes 1 serving. Serve at mealtime only.

Each serving is equivalent to: 1 serving Bread

Curried Toast or Croutons

1 teaspoon margarine   pinch salt and pepper
⅛ teaspoon curry powder   1 slice white bread

In small bowl combine margarine, curry powder, salt and pepper. Spread over bread slice. Place on baking sheet; bake at 375°F, Gas Mark 5, for 7 minutes or until bread is crisp and golden. Serve hot, or cut into cubes and store in airtight container. When ready to use, reheat in oven to crisp. Makes 1 serving. Serve at mealtime only.

Each serving is equivalent to: 1 serving Fat; 1 serving Bread

Toast Cups—I

Use as shells, for 'creamed' fillings or salads.

6 thin slices white bread (see page 77)

Trim crust from bread. Reserve crust. Press one thin bread slice into each of 6 patty tins (3-inch diameter). Bake for 10 to 12 minutes at 350°F, Gas Mark 4, or until golden brown. Make crumbs from crusts by processing them in blender. Use crumbs, evenly divided, as topping for filled toast cups. Makes 3 servings, 2 toast cups each. Use at mealtime only.

Each serving is equivalent to: 1 serving Bread

Variation:

Miniature Toast Cups (for hors d'oeuvres)—Use the small patty tins (1½-inch diameter). Cut thin bread slices into quarters before proceeding. Makes 3 servings, 8 toast cups each.

Toast Cups—II

6 thin slices white bread (see page 77)
2 fl oz water

½ teaspoon vanilla flavouring
artificial sweetener to equal 1 teaspoon sugar, or to taste

Press each thin slice of bread into a patty tin (3-inch diameter). Combine remaining ingredients. Sprinkle bread with flavoured water. Bake for 12 to 14 minutes at 350°F, Gas Mark 4, or until golden brown. Makes 3 servings, 2 toast cups each. Use at mealtime only.

Each serving is equivalent to: 1 serving Bread

8-Inch Pie Crust

3 tablespoons water
¼ teaspoon vanilla flavouring

2 slices currant or white bread, made into crumbs

In a mixing bowl combine water and flavouring. Add breadcrumbs and stir with fork until crumbs are evenly moistened. Press into 8-inch pie dish. Bake at 400°F, Gas Mark 6, for 10 to 12 minutes. Cool. Divide evenly. Makes 2 or 4 servings. Use at mealtime only.

Each serving is equivalent to: 2 servings—1 serving Bread. 4 servings—½ serving Bread

9-Inch Pie Crust

2 tablespoons skim milk
¼ teaspoon vanilla flavouring

3 slices currant or white bread, toasted and made into crumbs

In mixing bowl, combine skim milk and flavouring. Add bread-crumbs and stir with fork until crumbs are evenly moistened. Press into 9-inch pie dish. Bake at 400°F, Gas Mark 6, for 10 to 12 minutes. Cool. Divide evenly. Makes 3 or 6 servings. Use at meal-time only.

Each serving is equivalent to: 3 servings—2 teaspoons Skim Milk; 1 serving Bread. 6 servings—1 teaspoon Skim Milk; ½ serving Bread

Oil Pie Crust

8 slices currant or white bread, made into crumbs

4 tablespoons vegetable oil
1 teaspoon vanilla flavouring

In bowl combine all ingredients. Mix well. Pat into 9 or 10-inch pie dish. Bake at 400°F, Gas Mark 6, for 10 minutes. Cool before filling. Divide evenly. Makes 8 or 16 servings. Use at mealtime only.

Each serving is equivalent to: 4 servings—2 serving Bread; 3 servings Fat: 8 servings—1 serving Bread; 1½ servings Fat. 16 servings—½ serving Bread; ¾ serving Fat

Bread Stuffing

There are dozens of ways to use this stuffing. Think of it as a filling for precooked green pepper, tomato, marrow or aubergine. Bake it in a casserole to accompany your Christmas bird. Or tuck it under your cooked chicken or fish just before serving.

2 oz celery, diced
8 fl oz Chicken Stock (see page 135)
2 slices day-old white bread, diced

salt and pepper to taste
¼ teaspoon thyme
¼ teaspoon savory

In saucepan cook celery in stock until celery is soft and stock is almost evaporated. Add bread and seasonings. Moisten with additional water, if stuffing is too dry. Heat and serve. Divide evenly.

Makes 2 servings. Serve at mealtime only.

Each serving is equivalent to: $^1/_3$ serving Vegetables; $^2/_3$ serving Something Extra (4 fl oz stock); 1 serving Bread

Instant 'Pizza'

1 English muffin, split and toasted
1½ oz (about 2 tablespoons)
   tomato purée
2 tablespoons water

¼ teaspoon oregano or Italian
   seasoning, or to taste
2 slices Mozzarella, Cheddar, or
   other hard cheese, 1 oz each

Mix tomato purée and water. Spread cut side of each muffin half with tomato mixture. Sprinkle each with ⅛ teaspoon oregano and top each with 1 oz cheese. Place under grill; grill just long enough to melt cheese. Makes 1 midday meal serving.

Each serving is equivalent to: 2 servings Bread (once-a-week selection); ¾ serving Bonus (1½ oz tomato purée); 2 oz Hard Cheese

Variations:

1. Omit 1 oz hard cheese. Arrange 1 oz drained canned tuna or sardines, flaked, on top of tomato purée on each muffin half. Sprinkle with oregano. Grate 1 oz hard cheese. Divide evenly over fish. Grill just until cheese melts. Makes 1 midday meal serving.

Each serving is equivalent to: 2 servings Bread (once-a-week selection); ¾ serving Bonus (1½ oz tomato purée); 2 oz Fish; 1 oz Hard Cheese.

2. Omit 1 oz hard cheese. Season tomato purée with minced chives or dried onion flakes to taste. Spread on muffin halves. Top each with ½ oz (about 1½ tablespoons) cooked, chopped, or sliced mushrooms and ½ oz grated hard cheese. Grill just until cheese melts. Makes 1 midday meal serving. Supplement as required.

Each serving is equivalent to: 2 servings Bread (once-a-week selection); ¾ serving Bonus (1½ oz tomato purée); $^1/_3$ serving Vegetables; 1 oz Hard Cheese.

3. Omit English muffin and use 2 thin slices white bread, toasted (see page 80). Proceed as above, in basic recipe. Makes 1 midday meal serving.

Each serving is equivalent to: 1 serving Bread; ¾ serving Bonus (1½ oz tomato purée); 2 oz Hard Cheese

Blackberry Muffins

1 slice currant bread, made into crumbs
1 oz nonfat dry milk
½ teaspoon baking powder
1 tablespoon water
½ teaspoon vanilla flavouring
1 standard egg, separated
5 oz blackberries

In bowl, combine first 3 ingredients. Add water, vanilla, egg yolk and blackberries. Stir to combine. In separate bowl beat egg white until stiff but not dry. Fold egg white into batter and pour into nonstick muffin tins. Bake at 350°F, Gas Mark 4, for 20 minutes. Makes 1 morning or midday meal serving. Supplement as required.

Each serving is equivalent to: 1 serving Bread; 1 serving Milk (10 fl oz skim milk); 1 Egg; 1 serving Fruit

Gingerbread

2 slices currant bread, made into crumbs
2 tablespoons flour
½ teaspoon cinnamon
⅛ teaspoon ginger
⅛ teaspoon nutmeg
10 fl oz skim milk
2 standard eggs, beaten
2 tablespoons margarine, melted

In bowl, combine first 5 ingredients. Stir in milk, eggs and margarine. Pour into small nonstick baking tin. Bake at 350°F, Gas Mark 4, for 40 minutes or until knife inserted in centre comes out clean. Divide evenly. Makes 2 morning or midday meal servings. Supplement as required.

Each serving is equivalent to: 1 serving Bread; 3 servings Something Extra (1 tablespoon flour); ½ serving Milk (5 fl oz skim milk); 1 Egg; 3 servings Fat

Prune Bread Custard

2 slices white bread, cut into cubes
10 fl oz skim milk
2 standard eggs, beaten
2½ fl oz prune juice
1 teaspoon vanilla flavouring

pinch salt
4 dried medium prunes, stoned
 and chopped
cinnamon to taste

Place half the bread cubes in each of 2 individual casseroles. Combine milk, eggs, prune juice, vanilla and salt in medium bowl. Divide evenly and pour over bread. Top each casserole with ½ of the chopped prunes. Sprinkle with cinnamon. Bake at 350°F, Gas Mark 4, for 45 minutes or until pudding is brown and knife inserted in centre comes out clean. Makes 2 morning or midday meal servings. Supplement as required.

Each serving is equivalent to: 1 serving Bread; ½ serving Milk (5 fl oz skim milk); 1 Egg; 1 serving Fruit

Chocolate Meringue Pie

1 tablespoon unflavoured gelatine
1 pint skim milk
artificial sweetener to equal 4
 teaspoons sugar, or to taste
¼ teaspoon salt
2 standard eggs, separated

1 tablespoon unsweetened cocoa,
 dissolved in 1 tablespoon water
½ teaspoon vanilla flavouring
8-inch Pie Crust (see page 81)
⅛ teaspoon cream of tartar

In saucepan sprinkle gelatine over milk to soften. Place over low heat and stir until gelatine dissolves. Remove from heat. Add sweetener to equal 2 teaspoons sugar, or to taste, and ⅛ teaspoon salt. In a bowl, beat egg yolks. Add a few teaspoons of hot milk mixture to beaten egg yolks, then stir yolks into milk. Blend in cocoa. Cook until mixture thickens slightly; remove from heat. Stir in vanilla. Pour into pie crust and refrigerate until firm. Beat egg whites with remaining sweetener and salt until frothy. Add cream of tartar and beat until mixture stands in stiff, glossy peaks. Spread over pie filling. Grill about 4 inches from heat for 30 seconds or until meringue is slightly browned. Serve at once or refrigerate and serve well chilled. Divide evenly. Makes 2 midday meal servings. Supplement as required.

Each serving is equivalent to: 2½ servings Something Extra (1½ teaspoons gelatine and 1½ teaspoons cocoa); 1 serving Milk (10 fl oz skim milk); 1 Egg; 8-inch Pie Crust (see page 81)

Variation:
Mocha Meringue Pie—Replace skim milk with 20 fl oz strong coffee. Reduce cocoa to 1¼ teaspoons, dissolved in 1¼ teaspoons water. Add 1½ teaspoons maple flavouring with the vanilla. Follow recipe as above. In equivalent listing, eliminate milk and change Something Extra to 1¾ servings (1½ teaspoons gelatine and ¾ teaspoon cocoa).

Chocolate Currant Cake with Apricot Sauce

4 standard eggs, separated
2 fl oz water
artificial sweetener to equal 5
   teaspoons sugar, or to taste
2 tablespoons plus 2 teaspoons
   unsweetened cocoa, dissolved in
   3 tablespoons water

4 slices currant bread, made into
   crumbs
Apricot Sauce (see following
   recipe)

Preheat oven to 350°F, Gas Mark 4. Line 9-inch round baking tin with foil; set aside. In mixing bowl combine egg yolks, water and sweetener. Beat for 5 minutes or until thick. Add cocoa and beat to combine. Fold in breadcrumbs. In separate bowl beat egg whites until stiff peaks form. Carefully fold whites into yolk mixture. Pour mixture into prepared baking tin; bake for 30 minutes or until firm. Remove from tin and cool on wire rack. To serve, top cake with ¾ of the Apricot Sauce. Divide into 4 equal portions and serve each portion with ¼ of remaining sauce. Makes 4 midday meal servings. Supplement as required.

Each serving is equivalent to: 1 Egg; 2 servings Something Extra (2 teaspoons cocoa); 1 serving Bread; Apricot Sauce (see following recipe)

Apricot Sauce

16 canned apricot halves with 8
   tablespoons juice, no sugar
   added

artificial sweetener to equal 1
   teaspoon sugar, or to taste
   (optional)

Dice apricots and set aside. In a small saucepan combine juice and sweetener; boil until liquid is reduced by ½. Stir in diced apricots. Cool. Divide evenly. Makes 4 servings.
   Each serving is equivalent to: 1 serving Fruit

Fruit Cake

4 oz nonfat dry milk
12 oz canned crushed pineapple,
   no sugar added, drained
   (reserve juice)
4 fl oz orange juice
10 oz cranberries, chopped
2 medium apples, peeled, cored,
   and grated

artificial sweetener to equal 4
   teaspoons sugar, or to taste
1 tablespoon lemon juice
1 teaspoon vanilla flavouring
8 slices currant bread, made into
   crumbs
¼ teaspoon cinnamon

Combine milk, pineapple juice and orange juice in a large bowl. Beat until frothy. Add remaining fruit, sweetener, lemon juice and vanilla. Combine breadcrumbs and cinnamon. Add to fruit mixture and mix well. Pour into 8 × 8 × 3-inch nonstick tin and bake at 350°F, Gas Mark 4, for 1 hour. Divide evenly. Makes 8 servings. Serve at mealtime only.
   Each serving is equivalent to: ½ serving Milk (5 fl oz skim milk); 1 serving Fruit; 1 serving Bread

Passover Recipes

For the Passover Holiday only, ½ board of egg, regular, or wholemeal matzo may be used in place of 1 slice of bread.

Apple Matzo Kugel (Pudding)

2 matzo boards, broken into pieces	1 teaspoon grated lemon rind
4 standard eggs, separated	artificial sweetener to equal 2
3 medium apples, peeled, cored	teaspoons sugar, or to taste
and grated	½ teaspoon salt
4 fl oz orange juice	¼ teaspoon cinnamon
1 teaspoon lemon juice	

In small bowl soak matzo in water until soft; drain in colander and squeeze dry. Transfer to medium bowl; add egg yolks, one at a time, mixing well after each addition. In a separate bowl combine grated apples, fruit juices, lemon rind, sweetener and seasonings; add to matzo mixture and stir well. Beat egg whites, in small bowl, until stiff but not dry; fold into matzo mixture. Place in 3-pint casserole and bake at 350°F, Gas Mark 4, for 1 hour or until top is browned. Divide evenly. Makes 4 midday meal servings. Supplement as required.

Each serving is equivalent to: 1 serving Bread; 1 Egg; 1 serving Fruit

Apple Orange Matzo Crumble

3 medium apples, peeled, cored	¼ teaspoon cinnamon
and diced	pinch ginger
4 fl oz orange juice	1 matzo board, made into crumbs
4 oz cooked pumpkin, mashed	⅛ teaspoon grated orange rind
artificial sweetener to equal 3	1 tablespoon plus 1 teaspoon
teaspoons sugar, or to taste	margarine, melted

Place apples and orange juice in medium saucepan, cook over medium heat until tender. Add pumpkin, artificial sweetener to equal 2 teaspoons sugar, or to taste, cinnamon and ginger; mix well. Divide evenly into 4 individual ovenproof puddings basins. In small bowl combine matzo crumbs, orange rind and remaining sweetener. Add margarine and mix until well blended. Divide crumb mixture evenly over fruit mixture. Bake at 425°F, Gas Mark 7, for 20 minutes. Serve hot or chilled. Makes 4 servings. Serve at mealtime only.

Each serving is equivalent to: 1 serving Fruit; 1 oz Limited Vegetable; ½ serving Bread; 1 serving Fat

Banana Pudding

2 matzo boards, broken into 2-inch
  pieces
4 standard eggs, beaten
12 fl oz water
2 oz nonfat dry milk

artificial sweetener to equal 2
  teaspoons sugar, or to taste
½ teaspoon vanilla flavouring
⅛ teaspoon cinnamon
½ teaspoon salt
2 medium bananas, sliced

Pour hot water over matzo in colander; drain. In medium bowl combine eggs, water, milk, sweetener, vanilla, cinnamon and salt. Fold in matzo and banana. Pour into 8 × 8 × 2-inch nonstick baking tin. Bake at 350°F, Gas Mark 4, for 50 minutes or until knife inserted in centre comes out clean. Serve warm or chilled. Divide evenly. Makes 4 midday meal servings. Supplement as required.

Each serving is equivalent to: 1 serving Bread; 1 Egg; ½ serving Milk (5 fl oz skim milk); 1 serving Fruit

Matzo Pie Crust

2 matzo boards, made into fine
  crumbs

2 tablespoons plus 2 teaspoons
  margarine
2 tablespoons water

Preheat oven to 375°F, Gas Mark 5. In medium bowl combine matzo crumbs and margarine. Using a fork or fingers, blend water into matzo. Press into sides and bottom of 8-inch pie dish. Bake for 8 to 10 minutes or until golden brown. Divide evenly. Makes 4 servings. Use at mealtime only.

Each serving is equivalent to: 1 serving Bread; 2 servings Fat

Passover Provençal Quiche

4 standard eggs, beaten	3 oz onion, diced
2 tablespoons margarine, melted	4 oz Cheddar cheese, diced
2 matzo boards	⅛ teaspoon garlic powder
8 oz tomatoes, peeled and sliced	salt and pepper to taste

Combine eggs and margarine in bowl. *Break one matzo board into quarters and soak in hot water in shallow pan until soft. Using spatula lift matzo from water. Gently press out moisture and place in 8 × 8 ×2-inch nonstick baking tin. Pour ¼ egg mixture over matzo. Arrange half of the tomato, onion and cheese over matzo. Season with half the garlic powder, salt and pepper. Repeat procedure from asterisk(*). Pour remaining egg mixture over top. Bake at 375°F, Gas Mark 5, for ½ hour or until knife inserted in centre comes out clean. Divide evenly. Makes 4 midday meal servings.

Each serving is equivalent to: 1 Egg; 1½ servings Fat; 1 serving Bread; ⅔ serving Vegetables; ¾ oz Limited Vegetables; 1 oz Hard Cheese

Spinach with Matzo

14 oz cooked spinach, chopped	4 oz cooked onion, chopped
10 oz cottage cheese	1 matzo board, made into crumbs
5 oz cooked mushrooms, chopped	¼ teaspoon onion powder
4 standard eggs, beaten	salt and pepper to taste

In large bowl combine all ingredients. Pour into 3-pint casserole; bake at 350°F, Gas Mark 4, for 40 minutes or until firm. Divide evenly. Makes 4 midday meal servings.

Each serving is equivalent to: 1⅔ servings Vegetables; 2½ oz Soft Cheese; 1 Egg; 1 oz Limited Vegetable; ½ serving Bread

Barbeque Fruit Sauce (page 285)   Coconut Bread Pudding (page 303)

Chinese Chicken with Green Peppers and Mushrooms (page 141)

Shrimp Chow Mein (page 326)

Cod Kebabs (page 327)

Sponge Cake

4 standard eggs, separated	1 teaspoon grated lemon rind
4 fl oz water	1 teaspoon vanilla flavouring
2 oz nonfat dry milk	2 matzo boards, made into crumbs
artificial sweetener to equal 9 teaspoons sugar, or to taste	

Preheat oven to 350°F, Gas Mark 4. In large bowl beat egg yolks until thick and lemon-coloured. Slowly add water, continuing to beat. One at a time add milk, artificial sweetener to equal 6 teaspoons sugar, or to taste, lemon rind and vanilla, beating after each addition. Fold in matzo crumbs. In medium bowl beat egg whites with remaining sweetener until stiff but not dry; fold into yolk mixture. Pour into 10-inch nonstick loaf tin. Bake for 35 minutes or until lightly browned. Remove from tin; cool. Divide evenly. Makes 4 midday meal servings. Supplement as required.

Each serving is equivalent to: 1 Egg; ½ serving Milk (5 fl oz skim milk); 1 serving Bread

Variation:

Mandelbrot—Prepare Sponge Cake adding ½ teaspoon almond flavouring with vanilla; slice into pieces about 1 inch thick. Arrange cut side down on a baking sheet; bake at 400°F, Gas Mark 6, for 10 minutes or until lightly toasted. Divide evenly.

Stuffed Fish Fillets

3 oz tomato, peeled and diced	1 matzo board, made into crumbs
1 oz mushrooms, chopped	4 fish fillets, 3 oz each
1 oz onion, finely chopped	salt, pepper and garlic powder to taste
3 tablespoons water	
2 tablespoons chopped parsley	lemon slices and parsley sprigs to garnish
1 garlic clove, crushed	
4 oz Cheddar cheese, diced	

In nonstick frying pan combine tomato, mushrooms, onion, water, parsley and garlic. Cook over medium heat, stirring occasionally, until onion is soft. Remove from heat. Stir in cheese and matzo crumbs; set aside. Sprinkle fish with salt, pepper, and garlic powder. Place each fillet in small individual ovenproof casserole. Spoon equal amounts of stuffing mixture over each fillet. Bake at 350°F, Gas Mark 4, for 20 minutes or until fish flakes easily at the touch of a fork. Garnish each serving with lemon slices and parsley sprigs. Makes 4 midday meal servings.

Each serving is equivalent to: $^1/_3$ serving Vegetables; ¼ oz Limited Vegetable; 1 oz Hard Cheese; ½ serving Bread; 2 oz Fish

Rules for Using Cereal

1. Amounts
   Women, Men and Teenagers: Ready-to-eat (not presweetened), 1 oz
   Uncooked, 1 oz
2. Select cereal at the morning meal only, up to 3 times weekly, if desired. When cereal is taken, bread may be taken at the morning meal or another meal. Cereal must be eaten with at least ½ serving of milk.
3. Approved ready-to-eat cereals include cornflakes, puffed wheat, sultana bran, wheat germ, bran etc. These may be used alone, or in any combination totalling 1 oz.
4. Examples of uncooked cereals are oatmeal and cream of wheat.
5. The following Choice Group items may be taken as Cereal Selections as well:
   cornmeal, 1 oz dry
   cracked wheat (Bulgur), 1 oz dry
   hominy grits, 6 oz cooked

Cooked Cereal with Fruit

Cook 1 oz uncooked cereal in 5 fl oz skim milk plus enough water to equal the amount of liquid indicated on package directions. Use a very low heat and stir constantly to avoid burning. Add seasoning as desired—pinch of salt, cinnamon. Just before cereal is done, stir in 4 stoned, diced, dried, medium prunes. Heat and serve. Other fruit may be substituted (see 'Fruit Servings' page 20). Makes 1 morning meal serving.

Each serving is equivalent to: 1 oz Cereal; ½ serving Milk (5 fl oz skim milk); 1 serving Fruit

Deep Dish Apple Pie

1 oz cornflakes, crushed
½ oz nonfat dry milk
artificial sweetener to equal 1
   teaspoon sugar, or to taste
¼ teaspoon vanilla flavouring.
⅛ teaspoon cinnamon

pinch nutmeg
3 tablespoons water
1 teaspoon margarine, melted
1 medium apple, peeled, cored and
   sliced
4 fl oz water

In medium bowl combine first 8 ingredients in order given. Press half of the cereal mixture in the bottom of small casserole. Set aside remaining mixture. In small saucepan combine apple and water. Cook until tender. Remove apple slices from saucepan with slotted spoon and reserve 3 tablespoons liquid. Layer apples in baking dish. Top with remaining crumbs and sprinkle with reserved liquid. Bake at 325°F, Gas Mark 3, for 20 minutes. Serve warm or chilled. Makes 1 morning meal serving.

Each serving is equivalent to: 1 oz Cereal; ½ serving Milk (5 fl oz skim milk); 1 serving Fat; 1 serving Fruit

Sesame Granola with Wheat Germ

4 oz nonfat dry milk
3 oz uncooked oatmeal
1 oz wheat germ
1 tablespoon plus 2 teaspoons flour
2 teaspoons sesame seeds
¼ teaspoon cinnamon
2 fl oz water

8 dried medium prunes, stoned
   and cut into small pieces
1 tablespoon plus 2 teaspoons
   vegetable oil
¼ teaspoon each vanilla and
   coconut flavouring (optional)

Combine nonfat dry milk, oatmeal, wheat germ, flour, sesame seeds and cinnamon in large bowl. In small saucepan combine water and prunes. Bring to boil; cook for 3 minutes. Remove from heat; stir

stir in oil and flavourings if desired. Combine with oatmeal mixture and spread in 13 × 9-inch baking tin. Bake at 325°F, Gas Mark 3, for 25 minutes, stirring occasionally. Allow to cool and store in a tightly closed container in refrigerator. Divide evenly. Makes 4 morning meal servings.

Each serving is equivalent to: 1 serving Milk (10 fl oz skim milk); 1 oz Cereal; 1¾ servings Something Extra (1¼ teaspoons flour and ½ teaspoon sesame seeds); ½ serving Fruit; 1¼ servings Fat

CHOICE GROUP

*

Can you believe—recipes for Mushroom and Barley Soup, Hot German Potato Salad, Pilaf, Risotto and Rice Stuffing to go with Christmas turkey! Here they are!

Rules for Using Choice Group

1. Omit 1 serving of bread and select one item from this list up to 3 times weekly, if desired:
   barley, 4 oz cooked
   buckwheat groats (kasha), 1 oz dry
   corn ear, 1 medium
   whole kernel or cream style, 3 oz
   cornmeal, 1 oz dry
   cracked wheat (Bulgur), 1 oz dry
   hominy grits, 6 oz cooked
   pasta, macaroni, spaghetti, or noodles, 3 oz cooked
   potato, fresh or canned, raw or cooked, 3 oz
   rice, white, brown or wild, 3 oz cooked
2. Choice Group items may be split evenly or split with ½ serving of bread, if consumed at the same meal. These combinations count as one of the three weekly Choice Group selections.
3. Canned Choice Group items containing sugar are 'illegal' except for canned corn.
4. Cornmeal, cracked wheat (Bulgur) and hominy grits may be taken as cereal selections as well as Choice Group items.

Barley and Vegetables

Use as a side dish.

6 fl oz Beef Stock (see page 157) 1 oz onion, chopped
2½ oz carrot, diced   4 oz cooked barley
2 oz white turnip, diced   salt and pepper to taste
1 oz celery, diced

Heat stock in a medium saucepan. Add vegetables and cook 15 minutes. Add barley; season with salt and pepper. Continue cooking until vegetables are tender and mixture becomes slightly thickened, stirring frequently. Serve hot. Makes 1 serving. Serve at mealtime only.

   Each serving is equivalent to: 1 serving Something Extra (6 fl oz stock); 1²/₃ servings Vegetable; 1 oz Limited Vegetable; 1 serving Choice Group

Mushroom and Barley Soup

1 pint 12 fl oz Beef Stock (see page   4 oz onion, diced
   157)   2 oz celery sticks, chopped
16 oz cooked barley, plus cooking   1 tablespoon chopped fresh parsley
   liquid   pinch nutmeg
14 oz mushrooms, thinly sliced   salt to taste
4 oz carrots, shredded

Combine all ingredients in large pot; cover and simmer slowly for 1½ hours, or until desired consistency. Divide evenly. Makes 4 servings. Serve at mealtime only.

   Each serving is equivalent to: 1¹/₃ servings Something Extra (8 fl oz stock); 1 serving Choice Group; 1²/₃ servings Vegetables; 1 oz Limited Vegetable

Boiled Corn

Drop 6 medium ears of husked corn into large pan of boiling salted water. Return water to boil, and cook corn for 5 minutes. Drain.

Serve hot with 1 teaspoon margarine for each ear. Sprinkle with salt, if desired. Makes 6 servings, 1 ear of corn each. Serve at mealtime only.

Each serving is equivalent to: 1 serving Choice Group; 1 serving Fat

'Cream' of Corn Soup

1 tablespoon margarine	pinch pepper and paprika
2 oz onion, finely diced	10 fl oz skim milk
1 tablespoon flour	6 oz canned cream style corn
⅛ teaspoon salt	1 tablespoon chopped fresh chives

Melt margarine in top of double boiler over boiling water. Add onion and cook for 4 minutes or until tender. Stir in flour, salt, pepper and paprika. Gradually add milk, and cook, stirring constantly, until thickened. Add corn; cook for 5 minutes, stirring frequently. Sprinkle with chives. Divide evenly. Makes 2 servings. Serve at mealtime only.

Each serving is equivalent to: 1½ servings Fat; 1 oz Limited Vegetable; 1½ servings Something Extra (1½ teaspoons flour); ½ serving Milk (5 fl oz skim milk); 1 serving Choice Group

Mamaliga

A Rumanian dish. It may be used as a breakfast cereal or served as a meat accompaniment in place of bread.

4 oz dry yellow cornmeal	1 teaspoon salt
8 fl oz cold water	1 pint 4 fl oz boiling water

In medium bowl combine cornmeal, cold water and salt. Gradually pour into boiling water in medium saucepan, stirring constantly. Return to boil, stirring constantly. Reduce heat; cover. Cook for 5 minutes, stirring occasionally For a thicker dish, let stand for 5 minutes before serving. Divide evenly. Makes 4 servings. Serve at mealtime only.

Each serving is equivalent to: 1 serving Choice Group or 1 oz Cereal

Variations:
1. Make a well in each serving of Mamaliga and add 1 oz crumbled feta cheese and 1 teaspoon margarine to each portion. Add garlic powder if desired. Makes 1 morning or midday meal serving. Supplement as required.

Each serving is equivalent to: 1 serving Choice Group; 1 oz Hard Cheese; 1 serving Fat

2. Stir 2½ oz cottage cheese into each serving of Mamaliga. Artificial sweetener and cinnamon may be added if desired. Makes 1 morning or midday meal serving. Supplement as required.

Each serving is equivalent to: 1 serving Choice Group; 2½ oz Soft Cheese

3. Mamaliga may be spooned into a loaf tin. It will firm up as it becomes cold. Slice and serve. To reheat Mamaliga, put 1 serving in individual casserole; top with 1 portion Ratatouille (see page 272), 1 serving vegetables, or 2 oz tomato purée mixed with 3 tablespoons water. Add 1 oz hard cheese, if desired. Cover; bake at 375°F, Gas Mark 5, for 20 to 30 minutes. Makes 1 midday meal serving. Supplement as required.

Each serving is equivalent to: 1 serving Choice Group; Ratatouille (see page 272) or 1 serving Vegetables or 1 serving Bonus (2 oz tomato purée); 1 oz Hard Cheese (optional)

Cornmeal Bread

A filling breakfast dish.

2 oz dry yellow cornmeal
¼ teaspoon salt
4 fl oz cold water
8 fl oz boiling water
1 oz nonfat dry milk
2 tablespoons flour

artificial sweetener to equal 1
    teaspoon sugar, or to taste
1 teaspoon baking powder·
2 standard eggs, beaten
2 tablespoons low-fat spread,
    melted
2 fl oz water

Stir cornmeal and salt into cold water in medium saucepan. Add boiling water; cook for 5 minutes. Remove from heat. In small bowl, combine remaining dry ingredients. Add eggs, low-fat spread and water, one at a time, mixing after each addition. Stir into cornmeal mixture. Pour into 8 × 8-inch baking tin. Bake at 425°F, Gas Mark 7, for 25 minutes or until firm. Divide evenly. Makes 2 morning or midday meal servings. Supplement as required.

Each serving is equivalent to: 1 serving Choice Group; ½ serving Milk (5 fl oz skim milk); 3 servings Something Extra (1 tablespoon flour); 1 Egg; 1½ servings Fat

Tamale Pie

The amount of chilli powder you use depends on how spicy you like your food.

6 oz green pepper, seeded and
  diced
2 oz onion, diced
1 garlic clove, crushed
12 oz cooked minced beef,
  crumbled, or boned cooked
  chicken, cut into strips
4 oz tomato purée
4 fl oz water

1 teaspoon chilli powder, or to
  taste
¾ teaspoon salt
½ teaspoon oregano
⅛ teaspoon cumin
pepper to taste
2 oz dry yellow cornmeal
4 fl oz cold water
8 fl oz boiling water

Cook green pepper, onion and garlic in large nonstick frying pan until browned. Add beef or chicken and tomato purée with 4 fl oz water; simmer for 5 minutes. Stir in chilli powder, ¼ teaspoon salt, oregano, cumin and pepper. Set aside. In a small saucepan combine cornmeal, cold water and remaining ½ teaspoon salt. Gradually add boiling water and cook, stirring constantly, for 5 minutes or until mixture thickens. Spread half the cornmeal mixture in 8 × 8-inch baking tin. Top with tomato mixture and spread with remaining cornmeal. Bake at 350°F, Gas Mark 4, for 30 minutes. Divide evenly. Makes 2 evening meal servings.

Each serving is equivalent to: 1 serving Vegetables; 1 oz Limited Vegetable; 6 oz 'Beef' Group or Poultry; 1 serving Bonus (2 oz tomato purée); 1 serving Choice Group

Cold Kasha or Bulgur Salad

4 oz dry buckwheat groats (kasha)
or cracked wheat (Bulgur)
4 oz drained canned water
chestnuts, sliced
4 oz cooked peas
4 oz tomato, peeled, seeded and
chopped
3 oz mushrooms, sliced
2½ oz cucumber, peeled, seeded
and chopped

1 oz celery, chopped
2 oz spring onions, chopped
2 tablespoons chopped fresh
parsley
½ oz drained canned pimiento,
chopped
Garlic French Dressing (see page
284)
lettuce

Cook buckwheat groats or cracked wheat in boiling salted water to
cover until tender. Drain. Place in bowl. Add all remaining ingredients except lettuce; mix well. Chill. Serve on bed of lettuce. Divide
evenly. Makes 4 servings. Serve at mealtime only.

Each serving is equivalent to: 1 serving Choice Group; 2½ oz
Limited Vegetable; 1 serving Vegetables; Garlic French Dressing
(see page 000)

Groats and Corn

1 oz dry buckwheat groats (kasha)
12 fl oz Chicken Stock (see page
135)

3 oz drained canned whole kernel
corn
salt and pepper to taste
2 teaspoons margarine

In medium saucepan cook buckwheat groats in boiling chicken
stock for 25 minutes or until groats are tender and stock is absorbed.
Stir in corn, salt and pepper, and heat. Remove from heat and stir
in margarine. Divide evenly. Makes 2 servings. Serve at mealtime
only.

Each serving is equivalent to: 1 serving Choice Group; 1 serving
Something Extra (6 fl oz stock); 1 serving Fat

Kasha or Bulgur

16 fl oz water or chicken bouillon
   (made with 3 stock cubes)
¼ teaspoon salt

dash pepper
4 oz dry buckwheat groats (kasha)
   or cracked wheat (Bulgur)

In medium saucepan combine water or bouillon, salt, and pepper. Bring to boil. Slowly stir in groats or cracked wheat. Cover and cook, stirring occasionally, over low heat for 10 to 15 minutes or until liquid is absorbed and grains are tender. Divide evenly. Makes 4 servings. Serve at mealtime only.

Each serving is equivalent to: ¾ serving Something Extra (¾ stock cube) (optional); 1 serving Choice Group

Variations:
Toasted Grains—Lightly brown the buckwheat groats or cracked wheat in shallow baking tin when the oven is in use. Stir grains so they don't burn. This takes only a few minutes and adds a roasted nutty flavour to the grains. Proceed as in above recipe.

Belila—A favourite Arabic breakfast is cracked wheat cooked until very soft in boiling water with a dash of cinnamon. Just before serving, it is sweetened. (Use artificial sweetener to equal 1 teaspoon sugar or to taste for each serving.) Serve with skim milk or natural unsweetened yogurt.

Pilaf

Use Beef Stock when serving Pilaf with meat, Chicken Stock when serving it with chicken.

12 fl oz Beef or Chicken Stock (see
   pages 157, 135)
5 oz carrots, diced
4 oz celery, diced

3 oz mushrooms, diced
4 oz dry buckwheat groats (kasha)
   or cracked wheat (Bulgur)

In medium saucepan combine stock and vegetables. Cover and cook for 20 minutes or until vegetables are tender. Remove from heat. Drain and measure liquid. Add enough water to measure 12 fl oz liquid. Return liquid to saucepan with vegetables. Bring to boil. Add kasha or Bulgur; reduce heat. Cover; cook for 10 to 15 minutes or until all liquid is absorbed. Divide evenly. Makes 4 servings. Serve at mealtime only.

Each serving is equivalent to: ½ serving Something Extra (3 fl oz stock); 1 serving Vegetables; 1 serving Choice Group

Quick Kasha Varnishkes

3 fl oz beef bouillon (made with ½ stock cube)
½ oz dry buckwheat groats (kasha)
1 oz mushrooms, sliced

1 oz onion, diced
1½ oz cooked bow-tie macaroni
1 teaspoon vegetable oil or margarine (optional)

In small saucepan bring stock to a boil. Add kasha; reduce heat. Cook until all liquid is absorbed. In small saucepan brown mushrooms and onion. Add kasha mixture and macaroni. Reheat, adding 1 or 2 tablespoons water, if necessary. Remove from heat. Stir in oil or margarine, if desired. Serve hot. Makes 1 serving. Serve at mealtime only.

Each serving is equivalent to: ½ serving Something Extra (½ stock cube); 1 serving Choice Group; ⅓ serving Vegetables; 1 oz Limited Vegetable; 1 serving Fat (optional)

Hominy Grits Three Ways

1. Hominy grits, like groats, is a word that stems from the Old English word for sand. Hominy grits is made from white or yellow corn. Prepare it according to package directions and, when thick and creamy, measure 6 oz per serving. Generally 3 to 4 tablespoons dry will make the right amount for each serving.   .

2. *Grits and Greens*: Steam 2 oz washed cabbage, kale, kohlrabi, spinach or turnip greens until soft. Season with seasoning salt and serve with 6 oz cooked hominy grits. Delicious as a side dish for pork. Makes 1 serving. Serve at mealtime only.

Each serving is equivalent to: $^2/_3$ serving Vegetables; 1 serving Choice Group

3. *Baked Grits and Cheese Casserole:* For each serving, transfer 6 oz cooked hominy grits to individual serving casserole, stir in ½ oz nonfat dry milk mixed with 4 tablespoons water, and top with 2 oz grated Cheddar, Parmesan cheese or other hard cheese. Bake at 350°F, Gas Mark 4, for 30 to 35 minutes or until top is brown and bubbly. Makes 1 midday meal serving.

Each serving is equivalent to: 1 serving Choice Group; ½ serving Milk (5 fl oz skim milk); 2 oz Hard Cheese

Cooking Noodles

Noodles are softer than macaroni, cook faster, and do not expand much during cooking. Prepare pasta according to package directions.

Variations on Basic Noodles:
1. Combine 3 oz hot cooked noodles, 2½ oz cottage cheese, 1 tablespoon margarine, 1 teaspoon toasted poppy seeds, a dash of Worcester sauce, salt, pepper and paprika. Makes 1 midday meal serving. Supplement as required.

Each serving is equivalent to: 1 serving Choice Group; 2½ oz Soft Cheese; 3 servings Fat; 1 serving Something Extra (1 teaspoon poppy seeds)

2. Combine 3 oz hot cooked noodles with 2 oz cooked diced onions and ¼ oz nonfat dry milk mixed with 2 tablespoons water. Makes 1 serving. Serve at mealtime only.

Each serving is equivalent to: 1 serving Choice Group; 2 oz Limited Vegetable; ¼ serving Milk (2½ fl oz skim milk)

3. Toss 3 oz hot cooked noodles with 1½ oz cooked ham and 1 oz grated hard cheese. Makes 1 midday meal serving.

Each serving is equivalent to: 1 serving Choice Group; 1½ oz 'Beef' Group (smoked); 1 oz Hard Cheese

4. Toss 3 oz hot cooked noodles with 3 oz cooked chopped spinach, 2½ fl oz natural unsweetened yogurt, and 1 teaspoon chives. Makes 1 serving. Serve at mealtime only.

Each serving is equivalent to: 1 serving Choice Group; 1 serving Vegetables; ½ serving Milk (2½ fl oz yogurt)

5. Combine 3 oz hot cooked noodles with 4 oz cooked chopped broccoli, 2½ oz cottage cheese, and 2 tablespoons chopped fresh parsley. Makes 1 midday meal serving. Supplement as required.

Each serving is equivalent to: 1 serving Choice Group; 1⅓ servings Vegetables; 2½ oz Soft Cheese

6. Arrange 3 oz cooked noodles in small baking tin. Dot with 2 teaspoons margarine. Bake at 350°F, Gas Mark 4, until brown. Makes 1 serving. Serve at mealtime only.

Each serving is equivalent to: 1 serving Choice Group; 2 servings Fat

7. Leftover noodles need not be wasted. Combine 1½ oz cooked noodles with ½ serving of cooked kasha, barley, (see 'Rules for Using Choice Group', page 95) . . . or whatever choice your refrigerator affords. Stir into 6 fl oz Chicken Stock (see page 135) or water with dissolved stock cube. Season to taste, if desired; freeze in small containers. Reheat in small saucepan as a hearty first course for midday or evening meal. As part of the morning meal, serve hot with 5 fl oz skim milk. Makes 1 serving. Serve at mealtime only.

Each serving is equivalent to: *Midday or evening meal*—1 serving Choice Group; 1 serving Something Extra (6 fl oz stock). *Morning meal*—1 serving Choice Group; 1 serving Something Extra (6 fl oz stock); ½ serving Milk (5 fl oz skim milk)

Baked Macaroni, Cheese and Cauliflower Casserole

8 oz cooked cauliflower florets
6 oz cooked elbow macaroni
4 oz drained canned mushrooms

salt and white pepper to taste
Creamy Cheese Sauce (see page 64)
paprika to garnish

In medium bowl combine all ingredients except paprika. Transfer to 2-pint shallow casserole. Sprinkle with paprika. Cover; bake at 350°F, Gas Mark 4, for 30 minutes. Uncover and bake for 5 minutes longer or until top begins to brown. Divide evenly. Makes 2 midday meal servings. Supplement as required.

Each serving is equivalent to: 2 servings Vegetables; 1 serving Choice Group; Creamy Cheese Sauce (see page 64)

Cold Macaroni Salad

12 oz cooked small tube macaroni
2 fl oz skim milk
6 oz green pepper, diced
4 oz onion, diced
4 oz tomato, diced
4 oz pickle, diced (reserve 2
    teaspoons brine)
9 fl oz natural unsweetened yogurt

4 tablespoons mayonnaise
1 beef stock cube, crumbled
1 garlic clove, crushed
¼ teaspoon salt
⅛ teaspoon white pepper
chopped fresh dill or chives to
    garnish

Place macaroni in large bowl and moisten with milk. Add diced vegetables and pickle. In small bowl combine yogurt, mayonnaise, reserved pickle brine, crumbled stock cube, garlic, salt and pepper. Pour over pasta mixture and toss to combine. Cover and refrigerate until chilled. Sprinkle with dill or chives. Divide evenly. Makes 4 servings. Serve at mealtime only.

Each serving is equivalent to: 1 serving Choice Group; ½ serving Milk (½ fl oz skim milk and 2¼ fl oz yogurt); $1^1/_{16}$ servings Vegetables; 1 oz Limited Vegetable; 3 servings Fat; ¼ serving Something Extra (¼ stock cube)

Noodle, Cheese and Prune Pudding

Cook the prunes with very little water so that when they are done, most of the liquid has evaporated, otherwise some of the sweet natural flavour of the fruit is lost in the liquid. We want it to stay in the fruit.

6 fl oz skim milk
6 dried medium prunes, cooked,
    stoned and chopped
artificial sweetener to equal 3
    teaspoons sugar, or to taste
1 tablespoon flour
¼ teaspoon cinnamon
1 lb 2 oz cooked noodles
15 oz cottage cheese

In medium bowl combine milk, prunes, sweetener, flour and cinnamon. Set aside. Combine noodles and cottage cheese in large bowl and transfer to 10 × 6 × 1¾-inch baking tin. Pour prune mixture over noodles. Bake at 375°F, Gas Mark 5, for 1 hour or until hot and bubbly. Divide evenly. Makes 6 midday meal servings. Supplement as required.

Each serving is equivalent to: $^1/_{10}$ serving Milk (1 fl oz skim milk); ¼ serving Fruit; ½ serving Something Extra (½ teaspoon flour); 1 serving Choice Group; 2½ oz Soft Cheese

Pasta Alfredo Style

Cook the pasta firm (al dente), and drain well. If the pasta is going to be used immediately, it is not necessary to rinse.

2 tablespoons margarine
2½ fl oz natural unsweetened
    yogurt
2 oz Parmesan cheese, grated
2 oz Cheddar cheese, diced
12 oz cooked spaghetti
salt and freshly ground pepper to
    taste
parsley sprigs and pimiento strips
    to garnish

Melt margarine in top of double boiler over hot water. Add the yogurt and cheese. Cook until cheese melts; add spaghetti. Mix well and season with salt and pepper. Serve hot. Garnish with parsley and pimiento. Divide evenly. Makes 4 midday meal servings. Supplement as required.

Each serving is equivalent to: 1½ servings Fat; ⅛ serving Milk (⅝ fl oz yogurt); 1 oz Hard Cheese; 1 serving Choice Group

Tips On Cooking Potatoes

Gently scrub potatoes under running water with a vegetable brush. Here are some tips on cooking potatoes which will help to prevent the loss of nutritional value:
1. When boiling, use as little water as possible.
2. Steaming potatoes is an excellent way to conserve their nutrients.
3. Leave skin on potatoes during cooking.
4. If potatoes are peeled before cooking, use a vegetable peeler, removing as thin a layer of skin as possible, since many of the nutrients are found close to the skin.
5. Peeled potatoes turn dark if not cooked right away. To keep them white, toss with a little lemon juice. Soaking in a bowl of cold water is not recommended as this usually results in a loss of vitamins.

Baked Potatoes

Pierce the skin of each 3 oz potato in several places with the prongs of a fork. This allows steam to escape and prevents the potato from bursting. Bake potatoes directly on oven rack or use a baking sheet. Oven temperature can range from 325°F, Gas Mark 3, to 450°F, Gas Mark 8. Potatoes are done when they feel soft. Baked potatoes can be wrapped in foil, frozen and reheated at 350°F, Gas Mark 4, for 1 hour. Serve at mealtime only. One potato (3 oz) is equivalent to 1 serving Choice Group.

Boiled Potatoes

In a covered saucepan cook potatoes in about 1 inch of salted water until tender. Check occasionally and add more water if necessary. Whole potatoes will take 30 to 40 minutes; cut up, 20 to 25 minutes. Weigh and serve 3 oz portions. Serve at mealtime only.
    Each serving is equivalent to: 1 serving Choice Group

Roast Potatoes

Prepare boiled potatoes and peel, or use drained canned potatoes. Pat dry and arrange in shallow nonstick baking tin; season with salt, pepper and paprika, and bake at 425°F, Gas Mark 7, turning occasionally until brown. Weigh and serve 3 oz portions. Serve at mealtime only.

Each serving is equivalent to: 1 serving Choice Group

Creamy Baked Potatoes

6 baked potatoes, 3 oz each
6 fl oz buttermilk
1 tablespoon chives
1½ teaspoons margarine, melted

½ teaspoon salt or to taste
pinch white pepper
paprika to garnish

Cut baked potatoes in half lengthwise. From one half of each, scoop out pulp, leaving a thin shell that maintains its shape. From other half, scoop out all the pulp and discard skin. In bowl, mash pulp and add remaining ingredients except paprika. Divide evenly and spoon into shells; sprinkle with paprika. Place on baking sheet, bake at 350°F, Gas Mark 4, for 25 minutes or until hot. Serve immediately. Makes 6 servings. Serve at mealtime only.

Each serving is equivalent to: 1 serving Choice Group; $^1/_{10}$ serving Milk (1 fl oz buttermilk); ¼ serving Fat

Curried Potato Soup

12 fl oz chicken bouillon (made
    with 2 stock cubes)
6 oz cooked potato, diced

Put the boullion into saucepan with the potato. Bring to boil, cover and simmer for 10 minutes or until potato is tender. Add the curry powder 2 to 3 minutes before the cooking time is completed. Serve sprinkled with parsley. Makes 2 servings. Serve at mealtime only.

Each serving is equivalent to: 1 serving Something Extra (1 stock cube); 1 serving Choice Group

Hot German Potato Salad

12 fl oz Ham Stock (see page 157)
4 fl oz water
1½ lbs peeled potatoes, cut into
   ¼-inch slices
4 oz onion, diced
1 oz celery, diced
1 tablespoon flour

2 fl oz cider vinegar
artificial sweetener to equal 2
   teaspoons sugar, or to taste
1½ teaspoons salt
½ teaspoon celery seed
¼ teaspoon pepper

In medium saucepan, bring stock and water to boil. Add potatoes; cook until tender but still firm. Using a slotted spoon, remove potatoes from stock; set aside. Add onion and celery to stock. Cook until vegetables are tender and stock is reduced to approximately 4 fl oz. In measuring jug dissolve flour in vinegar; add sweetener and seasonings. Stir into stock in saucepan; cook until thickened. Pour over potatoes and toss gently. Serve at once. Divide evenly. Makes 8 servings. Serve at mealtime only.

Each serving is equivalent to: ⅝ serving Something Extra (1½ fl oz stock and ⅜ teaspoon flour); 1 serving Choice Group; ½ oz Limited Vegetable; ⅛ oz Vegetables

Oven-Baked Potato Fans (in foil)

Make this when your oven is in use. For each serving, place a 3 oz scrubbed potato on a board and with a sharp knife, slice down at ¼-inch intervals, almost through to the bottom. Place each potato on a square of heavy duty aluminum foil. For each potato melt 1 teaspoon margarine in small flameproof pan. Remove from heat; add salt, pepper, chives and paprika to taste. Brush one portion mixture into slices of each potato. Wrap tightly in foil. Bake at 400°F, Gas Mark 6, for 45 minutes or until potato is tender. Open at the table and eat out of the foil. Serve at mealtime only.

Each serving is equivalent to: 1 serving Choice Group; 1 serving Fat

Potato Bake

6 oz peeled potato, grated
2 standard eggs
1 tablespoon plus 1 teaspoon
   margarine, melted

1½ oz onion, grated
½ teaspoon salt
⅛ teaspoon baking powder
pinch white pepper

Place potato in strainer and squeeze out excess moisture. Beat eggs in bowl until thick. Stir in potatoes and remaining ingredients. Place in shallow nonstick 1-pint casserole. Bake at 350°F, Gas Mark 4, for 50 minutes or until golden. Divide evenly. Makes 2 midday meal servings. Supplement as required.

Each serving is equivalent to: 1 serving Choice Group; 1 Egg; 2 servings Fat; ¾ oz Limited Vegetable

Potato Yogurt Salad

10 fl oz natural unsweetened
   yogurt
2 teaspoons prepared mustard
2 teaspoons prepared horseradish
1½ lbs peeled cooked potatoes,
   cubed

6 oz cucumber, peeled and sliced
2 oz celery, thinly sliced
2 tablespoons dried onion flakes,
   reconstituted
1 tablespoon chopped fresh chives

In small bowl combine yogurt, mustard and horseradish. Combine remaining ingredients in large bowl. Pour yogurt mixture over salad and toss to combine. Refrigerate until chilled. Divide evenly. Makes 8 servings. Serve at mealtime only.

Each serving is equivalent to: ¼ serving Milk (1¼ fl oz yogurt); 1 serving Choice Group; ⅓ serving Vegetables

Puréed Potatoes

For a planned leftover, you can boil extra potatoes and put them through food mill or potato masher, then freeze in 3 oz patties and reheat on foil with oven meal.

1 lb 2 oz peeled potatoes
1¼ teaspoons salt
6 fl oz skim milk

3 tablespoons margarine, at room
   temperature
pinch nutmeg, or to taste

Slice or quarter potatoes and place in saucepan. Add boiling water to cover and 1 teaspoon salt. Return to boil, lower heat, and simmer for 20 minutes or until potatoes are tender. Drain. Put potatoes through food mill or potato masher. Heat milk in medium saucepan. Slowly stir in potatoes. Continue stirring until well heated through. Remove from heat; stir in margarine, remaining ¼ teaspoon salt and nutmeg. Divide evenly. Makes 6 servings. Serve at mealtime only.

Each serving is equivalent to: 1 serving Choice Group; $^1/_{10}$ serving Milk (1 fl oz skim milk); 1½ servings Fat

Variation: Cook 9 oz shredded cabbage or cauliflower florets in boiling salted water to cover until very tender, for 20 minutes. Drain and combine with Puréed Potatoes. Season with additional salt and sprinkle with white pepper. A treat with ham or roast beef. Divide evenly. Makes 6 servings. Serve at mealtime only. Add ½ serving Vegetables to equivalent listing.

Basic Rice

Rice may be cooked on top of stove or in the oven; cooking times and amounts will vary according to the brand of rice; however, follow package directions. When cooked, be sure to measure 3 oz servings. Here's one cooking method.

1¼ pints water
8 oz uncooked rice
1 teaspoon salt

In saucepan combine all ingredients. Bring to boil; reduce heat, cover and simmer for 20 to 30 minutes. Remove from heat and let stand for 15 to 20 minutes. Measure 3 oz cooked rice for each serving. Serve at mealtime only.

Each serving is equivalent to: 1 serving Choice Group

Reheating—Combine 6 oz cooked rice with 2 tablespoons water in saucepan. Cover and cook over low heat for 4 minutes or until thoroughly heated. Divide evenly. Makes 2 servings. Serve at mealtime only.

Each serving is equivalent to: 1 serving Choice Group

Brown Rice—Use the same measurements as in basic recipe. Simmer, covered, for 45 minutes or until all water is absorbed. Measure 3 oz cooked brown rice for each serving. Serve at mealtime only. To reheat, follow preceding method.

Each serving is equivalent to: 1 serving Choice Group

Curried Rice and Prune Salad

6 oz cooked rice
1 teaspoon lemon juice
1 teaspoon vegetable oil
½ teaspoon curry powder
6 oz green pepper, seeded and
    finely diced

8 dried medium prunes, cooked,
    stoned and chopped
5 fl oz natural unsweetened yogurt
5 teaspoons mayonnaise
salt to taste
lettuce leaves or watercress

Combine all ingredients, except lettuce or watercress, in bowl in order given. Mix well; press mixture gently into 1-pint mould; chill. Turn out on plate. Surround with lettuce or watercress. Divide evenly. Makes 2 servings. Serve at mealtime only.

Each serving is equivalent to: 1 serving Choice Group; 3 servings Fat; 1 serving Vegetables; 1 serving Fruit; ½ serving Milk (2½ fl oz yogurt)

Crunchy Tangerine Salad

6 oz cooked rice
2 large tangerines, peeled and
    sectioned
2 oz cooked peas

2 oz drained canned water
    chestnuts, diced
Tangy French Dressing (see page
    314)
salt to taste

Combine all ingredients in bowl in order given. Divide evenly. Makes 2 servings. Serve at mealtime only.

Each serving is equivalent to: 1 serving Choice Group; 1 serving Fruit; 2 oz Limited Vegetable; Tangy French Dressing (see page 314)

Minted Rice

Serve with lamb.

12 oz cooked rice
1 tablespoon chopped fresh parsley
2 teaspoons finely chopped fresh mint, or 1 teaspoon dried mint

salt to taste
2 teaspoons margarine

In medium saucepan combine rice, parsley, mint and salt. Cook, stirring constantly, until heated through. Add a little water if necessary to prevent sticking. Remove from heat, stir in margarine. Divide evenly. Makes 4 servings. Serve at mealtime only.

Each serving is equivalent to: 1 serving Choice Group; ½ serving Fat

Mushroom Risotto

½ oz dried mushrooms
6 oz onion, diced
½ teaspoon turmeric

salt and pepper to taste
1 lb 2 oz cooked rice

In bowl soak mushrooms in hot water to cover for 20 minutes. Drain and reserve liquid. Cut off and discard stems; chop mushroom caps. Brown onion in preheated nonstick frying pan. Add chopped mushrooms and mushroom liquid, turmeric, salt and pepper. Heat to evaporate liquid. Stir in rice and reheat. Divide evenly. Makes 6 servings. Serve at mealtime only.

Each serving is equivalent to: ⅙ serving Vegetables; 1 oz Limited Vegetables; 1 serving Choice Group

Toasted Rice and Vermicelli

For a nutty flavour, start with 8 oz uncooked white rice. Spread rice in thin layer in shallow baking pan. Bake at 350°F, Gas Mark 4, to 425°F, Gas Mark 7, whenever oven is on, for 10 to 20 minutes or until rice is brown. Store in airtight container and cook, following package directions like ordinary white rice.

Break 8 oz uncooked vermicelli or fine egg noodles into ½-inch lengths. Follow above instructions for toasting. Check frequently, as this burns easily. When ready to cook, follow package directions for vermicelli or egg noodles.

4 oz onion, diced
1 garlic clove, crushed
6 oz cooked vermicelli, made from
   toasted vermicelli (see above)
6 oz cooked rice, made from
   toasted rice (see above)

3 fl oz Chicken Stock (see page
   135)
3 tablespoons chopped fresh
   parsley

In preheated saucepan brown the onion and garlic, stirring to prevent scorching. Add vermicelli, rice, Chicken Stock, and parsley. Simmer uncovered until mixture is almost dry, stirring occasionally. Divide evenly. Makes 4 servings. Serve at mealtime only.

Each serving is equivalent to: 1 oz Limited Vegetable; 1 serving Choice Group; ⅛ serving Something Extra (¾ fl oz stock)

Basic Wild Rice

1½ pints water
1 teaspoon salt
8 oz uncooked wild rice

In saucepan bring water and salt to boil. Stir in rice and return to boil. Reduce heat, cover and simmer for 40 minutes or until tender. Do not overcook; drain any excess liquid. Measure 3 oz cooked rice for each serving. Serve at mealtime only.

Each serving is equivalent to: 1 serving Choice Group

Wild Rice Stuffing

serve with chicken
3 oz green pepper, seeded and
  chopped
2 oz celery, chopped
2 oz onion, chopped

1½ oz mushrooms, sliced
6 fl oz chicken bouillon (made with
  1 stock cube)
1½ lbs cooked wild rice
1 teaspoon sage

In medium saucepan cook green pepper, celery, onion and mushrooms in bouillon until soft. Add wild rice and sage; mix well. Transfer to 3-pint baking dish and bake at 350°F, Gas Mark 4, for ½ hour. Divide evenly. Makes 8 servings. Serve at mealtime only.

Each serving is equivalent to: ¼ serving Vegetables; ¼ oz Limited Vegetable; ⅛ serving Something Extra (⅛ stock cube); 1 serving Choice Group

Wild Rice Casserole

Wild rice, the grain of a water reed, has a unique flavour. Use it by itself if you're feeling extravagant, or stretch it by mixing it with cooked brown rice, cooked Bulgur, or cooked egg noodles. For seasonings try dried chives, parsley or marjoram.

12 oz cooked wild rice
6 oz mushrooms, sliced
2 teaspoons flour
5 fl oz skim milk
1 teaspoon dried onion flakes,
  reconstituted in 2 teaspoons
  water

1 small bay leaf
¼ teaspoon thyme
pinch nutmeg
salt and pepper to taste
4 fl oz Chicken Stock* (optional,
  see page 135)

In a 3-pint ovenproof casserole combine wild rice and mushrooms. Sprinkle with flour and mix well. In small saucepan, scald milk with onion flakes and bay leaf. Remove and discard bay leaf; add milk to mushroom-rice mixture. Cook, stirring often, until rice mixture thickens slightly. Season with thyme, nutmeg, salt and pepper. Bake at 350°F, Gas Mark 4, for 15 to 20 minutes. To adjust consistency, add stock if desired. Serve hot. Divide evenly. Makes 4 servings. Serve at mealtime only.

Each serving is equivalent to: 1 serving Choice Group; ½ serving Vegetables; ½ serving Something Extra (½ teaspoon flour); ⅛ serving Milk (1¼ fl oz skim milk)

Note: If Chicken Stock is used, add an additional ⅙ serving Something Extra (1 fl oz stock) to equivalent listing.

Ham and Wild Rice Salad

A delicious midday meal using leftovers.

3 oz cooked wild or white rice
½ teaspoon cider vinegar
salt and pepper to taste
1 tablespoon mayonnaise
2 oz cooked peas
1½ oz cooked ham, diced

1 oz Cheddar cheese, grated, or 1 standard egg, hard-boiled and chopped
½ oz pickled cucumber, chopped
1 teaspoon chives

In bowl combine rice, vinegar, salt and pepper. Stir in mayonnaise. Add remaining ingredients; toss. Chill. Makes 1 midday meal serving.

Each serving is equivalent to: 1 serving Choice Group; 3 servings Fat; 1 oz Limited Vegetable; 1½ oz 'Beef' Group (smoked); 1 oz Hard Cheese; 1 Egg ⅙ serving Vegetables

MILK

*

Milk shakes? Mousses? Puddings? The names sound sinful on the Weight Watchers Food Programme—but they're all here, prepared our way, with lots of delicious flavours.

We've brought you recipes such as Peach Drink, Apple-Strawberry Whisk, Brandylike Alexander, and we tell you how to make yogurt at home, with ribbons of fruit folded in for the perfect snack food.

Rules for Using Milk

1. Amounts
   Women and Men: 2 servings daily
   Teenagers: 3 to 4 servings daily
2. Select servings at any time:
   milk, skim, ½ pint (10 fl oz)
   buttermilk, ½ pint (10 fl oz)
   yogurt, natural unsweetened, ¼ pint (5 fl oz)
3. The skim milk we allow is the instant nonfat dry milk, reconstituted according to label directions; or commercially prepared liquid skim milk with no whole milk solids added.
4. You may use your milk at any time—at meals, as snacks, in coffee or tea, or in our popular milk shakes and whipped toppings—but you must consume the amount allotted to you in your Menu Plan.
5. Mix-and-match your milk, if you like. For example, a woman may use 1 serving skim milk (10 fl oz) and 1 serving natural, sweetened yogurt (5 fl oz) to complete the daily requirement.

Brandylike Alexander

4 fl oz water
1 oz nonfat dry milk
1½ teaspoons brandy or rum
  flavouring

artificial sweetener to equal 2
  teaspoons sugar, or to taste
4 to 5 ice cubes
nutmeg to taste

Combine all ingredients except nutmeg in blender container. Blend until frothy. Divide evenly into 2 stemmed glasses. Top each with a pinch of nutmeg. Makes 2 servings.

Each serving is equivalent to: ½ serving Milk (5 fl oz skim milk)

Cappuccino Chiller

16 fl oz double-strength coffee
1 pint skim milk

cinnamon to taste
8 cinnamon sticks, optional

Refrigerate coffee in large container for 30 minutes. Add milk; chill. Divide evenly into 8 tall glasses. Add ice if desired. Sprinkle each with cinnamon. Garnish each with a cinnamon stick if desired. Makes 8 servings.

Each serving is equivalent to: ¼ serving Milk (2½ fl oz skim milk)

Hot Chocolate

12 fl oz water
2 teaspoons unsweetened cocoa
2 oz nonfat dry milk

artificial sweetener to equal 4
  teaspoons sugar, or to taste

Bring water to the boil in small saucepan; stir in cocoa until dissolved. Remove from heat. Stir in remaining ingredients, using a wire whisk, or transfer to blender container and blend until smooth. Divide evenly. Makes 2 servings.

Each serving is equivalent to: 1 serving Something Extra (1 teaspoon cocoa); 1 serving Milk (10 fl oz skim milk)

Chocolate Milk Shake

10 fl oz skim milk
artificial sweetener to equal 1
    teaspoon sugar, or to taste
1½ teaspoons unsweetened cocoa

½ teaspoon instant coffee
½ teaspoon vanilla flavouring
3 ice cubes

Combine all ingredients except ice cubes in blender container; blend until frothy. Add ice cubes one at a time, blending after each addition. Serve in tall glass. Makes 1 serving.

Each serving is equivalent to: 1 serving Milk (10 fl oz skim milk); 1½ servings Something Extra (1½ teaspoons cocoa)

Variations:
Double-Strength Milk Shake—Use 2 oz nonfat dry milk and 10 fl oz water to replace 10 fl oz skim milk. Continue as above. Flavouring may be varied to taste. Add 1 serving Milk (10 fl oz skim milk) to equivalent listing.

Super Milk Shake—Use 1 oz nonfat dry milk and 8 fl oz any flavour low-calorie carbonated beverage in place of 10 fl oz skim milk. Flavouring and sweetener may be omitted. Proceed as in basic recipe.

Fruit Shake—Omit cocoa and coffee from basic recipe. Add one of the following: ½ medium banana, 5 oz strawberries, 1 medium peach, stoned, or any other desired fruit (see 'Fruit Servings,' page 20). Blend as in basic recipe above.

Each serving is equivalent to: 1 serving Milk (10 fl oz skim milk); 1 serving Fruit

Orange Shake—In blender container, blend the following: 10 fl oz skim milk, 4 fl oz orange juice, 1 medium orange, peeled and cut up, 2 tablespoons lemon juice, artificial sweetener to equal 1 teaspoon sugar, or to taste, and 4 ice cubes. Divide evenly. Makes 2 servings.

Each serving is equivalent to: ½ serving Milk (5 fl oz skim milk); 1 serving Fruit

Peach Drink

4 oz canned sliced peaches, no
    sugar added
1 oz nonfat dry milk

3 fl oz water
1 fl oz low-calorie orange-flavoured
    carbonated beverage

Combine all ingredients in blender container. Process until well blended, about 20 seconds. Serve in a tall glass, over ice. Makes 1 serving.

Each serving is equivalent to: 1 serving Fruit; 1 serving Milk (10 fl oz skim milk)

Tangy Strawberry Shake

5 fl oz buttermilk
2½ oz strawberries

artificial sweetener to equal 1
    teaspoon sugar, or to taste
    (optional)
¼ teaspoon lemon juice

Combine all ingredients in blender container. Blend until smooth. Pour into a tall glass. Serve immediately. Makes 1 serving.

Each serving is equivalent to: ½ serving Milk (5 fl oz buttermilk); ½ serving Fruit

Tiger Tiger

1 oz nonfat dry milk
6 fl oz water
2 tablespoons frozen orange juice
    concentrate

1 teaspoon safflower oil
½ teaspoon vanilla flavouring
3 ice cubes (optional)

Combine all ingredients except ice cubes in blender container and blend at low speed. If desired, add ice cubes, one at a time, and blend until smooth. Divide evenly. Makes 2 servings. Serve at mealtime only.

Each serving is equivalent to: ½ serving Milk (5 fl oz skim milk); ½ serving Fruit; ½ serving Fat

Apple-Berry Cheese Mousse

2 tablespoons unflavoured gelatine	2 medium apples, cored, peeled
2 fl oz cold water	and quartered
2 fl oz boiling water	artificial sweetener to equal 2 to 3
10 oz cottage cheese	teaspoons sugar, or to taste
5 fl oz buttermilk	5 oz frozen blackberries or
2 slices white bread	blueberries, no sugar added

In blender container sprinkle gelatine over cold water to soften. Add boiling water; blend until dissolved. Add remaining ingredients except berries, and blend until smooth. Pour mixture into 9 × 9 × 2-inch baking dish. Top with berries. Place in refrigerator until firm. Divide evenly. Makes 2 midday meal servings.

Each serving is equivalent to: 2 servings Something Extra (1 tablespoon gelatine); 5 oz Soft Cheese; ¼ serving Milk (2½ fl oz buttermilk); 1 serving Bread; 1½ servings Fruit

Apple-Strawberry Whisk

1 tablespoon unflavoured gelatine	artificial sweetener to equal 4
2 fl oz cold water	teaspoons sugar, or to taste
3 fl oz boiling water	¼ teaspoon strawberry flavouring
2 oz nonfat dry milk	8 to 10 ice cubes
2½ oz strawberries (reserve 2	½ medium apple, peeled, cored
strawberries)	and sliced

In blender container sprinkle gelatine over cold water to soften. Add boiling water; blend until dissolved. Add milk, strawberries, sweetener and flavouring. Blend until smooth. Add ice cubes, two at a time, blending after each addition. Fold apple into mixture; divide evenly into 2 dessert glasses. Top each with a whole strawberry and chill. Makes 2 servings.

Each serving is equivalent to: 1 serving Something Extra (1½ teaspoons gelatine); 1 serving Milk (10 fl oz skim milk); ½ serving Fruit

Blackberry Pudding

1 tablespoon unflavoured gelatine	5 fl oz buttermilk
2 fl oz cold water	artificial sweetener to equal 4
2 fl oz boiling water	teaspoons sugar, or to taste
10 oz fresh or frozen blackberries	few drops lemon or vanilla
or blueberries, no sugar added	flavouring

In blender container sprinkle gelatine over cold water to soften. Add boiling water and blend until dissolved. Add 5 oz berries and remaining ingredients; blend until smooth. Fold in remaining berries. Divide evenly into 2 dessert glasses. Chill. Makes 2 servings.

Each serving is equivalent to: 1 serving Something Extra (1½ teaspoons gelatine); 1 serving Fruit; ¼ serving Milk (2½ fl oz buttermilk

Cinnamon Peach Dessert

1 oz nonfat dry milk	1 medium peach, peeled, stoned
6 fl oz water	and diced
2 teaspoons unflavoured gelatine	¼ teaspoon brandy flavouring
artificial sweetener to equal 2 to 3	pinch cinnamon
teaspoons sugar, or to taste	

Mix dry milk with water. In saucepan sprinkle gelatine over milk to soften; add sweetener. Heat, stirring constantly, until gelatine has dissolved. DO NOT BOIL. Remove from heat; add peach and flavouring. Cool. When on the point of setting, whisk well with rotary or electric beater. Pour into small dish; sprinkle with cinnamon and chill for 1 hour. Makes 1 serving.

Each serving is equivalent to: $1^1/_3$ servings Something Extra (2 teaspoons gelatine); 1 serving Milk (10 fl oz skim milk); 1 serving Fruit

Iced Borscht (page 245)

Pineapple Cole Slaw (page 323)

Bulgur Salad (page 100) and Pasta Alfredo Style (page 106)

Fruit Cottage Cheese Ring (page 60)

Coriander Lamb (page 325)

Beef with Peppers and Tomatoes (page 162)

Orange Custard

2 oz nonfat dry milk
16 fl oz water
4 standard eggs
½ teaspoon grated orange rind
¼ teaspoon cinnamon

⅛ teaspoon nutmeg
3 teaspoons artificial sweetener to
    equal 3 teaspoons sugar, or to
    taste

Scald milk in a saucepan, remove from heat, allow to stand for a few minutes. Add remaining ingredients, and whisk well together. Divide evenly into 4 individual ovenproof custard cups. Place in shallow pan containing 1 inch water. Bake at 350°F, Gas Mark 4, for 25 minutes or until a knife inserted in the centre comes out clean. Makes 4 morning or midday meal servings. Supplement as required.

Each serving is equivalent to: ½ serving Milk (5 fl oz skim milk); 1 Egg

Frozen Dessert

1 tablespoon unflavoured gelatine
2 fl oz cold water
2 fl oz boiling water
1 oz nonfat dry milk

artificial sweetener to equal 2 to 3
    teaspoons sugar, or to taste
½ teaspoon vanilla or other
    flavouring
6 to 8 ice cubes

In blender container sprinkle gelatine over water to soften. Add boiling water; blend to dissolve gelatine. Add milk, sweetener and flavouring. Blend until smooth. Add ice cubes, one at a time, blending after each addition. Makes 1 serving.

Each serving is equivalent to: 2 servings Something Extra (1 tablespoon gelatine); 1 serving Milk (10 fl oz skim milk)

Frozen Peach 'Cream'

2 oz nonfat dry milk
12 fl oz water
2 standard eggs, beaten
½ teaspoon vanilla flavouring

artificial sweetener to equal 4
   teaspoons sugar, or to taste
2 medium peaches, peeled and
   stoned

In bowl combine dry milk and water; pour $^2/_3$ mixture into saucepan and scald. Remove from heat. Stir in beaten eggs. Return to low heat; cook, stirring constantly, until thickened. Remove from heat and pour into blender container. Add remaining milk mixture, vanilla, artificial sweetener and 1 peach. Blend until smooth. Dice remaining peach; add to mixture. Pour into freezer trays and freeze until almost firm. Remove from freezer; transfer to bowl and beat. Serve immediately. Makes 2 midday meal servings. Supplement as required.

Each serving is equivalent to: 1 serving Milk (10 fl oz skim milk); 1 Egg; 1 serving Fruit

Hawaiian Mousse

2 tablespoons unflavoured gelatine
1 pint 4 fl oz water
3 oz nonfat dry milk
½ teaspoon rum flavouring
½ teaspoon coconut flavouring

¼ teaspoon vanilla flavouring
artificial sweetener to equal 2
   teaspoons sugar, or to taste
12 oz canned crushed pineapple,
   no sugar added

In medium saucepan sprinkle gelatine over 8 fl oz water; heat, stirring until gelatine is dissolved. Pour gelatine mixture into blender container; add remaining water, dry milk, flavourings and sweetener. Blend at low speed until smooth. Add pineapple, blend at medium speed until smooth. Pour into 3-pint mould. Chill. Turn out. Divide evenly. Makes 6 servings.

Each serving is equivalent to: $^2/_3$ serving Something Extra (1 teaspoon gelatine); ½ serving Milk (5 fl oz skim milk); ½ serving Fruit

Hot Lemon Custard

A delicious sauce over fruit.

2 standard eggs, well beaten
artificial sweetener to equal 1
   teaspoon sugar, or to taste
¼ teaspoon lemon flavouring

1 oz nonfat dry milk
8 fl oz water
2 Baked Apples (see page 23)

In bowl combine eggs, sweetener and flavourings; mix well. Combine milk and water in top of double boiler; heat over boiling water until milk forms tiny bubbles round the edges. Gradually stir milk into beaten eggs. Return to double boiler and heat until mixture thickens. Do not overcook. Divide evenly and serve each portion over one Baked Apple. Makes 2 midday meal servings. Supplement as required.

Each serving is equivalent to: 1 Egg; ½ serving Milk (5 fl oz skim milk); 1 serving Fruit

Pears With Chocolate Sauce

1 tablespoon plus 1 teaspoon
   unsweetened cocoa
2 tablespoons water
2 teaspoons cornflour
1½ oz nonfat dry milk, dissolved
   in 6 fl oz water

artificial sweetener to equal 2
   teaspoons sugar, or to taste
12 canned pear halves with 12
   tablespoons juice, no sugar
   added

Combine cocoa, water, and cornflour in a small saucepan and stir until completely dissolved. Add milk and cook, stirring constantly, until mixture comes to a boil. Remove from heat; add sweetener. Cover and chill. Place 2 pear halves and 2 tablespoons juice in each of 6 dessert dishes. Top each with equal amounts of sauce. Makes 6 servings.

Each serving is equivalent to: 1 serving Something Extra (⅔ teaspoon cocoa and ⅓ teaspoon cornflour); ¼ serving Milk (2½ fl oz skim milk); 1 serving Fruit

Strawberry-Orange Soufflé

8 fl oz orange juice
12 fl oz water
1 tablespoon unflavoured gelatine
few drops strawberry flavouring
artificial sweetener to equal 6
teaspoons sugar, or to taste
2 oz nonfat dry milk
2 tablespoons lemon juice

In medium saucepan combine orange juice and 4 fl oz water. Bring to boil. Remove from heat, sprinkle in gelatine, flavouring and sweetener. Stir to dissolve gelatine. Dissolve nonfat dry milk in 8 fl oz water; mix with gelatine and lemon juice. Chill until syrupy, then whisk well until thick and foamy. Divide evenly into 4 individual soufflé dishes. Chill until set. Makes 4 servings, 1 soufflé each.

Each serving is equivalent to: ½ serving Fruit; ½ serving Something Extra (¾ teaspoon gelatine); ½ serving Milk (5 fl oz skim milk)

Courgette Soup

1½ lbs courgettes, diced
4 oz onion, diced
3 teaspoons chicken stock powder
½ bay leaf
2 pints water
4 oz nonfat dry milk
1 teaspoon Worcester sauce
pinch nutmeg
salt and white pepper to taste

In large saucepan combine courgettes, onion, stock powder and bay leaf. Stir together over low heat for 10 minutes. Add water. Bring to boil. Reduce heat. Simmer 10 minutes. Remove from heat. Discard bay leaf. Place in blender container; blend until smooth. Return mixture to saucepan. Bring to boil. Add dry milk, Worcester sauce and nutmeg. Stir until dry milk has dissolved. Season to taste. Heat thoroughly but DO NOT BOIL. Divide evenly. Makes 4 servings.

Each serving is equivalent to: 2 servings Vegetables; 1 oz Limited Vegetable; ¾ serving Something Extra (¾ teaspoon stock powder); 1 serving Milk (10 fl oz skim milk)

Homemade Yogurt

2 pints less 2 tablespoons skim
milk (or reconstituted nonfat
dry milk)

1 tablespoon natural unsweetened
yogurt

In a large saucepan, heat milk to 110° to 115°F (or lukewarm) over
direct heat. (For better control, use the top of a double boiler over
boiling water.) Add yogurt and mix well with a wire whisk. Divide
evenly into yogurt-maker containers and blend, following manufacturer's instructions. When thick and creamy, place in refrigerator
until chilled. Divide evenly. Makes 4 servings.

Each serving is equivalent to: 1 serving Milk (5 fl oz yogurt).

Tips on controlling homemade yogurt: For a less tangy yogurt,
refrigerate as soon as it is thick. Check every 2 hours. For tart
yogurt do not refrigerate as promptly.

Cucumber and Yogurt Salad

A cooling salad for a hot summer day. Serve with a barbecued
kebab.

6 oz cucumber, peeled, seeded and
diced
10 fl oz natural unsweetened
yogurt

1 tablespoon chopped fresh mint
½ garlic clove, crushed
¼ teaspoon salt

Combine all ingredients in a bowl. Divide evenly. Makes 4 servings.

Each serving is equivalent to: ½ serving Vegetables; ½ serving
Milk (2½ fl oz yogurt)

Labneh

An Israeli treat.

5 fl oz natural unsweetened yogurt
1 teaspoon sesame oil

1 teaspoon chopped mint
pinch salt

Place yogurt in serving dish. Sprinkle with remaining ingredients. Serve chilled as a dip with raw vegetables. Makes 1 serving. Serve at mealtime only.

Each serving is equivalent to: 1 serving Milk (5 fl oz yogurt); 1 serving Fat

Yogurt Combinations—Delicious Snacks

1. Reserve juice from 1 serving drained canned fruit, no sugar added. Add fruit, crushed or puréed, to 10 fl oz natural unsweetened yogurt. In saucepan cook reserved fruit juice until reduced to about 1 teaspoon and stir into yogurt mixture. Makes 1 serving.

Each serving is equivalent to: 1 serving Fruit; 2 servings Milk (10 fl oz yogurt)

2. In bowl, mash 1 very ripe medium banana. Add 10 fl oz natural unsweetened yogurt and spoon equal amounts of mixture into each of 2 dessert dishes. Chill in freezer. Before serving sprinkle with cinnamon or instant coffee if desired. Makes 2 servings.

Each serving is equivalent to: 1 serving Fruit; 1 serving Milk (5 fl oz yogurt)

3. In saucepan cook 4 dried medium prunes in a little water until very soft. Continue cooking until almost all liquid is evaporated. Stone prunes and purée. In bowl combine prunes with 10 fl oz natural unsweetened yogurt. Divide evenly into 2 dessert dishes. Chill and serve. Makes 2 servings.

Each serving is equivalent to: ½ serving Fruit; 1 serving Milk (5 fl oz yogurt)

4. In bowl whip 2 fl oz frozen orange juice concentrate with 10 fl oz natural unsweetened yogurt. Transfer to freezer tray and freeze to soft mush. Return to bowl and beat. Refreeze until consistency of sorbet. Divide evenly. Makes 2 servings.

Each serving is equivalent to: 1 serving Fruit; 1 serving Milk (5 fl oz yogurt)

Yogurt Milk Shake

5 fl oz skim milk
5 oz blackberries or blueberries
2½ fl oz natural unsweetened
   yogurt

artificial sweetener to equal 1
   teaspoon sugar, or to taste
¼ teaspoon vanilla flavouring
3 ice cubes

Combine all ingredients, except ice cubes, in blender container. Blend until smooth. Add ice cubes. Blend until frothy. Serve at once. Makes 1 serving.

Each serving is equivalent to: 1 serving Milk (5 fl oz skim milk and 2½ fl oz yogurt); 1 serving Fruit

Yogurt Pineapple Sorbet

10 fl oz natural unsweetened
   yogurt
8 oz canned crushed pineapple, no
   sugar added

artificial sweetener to equal 2
   teaspoons sugar, or to taste
4 mint sprigs

Place yogurt in freezer tray; freeze until soft crystals form. Remove from freezer and transfer to bowl; beat well. Add fruit and sweetener; stir to combine. Return mixture to freezer tray; refreeze until soft crystals form. Remove from freezer and transfer to bowl; beat well and return to freezer. When chilled to firm consistency, divide evenly into 4 dessert glasses. Garnish with mint. Makes 4 servings.

Each serving is equivalent to: ½ serving milk (2½ fl oz yogurt); ½ serving Fruit

POULTRY, VEAL AND GAME

*

Some rewarding taste adventures await you here. Our test kitchen experts have created and adapted a number of unusual poultry, veal and game dishes; Chicken Curry in Cantaloupe, Foil-Baked Chicken Rolls, Chicken Pilaf, Easy Chicken Mousse, Apple-Glazed Veal, Turkey Terrapin and many others.. We also show you how to make a flavoursome stock. In short, some good things for you and your family appear in these pages.

Rules for Using Poultry, Veal and Game

1. Amounts (net cooked weight):
   Women, Men and Teenagers: 1 oz at the morning meal
   3 to 4 oz at the midday meal
   Women and Teenagers: 4 to 6 oz at the evening meal
   Men: 6 to 8 oz at the evening meal
2. The range of 3 to 4 oz of poultry, veal and game at the midday meal, and 4 to 6 oz for Women and Teenagers (6 to 8 oz for Men) at the evening meal, provides flexibility. It is a way to individualise the Food Plan to meet your specific needs.
3. If smoked poultry or game is selected, use the lower end of the serving range.
4. Select chicken, turkey, other poultry (not duck or goose), veal, or wild game. Serve poultry with skin removed.
5. As a 'rule of thumb', for each serving of poultry, veal or game, allow 2 oz for shrinkage in cooking and 2 oz for bone. When splitting an item from the poultry, veal and game category, for each

half-serving, allow 1 oz for shrinkage in cooking and 1 oz for bone. Weigh the serving after cooking, whenever possible.

6. *Cooking Procedures:*

Poultry and Game

May be boiled, poached, grilled, dry-fried, roasted or baked. Remove skin before eating.

If boiled with the skin, do not consume liquid. If boiled without the skin, liquid may be consumed. Refrigerate liquid; remove congealed fat. 6 fl oz equal one serving of bouillon or stock.

If skin is removed, poultry (or game) may be browned in a nonstick frying pan, or baked in a casserole with either raw or cooked ingredients. All ingredients may be consumed.

Veal

May be boiled, grilled, dry-fried, roasted or baked.

If boiled, liquid may be consumed. Refrigerate liquid; remove congealed fat. 6 fl oz equal one serving of bouillon or stock.

If browned in a nonstick frying pan: (a) transfer veal to another pan before adding raw or cooked ingredients; or (b) wipe pan clean before adding other ingredients.

If cooked in liquid (e.g. tomato juice or bouillon), veal must be removed from liquid with a slotted spatula. Whatever adheres to the veal may be consumed. Discard all other liquid.

Cooked veal may be used with added ingredients (e.g. casseroles, stews etc.). Liquid and added ingredients may be consumed.

Raw minced veal may be combined with other ingredients such as fruit, eggs, cheese, bread, Choice Group items, milk, vegetables and items from all categories in the Optional section only if boiled or baked (not grilled) on a rack.

Basic Roast Chicken

6 fl oz chicken bouillon (prepared with 1 stock cube)
1 tablespoon finely chopped celery
1 tablespoon dried onion flakes

1 teaspoon dried sweet pepper flakes
salt and pepper to taste
5 to 6 lb chicken

In small saucepan combine first 5 ingredients and simmer for 15 minutes. Place chicken breast side up, on rack in shallow, uncovered roasting pan. Roast at 325°F, Gas Mark 3, allowing about 20 minutes per lb. If meat thermometer is used, insert into centre of the inner thigh muscle. Cook to an internal temperature of 180° to 185°F. Baste frequently with stock mixture. Remove skin and weigh portions. Makes about 8 evening meal servings.

Each serving is equivalent to: ⅛ serving Something Extra (⅛ stock cube); 6 oz Poultry

Grilled Chicken

2½ to 3 lb chicken, cut in halves, quarters or pieces   **salt and pepper to taste**

Sprinkle chicken with salt and pepper. Place skin side down on rack in grill pan. Grill 3 to 6 inches from source of heat. Grill for 20 to 25 minutes, turn and grill for 15 to 20 minutes or until fork-tender. Remove skin. Weigh portions and serve. Makes 4 evening meal servings.

Each serving is equivalent to: 6 oz Poultry

Variations:

1. Combine 2 fl oz Chicken Stock (see page 135), 2 tablespoons chopped fresh tarragon and 2 teaspoons lemon juice. Pour over chicken and let stand for 1 hour. Drain before grilling. Heat marinade and serve with chicken. Add $^{1}/_{12}$ serving Something Extra (½ fl oz stock) to equivalent listing.

2. For each serving, spread 1 teaspoon low-calorie Italian or herb dressing over chicken before grilling. Add 1 teaspoon Speciality Food to equivalent listing.

3. Season chicken with garlic, lemon juice, salt, pepper and paprika before grilling.

Pan-Grilled Chicken

Remove skin from cut-up chicken. If desired bone and pound pieces flat so they brown evenly. Preheat nonstick frying pan. Add chicken and brown on all sides over moderate heat. Reduce heat and continue cooking, uncovered, turning the chicken frequently until cooked to desired degree of tenderness. Pan-grilled chicken is the basis for many different dishes.

Poached Chicken

Poaching is an excellent method for cooking skinned and boned chicken breasts and other skinned chicken portions. In wide shallow saucepan, bring to boil enough water to cover chicken. Reduce heat. Add chicken in one layer; cover and simmer until chicken is done, approximately 20 to 30 minutes, depending on size of chicken pieces. Remove chicken from liquid; serve or chill for later use. Poaching liquid may be chilled until fat congeals. Remove and discard fat. Liquid can be used in recipes calling for chicken stock.
   6 fl oz of liquid is equivalent to: 1 serving Something Extra

Poached Chicken in Sauce

Basic White Sauce (see page 278)
⅛ teaspoon nutmeg
⅛ teaspoon Worcester sauce
1 lb cooked broccoli florets

8 oz skinned and boned poached chicken
4 oz Cheddar or other hard cheese, grated

Combine Basic White Sauce, nutmeg and Worcester sauce; set aside. In ovenproof dish arrange broccoli and chicken. Pour sauce over chicken and top with cheese. Bake at 400°F, Gas Mark 6, for approximately 15 minutes or until chicken and sauce are hot and cheese is melted and bubbly. Divide evenly. Makes 4 midday meal servings.

Each serving is equivalent to: Basic White Sauce (see page 28); 1⅓ servings Vegetables; 2 oz Poultry; 1 oz Hard Cheese

Roast Chicken

5 to 6 lb chicken
salt and pepper to taste
6 fl oz Chicken Stock (see page 135) or

2 tablespoons plus 2 teaspoons low-calorie salad dressing
¼ teaspoon paprika

Wash and dry chicken. Remove skin. Sprinkle neck, body cavities and surface with salt and pepper. Place chicken in shallow pan. Combine stock or salad dressing with paprika and brush 1 tablespoon over chicken. Roast at 375°F, Gas Mark 5, for approximately 30 minutes per pound. Baste every 20 minutes with paprika mixture. Chicken is done when drumstick meat feels soft when pressed between fingers and leg twists easily out of thigh joint. Carve and weigh portions. Makes about 8 evening meal servings.

Each serving is equivalent to: 6 oz Poultry; ⅛ serving Something Extra (¾ fl oz stock) or 1 teaspoon Speciality Food

Simmered Chicken

5 to 6 lb chicken, skinned and cut in pieces
1¼ pints water
4 oz onion, sliced
2 oz carrots, sliced

2 oz celery stalks, chopped
1 teaspoon salt
3 peppercorns

In large saucepan combine chicken, water, onion, carrots, celery and salt. Bring to boil, then reduce heat and simmer for 15 minutes. Remove any scum that forms on surface. Cover and continue simmering for 1 hour; add peppercorns and continue simmering for another hour or until meat is tender. Do not boil rapidly as this toughens the meat. Remove chicken from liquid and use immediately if desired or chill and use in recipes calling for cooked chicken. Weigh portions. Makes about 8 evening meal servings.

Each serving is equivalent to: 6 oz Poultry

If desired, strain and refrigerate cooking liquid. Remove and discard congealed fat. Use liquid in recipes which call for chicken stock.

6 fl oz liquid is equivalent to: 1 serving Something Extra

Note: If vegetables are consumed, add $1/6$ serving Vegetables and ½ oz Limited Vegetable to equivalent listing.

Chicken Stock

2 chicken carcasses	**3 parsley sprigs**
3½ pints water	**1 bay leaf**
1 celery stick with leaves, sliced	**¼ teaspoon thyme**
6 peppercorns	**salt to taste**

Combine all ingredients in large saucepan. Bring to boil; reduce heat. Simmer for 1½ hours. Strain and remove solids. Refrigerate liquid; remove congealed fat. Divide into 6 fl oz portions.

Each serving is equivalent to: 1 serving Something Extra (6 fl oz stock)

Variations:

Thickened Stock—In small saucepan mix 2 tablespoons flour with 2 tablespoons water; stir in 12 fl oz Chicken Stock. Cook, stirring constantly, until thickened. Reduce heat and simmer for 7 minutes. Use as a sauce for cooked poultry. Divide evenly. Makes 4 servings.

Each serving is equivalent to: 2 servings Something Extra (1½ teaspoons flour and 3 fl oz stock)

Indian Style Stock—In small saucepan combine 16 fl oz Chicken Stock, 1 cinnamon stick and 2 crushed cardamom seeds. Simmer, covered, for 15 minutes. Strain to remove solids. Divide evenly. Makes 4 servings.

Each serving is equivalent to: $2/3$ serving Something Extra (4 fl oz stock)

Double-Strength Chicken Stock—To each 6 fl oz of hot Chicken Stock, add 1 teaspoon chicken stock powder.

Each serving is equivalent to: 2 servings Something Extra (6 fl oz stock and 1 teaspoon stock powder)

Extra-Strength Chicken Stock—For each serving, in saucepan simmer 6 fl oz Chicken Stock until it is reduced by half.

Each serving is equivalent to: 1 serving Something Extra (6 fl oz stock)

Garnishes—(1) Float slices of lemon or shreds of colourful rind on 6 fl oz hot stock.

(2) Add ½ oz shredded lettuce to 6 fl oz hot Chicken Stock before serving.

Each serving is equivalent to: $^1/_6$ serving Vegetables; 1 serving Something Extra (6 fl oz stock)

Tomato-Chicken Stock—Combine 6 fl oz Chicken Stock, 3 oz tomato, peeled, seeded and diced, and herbs to taste in small saucepan. Heat thoroughly. Try fresh or dried chives, dill, mint, parsley, rosemary, or tarragon.

Each serving is equivalent to: 1 serving Something Extra (6 fl oz stock); 1 serving Vegetables

Chicken Stock with Seeds—Sprinkle 6 fl oz hot Chicken Stock with 1 teaspoon caraway, poppy or sesame seeds just before serving. Toast the sesame seeds if desired.

Each serving is equivalent to: 2 servings Something Extra (6 fl oz stock and 1 teaspoon seeds)

Storing Stock

Refrigerate stock up to 2 days, or freeze in freezer containers in 6 fl oz or 12 fl oz containers. If freezing in glass jars, leave room for expansion.

Thrift Tips

Keep a small container in your freezer for trimmings from celery, mushrooms, and other vegetables. Use in preparation of stock.

Chicken in the Pot

For each serving combine 6 fl oz Chicken Stock (see page 135), 1 oz diced celery and 1 oz diced carrots in saucepan. Cover and simmer until vegetables are tender. Add 3 oz cooked diced chicken; continue cooking for 5 minutes. If desired, add 3 oz cooked rice or noodles. Makes 1 evening meal serving. Supplement as required.

Each serving is equivalent to: 1 serving Something Extra (6 fl oz stock); $^2/_3$ serving Vegetables; 3 oz Poultry; 1 serving Choice Group (optional)

Chicken Soup with Vegetables

3½ pints water
1 lb chicken pieces, skinned
4 oz carrots, sliced
4 oz celery, sliced
2 oz onion, diced

3 parsley sprigs
1 bay leaf
¼ teaspoon thyme
salt and freshly ground pepper to taste

Combine all ingredients except salt and pepper in a saucepan. Simmer for 1 hour. Season with salt and pepper. Discard parsley and bay leaf. Refrigerate soup; remove and discard congealed fat.* Measure 1 pint 4 fl oz liquid. Remaining liquid can be frozen to be used at another time; 6 fl oz is equivalent to 1 serving bouillon or stock. Combine measured liquid with solids in saucepan. Bring to boil; lower heat. Simmer until chicken and vegetables are heated throughout. Divide evenly into large soup bowls. Makes 2 midday meal servings.

Each serving is equivalent to: 4 oz Poultry; 1⅓ servings Vegetables; 1 oz Limited Vegetable; 2 servings Something Extra (12 fl oz stock)

California Orange Chicken Salad

8 oz cooked chicken, diced
10 oz cottage cheese
2 medium oranges, peeled and
    diced
4 oz drained canned water
    chestnuts, sliced
2 oz celery, diced

2 tablespoons mayonnaise
1 tablespoon grated fresh orange
    rind
½ teaspoon salt
⅛ teaspoon white pepper
4 large lettuce leaves

*If fat is difficult to remove, line a strainer with 4 layers of muslin or a wet heavy paper towel. Place strainer over a bowl. Pour liquid with fat through muslin or towel. Discard fat.

In bowl combine all ingredients except lettuce. Form lettuce into 4 cups; divide chicken mixture evenly into 4 lettuce cups. Makes 4 midday meal servings.

Each serving is equivalent to: 2 oz Poultry; 2½ oz Soft Cheese; ½ serving Fruit; 1 oz Limited Vegetable; ⅙ serving Vegetables; 1½ servings Fat

Variations:
1. Omit cottage cheese and use 4 oz diced Cheddar cheese. Season with ⅛ teaspoon hot sauce. Serve with sliced radishes. Substitute 1 oz Hard Cheese for 2½ oz Soft Cheese in equivalent listing.

2. Omit oranges and use 2 medium apples, peeled, cored, diced and sprinkled with lemon juice. Add 9 oz blanched chopped bean sprouts and 3 oz dill pickle, diced. Increase mayonnaise to 4 tablespoons.

Each serving is equivalent to: 2 oz Poultry; 2½ oz Soft Cheese; ½ serving Fruit; 1 oz Limited Vegetable; 1⅙ servings Vegetables; 3 servings Fat

Chicken Curry in Cantaloupe

6 oz poached chicken, diced
¼ recipe Curry Sauce (1 serving, see page 278)

1 oz drained canned water chestnuts, diced
½ medium cantaloupe melon

In bowl combine chicken, Curry Sauce and water chestnuts; set aside. Using a melon baller, scoop out all of the pulp from cantaloupe, leaving rind intact. Fill rind with chicken mixture and garnish with melon balls. Serve chilled. Makes 1 evening meal serving.

Each serving is equivalent to: 6 oz Poultry; Curry Sauce (see page 278); 1 oz Limited Vegetable; 1 serving Fruit

Easy Chicken Mousse

1 tablespoon unflavoured gelatine
4 fl oz water
6 fl oz Double-Strength Chicken
Stock (see page 135)
4 tablespoons mayonnaise
1 tablespoon lemon juice
¼ teaspoon white pepper
salt to taste

10 fl oz natural unsweetened
yogurt
1 lb cooked chicken, diced
2 oz celery, diced
6 oz cooked asparagus spears,
chilled
4 oz drained canned pimiento, cut
in strips

In saucepan sprinkle gelatine over water to soften. Heat, stirring constantly until gelatine is dissolved. In bowl combine stock, mayonnaise, lemon juice, pepper and salt; stir in gelatine mixture and milk; refrigerate until consistency of unbeaten egg whites, about 15 minutes. Fold in chicken and celery. Pour into large ring mould. Chill until firm. Turn out on serving plate. Fill centre with asparagus. Garnish with pimientos. Divide evenly. Makes 4 midday meal servings.

Each serving is equivalent to: 1 serving Something Extra (¾ teaspoon gelatine and 1½ fl oz Double-Strength Stock); 3 servings Fat; ½ serving Milk (2½ fl oz yogurt); 4 oz Poultry; 1 serving Vegetables

Chicken and Egg Loaf

12 oz cooked chicken
3 oz carrots, sliced
1 standard egg, hard-boiled
1 oz canned pimiento
3 slices white bread, made into
crumbs
5 standard eggs, beaten

2 teaspoons lemon juice
½ teaspoon salt
¼ teaspoon hot sauce
⅛ teaspoon white pepper
1½ recipes Tomato Sauce (6
servings, see page 288)

Put chicken, carrots, hard-boiled egg, and pimiento through mincer. Stir in the breadcrumbs, beaten eggs, lemon juice, salt, hot sauce and pepper. Transfer to nonstick loaf tin. Bake at 350°F, Gas Mark 4, for 30 minutes or until firm. Slice and serve with Tomato Sauce. Divide evenly. Makes 6 midday meal servings.

Each serving is equivalent to: 2 oz Poultry; $\frac{1}{6}$ serving Vegetables; 1 Egg; ½ serving Bread; Tomato Sauce (see page 288)

Chicken and Sardine Acapulco

A Mexican dish inspired this recipe for combining leftovers.

1 oz onion, diced	2 oz drained canned sardines,
1 small garlic clove, crushed	flaked
3 oz tomato, chopped	½ hot chilli pepper, seeded and
2 fl oz Chicken Stock (see page	minced
135)	salt and pepper to taste
1 teaspoon chopped fresh parsley	shredded lettuce to garnish
2 oz cooked chicken, diced	

Brown onion and garlic in nonstick frying pan. Add tomato, stock and parsley, and cook for 10 minutes. Add chicken, sardines and chilli pepper. Simmer, uncovered, for 15 minutes or until chicken is well heated through. Season with salt and pepper. Serve garnished with lettuce. Makes 1 midday meal serving.

Each serving is equivalent to: 1 oz Limited Vegetable; 1 serving Vegetables; $\frac{1}{3}$ serving Something Extra (2 fl oz stock); 2 oz Poultry; 2 oz Fish

Chicken Pilaf

12 fl oz Chicken Stock (see page	3 oz peeled potato, cut into ½-inch
135)	dice
3 oz cooked brown rice	pinch cinnamon
8 canned plums with 8 tablespoons	pinch cumin
juice, no sugar added, stoned	12 oz poached chicken, diced
and diced	

In medium saucepan combine all ingredients except chicken. Cover and simmer for 30 minutes or until potato is tender. Add chicken and heat until chicken is thoroughly hot. Divide evenly. Makes 2 evening meal servings.

Each serving is equivalent to: 1 serving Something Extra (6 fl oz stock); 1 serving Choice Group; 2 servings Fruit; 6 oz Poultry

Poached Chicken with Yogurt

Tart and refreshing on a summer day.

5 fl oz natural unsweetened yogurt
1 tablespoon plus 2 teaspoons flour
6 fl oz Chicken Stock (see page 135)
4 fl oz water
1 oz spring onions, diced

1 tablespoon lemon juice
½ teaspoon salt
6 oz cucumber, peeled and diced
12 oz poached chicken breasts, cut into 1½-inch pieces

In small bowl combine yogurt and flour. Set aside. In saucepan combine remaining ingredients except cucumber and chicken. Bring to boil. Reduce heat. Stir in yogurt mixture. Simmer, stirring constantly, until sauce is thickened. Add cucumber. Heat thoroughly. Serve over chicken. Divide evenly. Makes 2 evening meal servings.

Each serving is equivalent to: ½ serving Milk (2½ fl oz yogurt); 3 servings Something Extra (2½ teaspoons flour and 3 fl oz stock) ½ oz Limited Vegetable; 1 serving Vegetables; 6 oz poultry

Chinese Chicken with Green Peppers and Mushrooms

1 lb skinned and boned chicken, cut into bite-size pieces
2 teaspoons cornflour
1 tablespoon plus 1 teaspoon soy sauce
½ oz dried mushrooms, reconstituted and quartered

6 oz green pepper, seeded and cut into squares
2 oz spring onions, chopped
2 tablespoons plus 2 teaspoons red wine vinegar
salt and pepper to taste
1 teaspoon chicken stock powder, dissolved in 4 fl oz hot water

In bowl toss together chicken and cornflour; add soy sauce and mix well. Set aside to marinate for 20 to 30 minutes. Heat nonstick frying pan; add chicken and marinade. Cook, stirring constantly, until chicken is well browned. Remove from pan and set aside. Add remaining ingredients to pan, except stock, and cook for 5 minutes. Add chicken and stock; cook, stirring constantly, until mixture boils. Reduce heat and simmer for 10 minutes. Makes 2 evening meal servings. Divide evenly.

Each serving is equivalent to: 6 oz Poultry; ½ serving Something Extra (1 teaspoon cornflour and ½ teaspoon stock powder); 1 serving Vegetables; 1 oz Limited Vegetable

Chicken Italian Style (Cacciatore)

2 lbs skinned and boned chicken breasts
6 oz green pepper, seeded and cut into strips
2 oz onion, sliced

1 garlic clove, crushed
8 fl oz water
4 oz tomato purée
1 teaspoon oregano
½ teaspoon salt

Brown chicken in large preheated nonstick frying pan. Add green pepper, onion and garlic; cook for 4 minutes. Add remaining ingredients; cover and simmer, stirring occasionally, for 40 minutes or until done. Divide evenly. Makes 4 evening meal servings.

Each serving is equivalent to: 6 oz Poultry; ½ serving Vegetables; ½ oz Limited Vegetable; ½ serving Bonus (1 oz tomato purée)

Chicken Indian Style (Korma)

2 lbs skinned and boned chicken breasts
4 oz onion, chopped
1 garlic clove, crushed
1 oz hot chilli pepper, chopped
½ teaspoon paprika

¼ teaspoon cardamom
¼ teaspoon coriander
¼ teaspoon cumin
5 fl oz water
1 oz tomato purée

Brown chicken in large preheated nonstick frying pan. Add remaining ingredients in order given. Cover and simmer, stirring occasionally, for 40 minutes or until chicken is tender. Divide evenly. Makes 4 evening meal servings.

Each serving is equivalent to: 6 oz Poultry; 1 oz Limited Vegetable; ¼ oz Vegetables; ⅛ serving Bonus (¼ oz tomato purée)

Foil-Baked Chicken Rolls

2 boned and skinned chicken
  breasts, 6 oz each
salt and freshly ground pepper to
  taste
2 teaspoons prepared mustard

2 teaspoons low-fat spread
2 teaspoons chopped fresh chives
2 teaspoons chopped fresh parsley
2 teaspoons lemon juice
½ teaspoon garlic powder

Pound chicken breasts until they are about ¼ inch thick. Season with salt and pepper. Place each breast on a 12 × 12-inch piece of aluminum foil. Combine remaining ingredients in small bowl. Divide evenly and spread over each chicken breast. Roll chicken breast, tucking ends in. Seal rolls in foil. Place in baking pan. Bake at 375°F, Gas Mark 5, for 30 minutes. Serve 1 foil packet per portion and open them at the table. Makes 2 midday meal servings.

Each serving is equivalent to: 4 oz Poultry; ½ serving Fat

Oven-Barbecued Chicken with Vegetables

An all-in-one oven meal if you bake potatoes and apples in the oven with the chicken. Vary chicken seasonings. Garlic, oregano or parsley adds a nice touch.

10 oz carrots, diced
8 oz celery, diced
4 oz onion, diced
1 roasting chicken, 2½ to 3 lbs,
  skinned and cut into quarters

salt, pepper, paprika and poultry
  seasoning to taste
4 tablespoons tomato ketchup
2 tablespoons prepared mustard

In large shallow casserole combine carrots, celery and onion. Season chicken pieces and place over vegetables. Combine ketchup and mustard and pour evenly over chicken. Bake at 375°F, Gas Mark 5, for 1 hour or until chicken is tender. Weigh portions of chicken and divide vegetables and sauce evenly. Makes 4 evening meal servings.

Each serving is equivalent to: 1½ servings Vegetables; 1 oz Limited Vegetable; 6 oz Poultry; 1½ servings Something Extra (1 tablespoon tomato ketchup)

Oven-'Fried' Chicken

2 slices white bread, made into
 crumbs
1 tablespoon flour
1 teaspoon dried parsley flakes
½ teaspoon poultry seasoning
½ teaspoon salt
½ teaspoon paprika

¼ teaspoon garlic powder
⅛ teaspoon freshly ground pepper
1 lb skinned and boned chicken or
 turkey breasts, cut into serving
 pieces
½ oz nonfat dry milk
2 tablespoons water

In bowl combine breadcrumbs, flour and seasonings. Mix dry milk and water. Dip chicken in milk and then in breadcrumb mixture to coat. Place in nonstick baking tin. Sprinkle evenly with any remaining crumbs and milk. Bake at 400°F, Gas Mark 6, for 15 to 20 minutes or until chicken is tender. Divide evenly. Makes 2 evening meal servings.

Each serving is equivalent to: 1 serving Bread; 1½ servings Something Extra (1½ teaspoons flour); 6 oz Poultry; ¼ serving Milk (2½ fl oz skim milk)

Variation:
Chicken Cheesey—To serve 4 for midday meal, use 4 skinned and boned chicken breasts, each weighing 3 oz. Prepare breadcrumb mixture as above; follow directions for coating breasts. Bake as above. When chicken is tender, put one 1 oz slice of Cheddar cheese on each breast and bake until cheese melts. Serve each portion with 1 tablespoon tomato ketchup, if desired.

Each serving is equivalent to: ½ serving Bread; 2¼ servings Something Extra (¾ teaspoon flour); 2 oz Poultry; ⅛ serving Milk (1¼ fl oz skim milk); 1 oz Hard Cheese; 1½ servings Something Extra (1 tablespoon tomato ketchup) (optional)

Roast Chicken with Spiced Cherry Sauce

12 oz frozen, stoned, sweet
  cherries, no sugar added
3 small chickens, 1¼ lbs each
salt, white pepper, garlic powder
  and paprika to taste
6 fl oz chicken bouillon made with
  stock cube
6 fl oz low-calorie orange-flavoured
  carbonated beverage

artificial sweetener to equal 1
  teaspoon sugar, or to taste
¼ cinnamon stick
¼ teaspoon lemon juice
1 clove
1 tablespoon cornflour, mixed with
  1 tablespoon water

Set cherries aside to thaw. Sprinkle chickens with salt, pepper, garlic powder and paprika. Place on a rack in roasting tin and roast at 350°F, Gas Mark 4, for ½ hour or until done. Baste occasionally with bouillon. While chickens are roasting, combine juice from cherries, orange drink, sweetener, cinnamon, lemon juice and clove in a medium saucepan. Add cornflour and stir. Place over medium heat; cook, stirring constantly, until mixture thickens. Add cherries; stir until coated with sauce and thoroughly heated. To serve, cut chickens in half and remove skin. Place each half on a dinner plate and top with ¹/₆ of the cherry sauce. Makes 6 evening meal servings.

Each serving is equivalent to: ½ serving Fruit; 6 oz Poultry; ²/₃ serving Something Extra (¹/₆ stock cube and ½ teaspoon cornflour)

Yogurt-Baked Chicken

2½ lbs chicken pieces, skinned
1 garlic clove, cut
10 fl oz natural unsweetened
  yogurt
4 oz drained canned small onions

2 tablespoons chopped fresh
  parsley
1 tablespoon water
¼ teaspoon sage
¼ teaspoon tarragon

Dry chicken pieces and rub with cut garlic clove. Place in shallow baking tin. Bake at 350°F, Gas Mark 4, for 45 minutes or until tender. Combine remaining ingredients in small bowl; spoon over chicken. Bake at 275°F, Gas Mark 1, for 20 minutes or until sauce is hot and bubbly. Divide evenly. Makes 4 evening meal servings.

Each serving is equivalent to: 6 oz Poultry; ½ serving Milk (2½ fl oz yogurt); 1 oz Limited Vegetable

Roast Turkey

Place turkey on a rack in a shallow roasting tin, breast side up. Roast at 325°F, Gas Mark 3. Allow about 20 minutes per lb for a bird under 12 lbs, and about 15 minutes per lb if larger. If a meat thermometer is used, insert into the centre of inner thigh muscle; when thermometer registers 180° to 185°F, turkey is done. Baste every half-hour with mixture of dried onion flakes, dried pepper flakes, and chopped celery cooked in 12 fl oz chicken bouillon. Remove skin and weigh portions.

Each serving is equivalent to: 4 to 6 oz Poultry; ⅛ serving Something Extra (¾ fl oz bouillon)

Turkey and Spaghetti Casserole

The perfect post-Christmas dinner dish.

6 oz tomato purée	artificial sweetener to equal ½
6 fl oz water	teaspoon sugar, or to taste
6 oz green pepper, seeded and	(optional)
diced	Mushroom White Sauce (see page
4 oz celery, diced	279)
1 teaspoon chicken stock powder	12 oz cooked thin spaghetti
1 garlic clove, crushed	1½ lbs cooked turkey, cubed
½ teaspoon basil	

In a medium saucepan combine tomato purée, water, green pepper, celery, stock powder, garlic, basil and sweetener if desired. Simmer for 15 to 20 minutes or until vegetables are tender. In large shallow casserole, spread ½ of the Mushroom White Sauce. Add ½ the spaghetti, turkey and tomato mixture. Repeat layers. Bake at 350°F, Gas Mark 4, for 30 minutes or until piping hot. Divide evenly. Makes 4 evening meal servings.

Each serving is equivalent to: ¾ serving Bonus (1½ oz tomato purée); 1 serving Vegetables; ¼ serving Something Extra (¼ teaspoon stock powder); Mushroom White Sauce (see page 279); 1 serving Choice Group; 6 oz Poultry

Turkey Casserole

12 oz green peppers, seeded and diced	½ teaspoon Worcester sauce
4 oz onion, finely chopped	¼ teaspoon dry mustard
3 oz mushrooms, sliced	8 oz cooked turkey, shredded
1 garlic clove, crushed	12 oz cooked elbow macaroni
¾ teaspoon paprika	4 oz Cheddar cheese, grated
	paprika to garnish

In nonstick frying pan combine green peppers, onion, mushrooms, garlic, paprika, Worcester sauce and dry mustard; cook until vegetables are soft. Add turkey and cook for 5 minutes longer. Place macaroni in large casserole. Pour turkey mixture over macaroni; sprinkle with cheese and paprika. Bake at 400°F, Gas Mark 6, for 25 minutes or until thoroughly heated. Divide evenly. Makes 4 midday meal servings.

Each serving is equivalent to: 1 oz Limited Vegetable; 1¼ servings Vegetables; 2 oz Poultry; 1 serving Choice Group; 1 oz Hard Cheese

Turkey Terrapin

This dish was originally made with turtle (terrapin), which accounts for the name.

10 fl oz skim milk	4 oz cooked turkey, diced
2 standard eggs, hard-boiled	4 oz drained canned water
2 tablespoons low-fat spread, melted	chestnuts, sliced
	1½ oz mushrooms, sliced
1 tablespoon flour	½ oz canned pimiento, diced
⅛ teaspoon allspice	salt and pepper to taste
⅛ teaspoon nutmeg	2 slices white bread, toasted

Heat milk in top of a double boiler over boiling water. Cut eggs in half. Remove yolks. In small bowl mash egg yolks; add margarine, flour, allspice and nutmeg; add to hot milk; cook until thickened and smooth. Chop egg whites and add to milk mixture with turkey, water chestnuts, mushrooms, pimiento, salt and pepper; cook until thoroughly heated. Divide evenly; serve each portion on 1 slice of toast. Makes 2 midday meal servings.

Each serving is equivalent to: ½ serving Milk (5 fl oz skim milk); 1 Egg; 1½ servings Fat; 1½ servings Something Extra (1½ teaspoons flour); 2 oz Poultry; 2 oz Limited Vegetable; ⅓ serving Vegetables; 1 serving Bread

Veal

Veal is actually young beef from a calf three to eight months old. It has a more delicate flavour and is lighter in colour than beef. Veal has less fat than beef and may toughen more quickly, but the cooking principles in 'How to Cook Meat' (see page 156), usually apply to veal as well.

Quick-and-Easy Vitello Tonnato

A summer salad.

5 oz drained canned tuna
1 oz drained canned anchovies
8 teaspoons mayonnaise
1 teaspoon lemon juice
½ teaspoon capers

pinch celery seed
6 oz cooked veal, sliced
freshly ground pepper to taste
lemon slices to garnish

In bowl combine tuna, anchovies, mayonnaise, lemon juice, capers and celery seed. Mash finely. Place veal in shallow container. Spread tuna mixture over veal and refrigerate for several hours or overnight. Sprinkle with pepper. Garnish top with slices of lemon. Divide evenly. Makes 2 evening meal servings.

Each serving is equivalent to: 3 oz Fish; 2 servings Fat; 3 oz Veal.

Variation: You can vary the amounts of fish and veal according to what you have, but do not exceed a combined total of 6 oz cooked weight per serving. Adjust equivalents accordingly.

Apple-Glazed Veal

2 lbs boned veal roast
4 fl oz beef bouillon (made from 1
  stock cube)
1 tablespoon soy sauce

¼ teaspoon salt
⅛ teaspoon pepper
Apple Topping (see following
  recipe)

Grill veal 3 inches from source of heat, turning to brown all sides. Transfer to baking tin. In measuring jug combine bouillon, soy sauce, salt and pepper; pour over veal. Bake at 350°F, Gas Mark 4, for 45 minutes. Add Apple Topping; cover and bake for 30 minutes longer or until veal is tender. Baste several times with pan juices. Divide evenly. Makes 4 evening meal servings.

Apple Topping

2 medium apples, peeled, cored
  and sliced

2 tablespoons frozen orange juice
  concentrate
½ teaspoon cinnamon

Combine all ingredients in small bowl and use as topping for veal. Makes 4 servings.

    Each serving is equivalent to: 6 oz Veal; $1/_6$ serving Something Extra (¼ stock cube); ¾ serving Fruit

Savoury Rolled Roast of Veal

Serve this with any desired sauce. (See 'Sauces and Salad Dressings' page 276.) Bake vegetables at the same time. Order a leg of veal for rolling, but don't ask the butcher to roll it. We're seasoning it first.

4 tablespoons chopped fresh
  parsley
4 garlic cloves, crushed
1 tablespoon dried onion flakes,
  reconstituted in 1 tablespoon
  water

3 lbs boned leg of veal
salt and pepper to taste
garlic powder to taste

In small bowl combine parsley, garlic and onion flakes. Sprinkle inside of veal with salt and pepper. Spread with parsley mixture. Roll the veal and tie with string. Season outside of veal with salt, pepper and garlic powder. Let stand for 1 hour if possible. Insert meat thermometer; place veal on a rack in roasting tin and roast at 350°F, Gas Mark 4 for 2 hours or until thermometer registers 170°F. Divide evenly. Makes 6 evening meal servings.

Each serving is equivalent to: 6 oz Veal

Variation: Spread veal evenly with a mixture of 1 tablespoon tomato ketchup and 1 tablespoon soy sauce 10 minutes before removing from oven. Add ¼ serving Something Extra (½ teaspoon tomato ketchup) to equivalent listing.

Buttermilk Veal Balls

1½ lbs ground veal
2 slices white bread, made into
 crumbs
4 fl oz buttermilk

¼ teaspoon garlic powder
⅛ teaspoon thyme
pinch salt and pepper

In a bowl combine all ingredients. Shape into balls 1½ inches in diameter. Place on a rack and bake at 375°F, Gas Mark 5, for 40 minutes or until browned. Divide evenly. Makes 4 midday meal servings.

Each serving is equivalent to: 4 oz Veal; ½ serving Bread; $^1/_{10}$ serving Milk (1 fl oz buttermilk)

Sweet-and-Sour Veal Balls in Cabbage

2 lbs ground veal
1 oz onion, grated
½ teaspoon salt
¼ teaspoon garlic powder
⅛ teaspoon pepper

12 oz cabbage, shredded
3 oz onion, sliced
2 tablespoons frozen orange juice
 concentrate
1 tablespoon lemon juice

In bowl combine veal, grated onion, salt, garlic powder and pepper. Mix well and shape into balls 1 inch in diameter. Place on rack in baking tin; bake at 350°F, Gas Mark 4, turning as necessary, to brown all sides. Place the shredded cabbage and sliced onion in medium saucepan. Add orange juice concentrate, lemon juice and enough water to cover. Bring to boil. Add veal balls, cover and simmer for 20 minutes or until cabbage is soft. Divide evenly. Makes 4 evening meal servings.

Each serving is equivalent to: 6 oz Veal; 1 oz Limited Vegetable; 1 serving Vegetables; ¼ serving Fruit

Veal-Stuffed Cannelloni

1 lb minced veal, shaped into 4
    patties
4 oz tomato purée
4 fl oz water
2 teaspoons basil
1 teaspoon oregano
½ teaspoon garlic powder, divided
salt and pepper to taste

6 oz cooked spinach, chopped
4 fl oz chicken bouillon (made with
    1 stock cube)
1 tablespoon chopped fresh parsley
pinch nutmeg
6 oz cooked cannelloni shells
    (approximately 6)

Cook veal patties in preheated nonstick frying pan until done. In small bowl crumble one patty and add tomato purée mixed with water, basil, oregano, ¼ teaspoon garlic powder, salt and pepper. Mix well. Set aside. Crumble remaining patties into medium bowl. Add all remaining ingredients except cannelloni shells; mix well. Divide mixture evenly and fill cannelloni shells. Place in an 8 × 8-inch baking dish. Top with veal sauce mixture. Cover. Bake at 350°F, Gas Mark 4, for 30 minutes. Divide evenly. Makes 2 evening meal servings.

Each serving is equivalent to: 6 oz Veal; 1 serving Bonus (2 oz tomato purée); 1 serving Vegetables; ⅓ serving Something Extra (½ stock cube); 1 serving Choice Group

Hawaiian Veal

1 lb stewing veal, cut into 1-inch cubes	½ medium pineapple, peeled, cored and diced
12 fl oz beef bouillon (made with 2 stock cubes)	3 oz mushrooms, sliced
1 tablespoon chopped fresh parsley	1 tablespoon cornflour, dissolved in 1 tablespoon water
¼ teaspoon dill seed	6 oz cooked rice
salt and pepper to taste	

Brown veal cubes in preheated nonstick frying pan. Transfer to medium saucepan. Add bouillon, parsley, dill seed, salt and pepper. Cover and simmer over low heat for 40 minutes or until veal is very tender. Add water if necessary to keep veal barely covered. Add pineapple and mushrooms; cover and simmer for 5 minutes or until mushrooms are cooked. Add cornflour and cook, stirring constantly, until thickened. Serve over rice. Divide evenly. Makes 2 evening meal servings.

Each serving is equivalent to: 6 oz Veal; 2½ servings Something Extra (1 stock cube and 1½ teaspoons cornflour); 1 serving Fruit; ½ serving Vegetables; 1 serving Choice Group

Italian Veal and Peppers

Any boned veal may be cut up and used for stewing if it is free of sinews. Boned veal shoulder is excellent.

1 lb stewing veal, cut into 1-inch cubes	1 garlic clove, crushed
4 oz tomato purée	½ teaspoon basil
4 fl oz water	½ teaspoon oregano
4 oz onion, sliced	freshly ground pepper to taste
1 teaspoon chicken stock powder	12 oz green peppers, seeded and cut into ½-inch strips

Brown veal in preheated nonstick frying pan. Remove veal and wipe pan clean. Replace veal and add all remaining ingredients except green peppers. Cover and cook over low heat for 45 minutes. Add peppers and continue cooking for 10 minutes longer or until veal and peppers are tender. Divide evenly. Makes 2 evening meal servings.

Each serving is equivalent to: 6 oz Veal; 1 serving Bonus (2 oz tomato purée); 2 oz Limited Vegetable; ½ serving Something Extra (½ teaspoon stock powder); 2 servings Vegetables

Veal Paprika

Good served with boiled potatoes or noodles.

1½ lbs stewing veal, cut into ½-
  inch cubes
4 oz onion, chopped
4 oz tomato purée
4 fl oz water
1 teaspoon paprika

¼ teaspoon salt
⅛ teaspoon garlic powder
⅛ teaspoon white pepper
2½ fl oz natural unsweetened
  yogurt

Brown veal in a preheated nonstick frying pan. Transfer to medium saucepan. Add onion and cook, stirring occasionally until onion is browned. Add tomato purée, water, paprika, salt, garlic powder and white pepper. Cover and simmer for 30 minutes or until veal is tender. Remove from heat; fold in yogurt. Divide evenly. Makes 4 midday meal servings.

Each serving is equivalent to: 4 oz Veal; 1 oz Limited Vegetable; ½ serving Bonus (1 oz tomato purée); ⅛ serving Milk (⅝ fl oz yogurt)

Quick-and-Easy Veal Marengo

This traditional dish is usually accompanied by rice or noodles.

1 tablespoon margarine
2 oz onion, diced
½ garlic clove, crushed
1 tablespoon flour
6 fl oz chicken bouillon
2 oz tomato purée

12 oz cooked veal, diced
3 oz mushrooms, sliced
¼ teaspoon thyme
¼ teaspoon tarragon
⅛ teaspoon grated orange rind
pinch pepper

Melt margarine in top of double boiler over boiling water. Add onion and garlic. Cook until onion is soft. Stir in flour and cook until blended; add bouillon and tomato purée. Cook, stirring constantly, until smooth and thickened. Stir in remaining ingredients; simmer for 10 minutes. Divide evenly. Makes 2 evening meal servings.

Each serving is equivalent to: 1½ servings Fat; 1 oz Limited Vegetable; 2 servings Something Extra (1½ teaspoons flour and 3 fl oz bouillon); ½ serving Bonus (1 oz tomato purée); 6 oz Veal; ½ serving Vegetables

Rabbit Stew

Chicken may also be prepared this way.

12 fl oz cider vinegar
12 fl oz water
4 oz onion, sliced
1 teaspoon salt
1 teaspoon ground cloves
3 bay leaves
¼ teaspoon crushed peppercorns,
   or more to taste

⅛ teaspoon allspice
2½ lbs rabbit, cut in pieces
6 fl oz chicken bouillon (made with
   1 stock cube)
¼ teaspoon gravy browning
2 teaspoons cornflour, dissolved in
   2 teaspoon water

In large bowl combine first 8 ingredients. Add rabbit; cover and refrigerate 1 to 2 days, turning occasionally. Remove rabbit; reserve marinade. Grill rabbit 4 inches from source of heat, turning once, for 12 minutes or until brown. Transfer rabbit and reserved marinade to large saucepan; cover and simmer for 1 hour or until tender. Remove rabbit and keep warm. Add bouillon and gravy browning to marinade. Stir in cornflour and cook, stirring constantly, until thickened. Strain sauce through double-layered muslin. Discard solids. Serve sauce with rabbit. Divide evenly. Makes 4 evening meal servings.

Each serving is equivalent to: 6 oz Game; ¾ serving Something Extra (¼ stock cube and ½ teaspoon cornflour)

'BEEF' GROUP

*

Beef, ham, lamb, pork, tongue, bologna, frankfurters, knackwurst, beef sausages and offal can provide hearty meals for you. Enjoy an excellent Old-Fashioned Pot Roast, Beef Chop Suey, Chilli for Four, and easy Lamb and Barley Stew, Swiss-Style Pot-au-Feu, and even Homemade Sausage. Money-saving and delicious recipes for Meat Loaf and a Quick-and-Easy Cassoulet are all included.

Rules for Using 'Beef' Group

1. Amounts (net cooked weight):
    Women, Men and Teenagers: 1 oz at the morning meal
    3 to 4 oz at the midday meal.
    Women and Teenagers: · 4 to 6 oz at the evening meal.
    Men: 6 to 8 oz at the evening meal.
2. The range of 3 to 4 oz of 'Beef' group at the midday meal and 4 to 6 oz for Women and Teenagers (6 to 8 oz for Men) at the evening meal provides flexibility. It is a way to individualise the Programme to meet your specific needs.
3. If smoked meat is selected, use the lower end of the serving range.
4. Select up to 3 times weekly, if desired, from beef, ham, lamb, pork and tongue.
5. Use lean meat. Remove visible fat before eating.
6. Select one of the following once a week, if desired, in place of a 'Beef' Group item:
    beef sausages   knackwurst
    bologna   offal
    frankfurters

155

7. As a 'rule of thumb', for each serving of a 'Beef' Group item allow 2 oz for shrinkage in cooking and 2 oz for bone. When splitting an item from the 'Beef' Group, for each half-serving allow 1 oz for shrinkage in cooking and 1 oz for bone. Weigh the serving after cooking, whenever possible.

8. Bologna, frankfurters, knackwurst and ham are precooked. Do not allow an additional 2 oz for shrinkage (with the exception of fresh beef sausage).

9. Whether a selection from the 'Beef' Group is taken by itself, or in combination with fish, poultry, meat, egg, cheese or dried peas/beans, it must be considered a 'Beef' Group meal.

10. *Cooking Procedures:*
May be boiled, grilled, baked, or roasted on a rack.

If boiled, liquid may be consumed. Refrigerate liquid; remove congealed fat. 6 fl oz equal one serving of bouillon or stock.

If grilled, baked or roasted on a rack, natural juices flowing from the meat during cutting may be consumed.

Cooked 'Beef' may be used with added ingredients (e.g. casseroles, stews, etc.) Liquid and added ingredients may be consumed.

Raw minced meat may be combined with other ingredients, such as fruit, eggs, cheese, bread, Choice Group items, milk, vegetables and items from all categories in the Optional Section only if boiled or baked (not grilled) on a rack.

How to Cook Meat

The most important thing to remember about cooking meat is that any cut can be delicious and tender if cooked properly. In most cases, the tenderness of the cut determines the preferred cooking method. Tender cuts are usually best when cooked by dry heat, such as roasting or grilling. Less tender cuts of meat are made tender by cooking with moist heat. Slow cooking in moisture softens the connective tissue, the part of the meat that cannot be made tender quickly.

Roasting—Good for tender cuts of beef, pork, and lamb.
Season with salt and pepper, if desired. Roasts may be seasoned

either before, during or after cooking, since salt only penetrates ¼ to ½ inch. Place meat on rack in open, shallow roasting tin. Insert a meat thermometer, if available, in the centre of largest muscle, not touching bone.

Do not add water, do not cover and do not baste. It is not necessary to preheat the oven. Roast at 300°F, Gas Mark 2, to 350°F, Gas Mark 4. Small roasts should be cooked at 350°F, Gas Mark 4, larger ones at lower temperatures. For browning, higher temperatures may be used. Roast to the desired degree of doneness. Then let roast stand for 15 to 20 minutes after removing it from the oven for easier carving. Slice and weigh servings.

Grilling—Good for tender beef steaks, lamb chops, pork chops, ham steaks, and minced meats.

Place meat on rack in grill pan and grill 2 to 5 inches from the heat, until top is brown. Season if desired. Turn and grill until done. Weigh and serve at once.

Cooking in Liquid (Boiling)—Good for less tender cuts of meat.

Place meat in large saucepan and cover with water. When meat is covered entirely, it can be cooked evenly without turning. Season with salt, pepper, herbs and spices if desired. Cover pan and simmer until tender. Remove meat; slice and weigh servings. If desired, strain and refrigerate cooking liquid. Remove and discard congealed fat. Use liquid in recipes which call for beef stock.

6 fl oz liquid is equivalent to: 1 serving Something Extra

Beef, Ham, Lamb, Veal Stock

Bones from beef, ham, lamb or veal can be used to make stocks. To make these strongly flavoured stocks, follow the directions for Chicken Stock (see page 135), but add 1 garlic clove and 1 tablespoon dried onion flakes. For added flavour and colour, brown bones on a rack, in a hot oven, before preparing the stock. Ham stock is an excellent base for split pea soup or any other soup made from dried peas/beans.

6 fl oz is equivalent to: 1 serving Something Extra

Boiled Beef

3 lbs boned beef topside
3½ pints water
1 to 2 teaspoons salt
bouquet garni (4 cloves, 2 sprigs
    thyme, 1 bay leaf tied in muslin)
1 lb 2 oz cabbage, cut in wedges

1 lb 2 oz peeled potatoes, diced
12 oz small white onions
9 oz white turnips, peeled and
    diced
9 oz carrots, sliced
3 oz celery with leaves, sliced

In large strong saucepan combine beef, water, salt and bouquet garni; cover and simmer for 2 to 3 hours or until beef is tender. Add more water if necessary. Drain and refrigerate liquid. Discard bouquet garni. Cool beef and refrigerate. Remove and discard congealed fat from liquid. In large pan combine 1 pint 16 fl oz liquid, beef and remaining ingredients. Simmer for 45 minutes or until vegetables are tender. Remove beef and vegetables from liquid; slice beef. Place on serving dish surrounded by vegetables. Divide beef and vegetables evenly. Divide liquid evenly into soup bowls. Makes 6 evening meal servings.

Each serving is equivalent to: 6 oz 'Beef' Group; $2^{1}/_{6}$ servings Vegetables; 1 serving Choice Group; 2 oz Limited Vegetable; 1 serving Something Extra (6 fl oz stock)

Beef Soup

3½ pints water
12 oz chuck steak
6 oz carrots, sliced
6 oz celery, sliced
2 oz onion, diced
3 parsley sprigs

3 parsley sprigs
1 bay leaf
1 garlic clove, crushed
salt and freshly ground pepper to
    taste

Combine all ingredients except salt and pepper in saucepan. Simmer for 1 hour. Season with salt and pepper. Transfer beef and liquid to bowl. Discard all remaining solids. Refrigerate beef and liquid. Remove and discard congealed fat.* Measure 12 fl oz liquid. Re-

*If fat is difficult to remove, line a strainer with 4 layers of muslin or a wet, heavy paper towel. Place strainer over a bowl. Pour liquid with fat through muslin or paper towel. Discard fat.

maining liquid can be frozen to be used at another time; 6 fl oz is equivalent to 1 serving bouillon or stock. Combine measured liquid with beef in saucepan. Bring to boil; reduce heat. Simmer until beef is completely heated through. Divide evenly into soup bowls. Makes 2 midday meal servings.

Each serving is equivalent to: 4 oz 'Beef' Group; 1 serving Something Extra (6 fl oz stock)

Old-Fashioned Pot Roast

2 lbs topside of beef
12 oz drained canned whole
  potatoes
12 fl oz tomato juice
8 oz onion, sliced
6 oz green pepper, seeded and
  diced
3½ oz carrots, shredded

2½ oz celery, diced
10 peppercorns, crushed
4 bay leaves
artificial sweetener to equal 3
  teaspoons sugar, or to taste
  (optional)
2 teaspoons salt
½ teaspoon paprika

Roast beef on a rack at 375°F, Gas Mark 5, for 45 minutes or until done. Place in large strong saucepan with remaining ingredients. Cover and simmer for 1 to 1½ hours, or until meat is very tender. Remove beef and potatoes; slice beef. Transfer 4 fl oz remaining mixture to blender container and blend until smooth. Return to pan and mix thoroughly. Divide beef evenly and place each portion on an individual serving plate with 3 oz potatoes. Divide sauce evenly and pour over each serving of beef and potatoes. Makes 4 evening meal servings.

Each serving is equivalent to: 6 oz 'Beef' Group; 1 serving Choice Group; ⅜ serving Bonus (3 fl oz tomato juice); 2 oz Limited Vegetable; 1 serving Vegetables

Sauerbraten

4 lbs topside of beef	2 oz carrots, sliced
1 tablespoon salt	1 oz celery, chopped
½ teaspoon freshly ground pepper	4 cloves
2 pints water	4 peppercorns
16 fl oz red wine vinegar	2 bay leaves
8 oz onion, sliced	

Season beef with salt and pepper. Place in large glass bowl. Add remaining ingredients. Cover and refrigerate for 4 to 6 days, turning meat several times daily. Remove meat; reserve marinade. Roast meat on rack at 375°F, Gas Mark 5, for 1 hour or until done. Place beef in large saucepan and add marinade. Bring to a boil; cover and simmer for 1½ to 2½ hours or until beef is tender. Remove beef; strain liquid and discard solids. Boil marinade until reduced to about 16 fl oz. Slice beef and serve with marinade. Divide evenly. Makes 8 evening meal servings.

Each serving is equivalent to: 6 oz 'Beef' Group

Barbecued Steak

1 oz dried onion flakes	3 lbs boned steak, cut into 1½-inch
2 tablespoons Worcester sauce	thick slices.
2 tablespoons lemon juice	1 tablespoon chopped fresh parsley
1 garlic clove, crushed	2 tablespoons margarine (optional)
¾ teaspoon salt	

In bowl combine first 5 ingredients; let stand for 10 minutes. Add beef. Cover and refrigerate for 2 to 6 hours. Remove steak from marinade and grill on a rack, basting with remaining marinade. Cook until done to taste. Sprinkle with parsley. Dot with margarine if desired. Divide evenly. Makes 6 evening meal servings.

Each serving is equivalent to: 6 oz 'Beef' Group; 1 serving Fat (optional)

Beef Chop Suey

Thinly sliced fore rib or top rib could replace the skirt steak in this and the recipes for Beef with Peppers and Tomatoes and Chinese Pepper Steak with Mushrooms.

2 lbs skirt steak
2 tablespoons soy sauce
4 fl oz water
4 oz onion, sliced
1½ oz fresh mushrooms, sliced
1½ oz carrots, sliced
1½ oz celery, sliced
1 teaspoon beef stock powder
artificial sweetener to equal ½
   teaspoon sugar, or to taste
salt to taste

2 oz fresh or rinsed canned bean
   sprouts
1½ oz canned bamboo shoots,
   sliced
½ oz dried mushrooms,
   reconstituted in warm water and
   sliced
1 tablespoon cornflour, dissolved in
   2 tablespoons water
4 oz tomato, cut into wedges

Preheat grill. Score steak and marinate in soy sauce for 10 minutes, turning once. Reserve marinade. Grill steak on a rack for 6 minutes; turn, grill for 4 minutes longer or until rare. Cool. Cut into strips. Set aside beef and juices from slicing. In nonstick frying pan over high heat combine water, onion, fresh mushrooms, celery, carrots and stock powder. Cook for 2 minutes, stirring occasionally. Add reserved marinade, sweetener and salt; mix well. When vegetables are tender-crisp add steak slices and juices, bean sprouts, bamboo shoots and dried mushrooms. Stir-cook for 2 minutes. Add cornflour; stir until mixture thickens. Add tomato wedges; mix well. Cook for 1 minute longer. Divide evenly. Makes 4 evening meal servings.

Each serving is equivalent to: 6 oz 'Beef' Group; 1 oz Limited Vegetable; 1 serving Vegetables; 1 serving Something Extra (¼ teaspoon stock powder and ¾ teaspoon cornflour)

Beef with Peppers and Tomatoes

2 lbs skirt steak
1 lb 2 oz green peppers, seeded
and sliced
4 oz onion, thinly sliced
2 garlic cloves, crushed
1 teaspoon beef stock powder
1 teaspoon salt
½ teaspoon pepper

2 fl oz soy sauce
2 fl oz water
½ teaspoon sherry flavouring
2 teaspoons cornflour
8 oz cut green beans
8 oz tomatoes, cut into wedges
parsley sprigs to garnish

Grill steak on a rack about 4 inches from source of heat for 15 minutes or until rare, turning once. Cut into thin slices; set aside. In nonstick frying pan combine green peppers, onion, garlic, stock powder, salt and pepper; sauté for 5 minutes, stirring occasionally. In small bowl combine soy sauce, water and flavouring. Add cornflour; stir to dissolve. Stir into vegetable mixture; cook until thickened. Add green beans. Cook until beans are tender-crisp. Place steak in serving dish. Top with vegetable mixture. Garnish with tomato wedges and parsley sprigs. Divide evenly. Makes 4 evening meal servings.

Each serving is equivalent to: 6 oz 'Beef' Group; 2¾ servings Vegetables; 1 oz Limited Vegetable; ¾ serving Something Extra (¼ teaspoon stock powder and ½ teaspoon cornflour)

Chinese Pepper Steak with Mushrooms

2 lbs skirt steak
2¼ lbs green peppers, seeded and
sliced
6 oz mushrooms, sliced
4 oz onion, sliced
1 garlic clove, crushed

1½ teaspoons salt
½ teaspoon ginger
¼ teaspoon pepper
12 fl oz beef bouillon (made with 2
stock cubes)
3 tablespoons soy sauce
2 tablespoons cornflour

Grill steak on rack for 12 minutes or until rare, turning once to brown both sides. In preheated nonstick frying pan or wok combine green peppers, mushrooms, onion, and garlic; cook for 3 minutes, stirring constantly. Add salt, ginger and pepper. In small bowl combine bouillon, soy sauce and cornflour; stir to dissolve corn-flour. Add to pan. Bring to a boil, stirring constantly until sauce is thickened and clear. Remove from heat. Slice steak; place equal amounts of steak on each of 4 plates and top each portion with ¼ of the vegetable mixture. Makes 4 evening meal servings.

Each serving is equivalent to: 6 oz 'Beef' Group; 3½ servings Vegetables; 1 oz Limited Vegetable; 2 servings Something Extra (½ stock cube and 1½ teaspoons cornflour)

Polynesian Beef

1½ lbs chuck steak, cut into 1-inch cubes
12 fl oz beef bouillon (made with 1 stock cube)
12 oz canned pineapple chunks, no sugar added, drained (reserve juice)
3 oz onion, grated
1 tablespoon soy sauce
1 tablespoon cider vinegar
1 garlic clove, crushed
½-inch slice fresh ginger root, mashed
¼ teaspoon salt
¼ teaspoon dry mustard
2 teaspoons cornflour, dissolved in 2 tablespoons water
9 oz cooked rice
1 tablespoon chopped fresh parsley

Grill beef on rack for 5 to 8 minutes, turning to brown all sides. In bowl combine bouillon, pineapple juice, onion, soy sauce, vinegar, garlic, ginger, salt and mustard. Add beef. Cover; refrigerate overnight. Transfer beef and marinade to saucepan and simmer for 30 minutes or until beef is tender. Stir in cornflour and simmer until thickened. Add pineapple; cook for 3 minutes. Divide evenly into 3 portions. Serve each portion over 3 oz hot rice. Sprinkle with parsley. Makes 3 evening meal servings.

Each serving is equivalent to: 6 oz 'Beef' Group; 1 serving Something Extra ($^1/_3$ stock cube and $^2/_3$ teaspoon cornflour); 1 serving Fruit; 1 oz Limited Vegetable; 1 serving Choice Group

Steak and Kidneys with Crust Topping

1 lb 2 oz cooked beef kidneys (see note)

1 lb 2 oz cooked beef, cut into ¾-inch cubes

3 tablespoons plus 1 teaspoon flour

2 beef stock cubes, crumbled ·

1 teaspoon salt

⅛ teaspoon pepper

14 fl oz water

4 oz onion, sliced

2 tablespoons Worcester sauce

¼ teaspoon thyme

3 slices white bread, made into crumbs

pinch salt

In saucepan sprinkle kidneys and beef with flour, crumbled stock cubes, salt and pepper. Add 12 fl oz water, onion, Worcester sauce and thyme. Bring to a boil, reduce heat and simmer, stirring often, until thickened. Place beef-kidney mixture in 3-pint casserole. Set aside. In bowl combine remaining 2 fl oz water, crumbs, and salt, stirring with a fork until crumbs are evenly moistened. Place mixture between two large sheets of greaseproof paper. Roll out in a shape to cover casserole. Remove from paper and place over steak-kidney mixture. Press crust to secure around sides of casserole. Bake at 325°F, Gas Mark 3, for 45 minutes or until top is lightly browned. Divide evenly. Makes 6 evening meal servings.

Each serving is equivalent to: 3 oz Kidneys; 3 oz 'Beef' Group; 2 servings Something Extra (1 ⅔ teaspoons flour and ⅓ stock cube); ⅔ oz Limited Vegetable; ½ serving Bread

Note: Wash beef kidneys; remove excess fat and sinew. Cut into ¾-inch slices. Place in covered saucepan with water to cover and simmer 1 hour or until tender. Drain and weigh.

Chilli Beef

Tie a checked napkin on the handle of the pot and bring it to the table. Serve steaming hot with a crisp green salad.

1 lb minced beef
1 pint 4 fl oz water
12 oz green peppers, seeded and
  diced
4 oz onion, chopped
2 oz celery, diced
1 oz chilli pepper, seeded and
  diced
½ garlic clove, crushed
3 oz canned tomatoes, chopped
  with liquid
4 oz tomato purée

1 tablespoon chilli powder, or to
  taste
½ teaspoon black pepper
¼ to ½ teaspoon cayenne pepper
  or a few drops hot sauce, or to
  taste
⅛ teaspoon cumin
2 cloves
1 bay leaf
salt to taste
1 lb drained canned dried red
  kidney or pinto beans

In saucepan combine beef and 1 pint water; simmer for 15 minutes or until beef loses its red colour. Strain and refrigerate liquid until fat congeals on top; remove fat and discard. Set aside 6 fl oz liquid. Freeze remaining liquid for later use. In saucepan combine the next 5 ingredients. Cook for 5 minutes. Add tomatoes, tomato purée, 4 fl oz water, seasonings, beans, reserved 6 fl oz liquid and beef. Simmer for 30 minutes. Divide evenly. Makes 4 evening meal servings.

Each serving is equivalent to: 3 oz 'Beef' Group; 1½ servings Vegetables; 1 oz Limited Vegetable; ½ serving Bonus (1 oz tomato purée); 4 oz Dried Beans; ¼ serving Something Extra (1½ fl oz stock)

Lasagne

1 lb 2 oz minced beef
4 oz onion, diced
4 tablespoons chopped fresh
  parsley
¾ teaspoon garlic powder
salt and white pepper to taste
8 oz tomato purée

8 fl oz water
6 fl oz beef bouillon (made with 1
  stock cube)
2 teaspoons oregano
15 oz skim milk ricotta cheese
1 lb 2 oz cooked lasagne

In bowl combine beef, onion, 2 tablespoons parsley, ¼ teaspoon garlic powder, salt and pepper. Shape into large patties and place on rack in baking tin. Bake at 400°F, Gas Mark 6, for 20 minutes or until firm. Cool; crumble. In saucepan combine beef, tomato purée, water, bouillon, oregano, ¼ teaspoon garlic powder, salt and pepper. Simmer for 25 minutes, stirring occasionally. Set aside. In separate bowl combine cheese, remaining 2 tablespoons parsley, ¼ teaspoon garlic powder, salt and pepper. Spread a thin layer of meat sauce in the bottom of an 8 × 8-inch baking tin. Arrange alternate layers of lasagne, cheese and meat sauce, ending with a layer of meat sauce. Bake at 350°F, Gas Mark 4, for 40 minutes. Allow to stand for 15 minutes before serving. Divide evenly. Makes 6 midday meal servings.

Each serving is equivalent to: 2 oz 'Beef' Group; ²/₃ oz Limited Vegetable; ²/₃ serving Bonus (¹/₃ oz tomato purée); ¹/₆ serving Something Extra (¹/₆ stock cube); 2½ oz Soft Cheese; 1 serving Choice Group

Meat Loaf

1 tablespoon unflavoured gelatine
6 fl oz beef bouillon (made with 1 stock cube)
6 oz cooked carrots, mashed
4 oz onion, grated
1 teaspoon salt
⅛ teaspoon dry mustard

pinch white pepper
1 lb minced beef
artificial sweetener to equal 1 teaspoon sugar, or to taste
½ teaspoon oregano
pinch garlic powder
freshly ground pepper to taste

In small saucepan sprinkle gelatine over bouillon to soften. Place over low heat and simmer, stirring constantly, until gelatine is dissolved. Remove from heat; set aside. In small bowl combine carrot, 2 oz onion, ½ teaspoon salt, dry mustard and white pepper. Set aside. In large bowl combine minced beef, sweeteners, oregano, garlic powder, pepper, remaining 2 oz onion, ½ teaspoon salt and 2 fl oz bouillon mixture. On sheet of greaseproof paper, form beef mixture into rectangle about ½ inch thick. Spread with carrot mixture to within 1 inch of edges. Roll up from narrow end. Slide off greaseproof paper, seam side down, onto rack in roasting tin. Brush remaining bouillon mixture over beef roll. Bake at 350°F, Gas Mark 4, for 1 hour or until beef is done to taste. Divide evenly. Makes 2 evening meal servings.

Each serving is equivalent to: 1 serving Something Extra (1½ teaspoons gelatine and ½ stock cube); 1 serving Vegetables; 2 oz Limited Vegetable; 6 oz 'Beef' Group

Simmered Meatballs

6 oz minced beef
2 standard eggs
2 slices white bread, made into
  crumbs
½ garlic clove, crushed (optional)

¼ teaspoon oregano (optional)
salt and freshly ground pepper to
  taste
2½ pints water

Combine all ingredients except water in bowl. Form into 10 meatballs of equal size. Place in saucepan with water. Simmer for 12 to 15 minutes or until meatballs are done to taste. Drain* Divide meatballs evenly. Makes 2 midday meal servings.

Each serving is equivalent to: 2 oz 'Beef' Group; 1 Egg; 1 serving Bread

Oriental Meatballs with Rice

1 lb lean minced beef
2 fl oz water
1 teaspoon garlic salt
½ teaspoon dry mustard
½ teaspoon ginger
6 oz cooked, celery, sliced
4 fl oz orange juice

1 tablespoon soy sauce
1 tablespoon red wine vinegar
artificial sweetener to equal 1
  teaspoon sugar, or to taste
6 oz cooked rice
chopped fresh parsley to garnish

Preheat grill. Combine first 5 ingredients in mixing bowl; blend well. Form into 16 equal balls. Place on rack in grill pan. Grill 3 to 4 inches from heat source, for 5 to 7 minutes or until brown; turn and brown other side. Place meatballs in saucepan. Combine celery, orange juice, soy sauce, vinegar and sweetener in blender container.

*Refrigerate liquid. Remove and discard congealed fat; 6 fl oz liquid is equivalent to 1 serving bouillon or stock. If fat is difficult to remove, place a strainer lined with 4 layers of muslin or a heavy wet paper towel over a bowl. Pour liquid through strainer. Discard fat.

Blend until smooth. Pour over meatballs. Heat and serve over rice. Garnish with chopped parsley. Divide evenly. Makes 2 evening meal servings.

Each serving is equivalent to: 6 oz 'Beef' Group; 1 serving Vegetables; ½ serving Fruit; 1 serving Choice Group

Hot-'n'-Spicy Meat Sauce

To serve over cooked pasta or cornmeal.

1½ lbs cooked minced beef, crumbled
1¼ pints water
2 oz canned tomatoes, puréed in food mixer or blender
8 oz tomato purée, mixed with 8 fl oz water
1 oz dried onion flakes
1 oz celery, finely chopped
3 tablespoons Worcester sauce
1 tablespoon chopped fresh parsley
artificial sweetener to equal 3

teaspoons sugar, or to taste
2 teaspoons garlic salt
2 teaspoons paprika
2 bay leaves
1 teaspoon chilli powder, or to taste
½ teaspoon oregano
½ teaspoon salt
¼ teaspoon cinnamon
¼ teaspoon pepper
¼ teaspoon thyme
chopped fresh parsley to garnish

Combine all ingredients, except garnish, in large saucepan. Simmer sauce, uncovered, for 2 hours or until thick. Remove bay leaves. Garnish with parsley. Serve hot. Divide evenly. Makes 4 evening meal servings.

Each serving is equivalent to: 6 oz 'Beef' Group; ¼ serving Vegetables; 1 serving Bonus (2 oz tomato purée)

Lamb and Barley Stew

2 lbs boned lamb, cut into 1-inch cubes
6 oz carrots, diced
4 oz onion, sliced
2 oz canned tomatoes
4 teaspoons chicken stock powder
½ teaspoon paprika

¼ teaspoon garlic powder
1 bay leaf
salt and pepper to taste
1¼ pints water
6 oz peeled potatoes, diced
8 oz cut green beans
8 oz cooked barley

Grill lamb on rack, turning to brown all sides; set aside. In large nonstick saucepan combine carrots, onion, tomatoes, stock powder, paprika, garlic powder, bay leaf, salt and pepper; sauté 5 minutes, stirring frequently. Add lamb and water. Bring to a boil; reduce heat. Simmer for 30 minutes or until lamb is tender. Add potatoes, green beans and barley, and cook covered for 1 hour or until potatoes are soft. Divide evenly. Makes 4 evening meal servings.

Each serving is equivalent to: 6 oz 'Beef' Group; $1\frac{1}{3}$ servings Vegetables; 1 oz Limited Vegetable; 1 serving Something Extra (1 teaspoon stock powder); 1 serving Choice Group

Moussaka

8 oz peeled aubergine, cut into ½-inch thick slices
8 oz onion, diced
8 oz canned tomatoes, chopped
4 fl oz water
3 oz tomato purée
2 tablespoons chopped fresh parsley
pinch cinnamon
pinch allspice
salt and pepper to taste
12 oz cooked minced lamb or beef, crumbled
½ recipe Basic White Sauce (2 servings, see page 278)

Brown aubergine slices on both sides in nonstick frying pan over high heat, pressing slices with back of spatula to release moisture. Set aside. In the same pan, brown the onions slightly. Add tomatoes, water, tomato purée, parsley, cinnamon, allspice, salt and pepper. Simmer for 5 minutes. Add crumbled meat and cook for 10 more minutes. In nonstick casserole place ½ the aubergine slices and ½ meat mixture; repeat layers. Spoon White Sauce on top. Bake at 375°F, Gas Mark 5, for 35 minutes or until top begins to brown. Divide evenly. Makes 2 evening meal servings.

Each serving is equivalent to: $2\frac{2}{3}$ servings Vegetables; 4 oz Limited Vegetable; ¾ serving Bonus (1½ oz tomato purée); 6 oz 'Beef' Group; Basic White Sauce (see page 278)

Quick-and-Easy Lamb Dinner

4 loin or chump lamb chops, about
  1 inch thick, 5 oz each
1 tablespoon dried onion flakes
1 teaspoon salt

½ teaspoon garlic powder
⅛ teaspoon pepper
2 tomatoes, 4 oz each, cut in half

Grill chops on rack 3 to 4 inches from source of heat for 6 to 7 minutes or until browned. In a small cup combine onion flakes, salt, garlic powder, and pepper. Turn chops and arrange tomato halves, cut side up, on grill rack. Sprinkle onion flake mixture over chops and tomatoes; grill for 5 to 6 minutes or until chops are done. Divide evenly. Makes 2 evening meal servings.

Each serving is equivalent to: 6 oz 'Beef' Group; $1^{1}/_{3}$ servings Vegetables

Savoury Lamb Succotash

8 oz cooked dried lima beans or
  butter beans
6 oz cooked lamb, diced
12 fl oz chicken bouillon (made
  with 1 stock cube)
3 oz canned tomatoes, chopped

3 oz peeled potato, diced
3 oz drained canned whole kernel
  corn
2 oz onion, diced
¾ teaspoon salt
¼ teaspoon thyme

Combine all ingredients in medium saucepan. Cover and cook for 1 hour or until sauce is very thick. Divide evenly. Makes 2 evening meal servings.

Each serving is equivalent to: 4 oz dried Beans; 3 oz 'Beef' Group; ½ serving Something Extra (½ stock cube); ½ serving Vegetables; 1 serving Choice Group; 1 oz Limited Vegetable

Roast Pork

Season lean shoulder, leg or loin of pork with salt, pepper and desired spices and herbs. Insert meat thermometer into thickest part of roast, not touching bone. Place on rack in roasting tin.

Roast at 350°F, Gas Mark 4, for 30 to 40 minutes per lb. Time will depend on the size and cut of meat. Pork is cooked when internal temperature registers 170°F on meat thermometer. Slice and weigh portions.

Homemade 'Sausage' with Hot Soup

1 lb 2 oz cooked pork, cut into 2-inch cubes
1½ slices white bread
4 tablespoons chopped fresh parsley
1½ oz shallots or onion
1 teaspoon salt
1 garlic clove
¼ teaspoon pepper
¼ teaspoon sage
¼ teaspoon savory
¼ teaspoon marjoram
pinch nutmeg
2½ pints Chicken or Beef Stock (see page 135 or 157)

Combine all ingredients except stock and put through mincer. Blend well and form into a loaf on piece of muslin. Wrap loaf in the muslin and twist ends to seal. Secure with string. Refrigerate overnight. Place in large saucepan or fish kettle with ends of muslin at edge of pot. Add stock and poach for 50 minutes. Remove 'sausage' from stock; refrigerate. Strain stock. Slice 'sausage' and serve evenly divided. Heat stock and divide evenly into 3 soup bowls. Makes 3 evening meal servings.

Each serving is equivalent to: 6 oz 'Beef' Group; ½ serving Bread; ½ oz Limited Vegetable; 2 ⅔ servings Something Extra (16 fl oz stock)

Paella

1½ teaspoons salt
1 teaspoon oregano
1 teaspoon lemon juice
¼ teaspoon freshly ground pepper
1 garlic clove, crushed
1 lb skinned and boned chicken
 breast, cut into 1-inch cubes
6 oz onion, chopped
6 oz green pepper, seeded and
 chopped
1 lb 2 oz cooked rice
9 oz fresh peas, or frozen small
 peas, thawed

9 oz drained canned artichoke
 hearts
8 fl oz boiling water
4 oz tomato purée, mixed with 4 fl
 oz water
¾ teaspoon capers
½ teaspoon ground coriander
½ teaspoon saffron or turmeric
6 oz cooked lobster
6 oz cooked shrimp
6 oz cooked pork, shredded
6 oz drained canned, mussels
shredded canned pimientos to
 garnish

In small cup combine salt, oregano, lemon juice, pepper and garlic to make a paste. Brown chicken, onion and green pepper in large heavy, preheated nonstick saucepan. Stir in seasoned paste. Add rice, peas, artichoke hearts, boiling water, tomato purée mixed with water, capers, coriander and saffron or turmeric; heat thoroughly. Stir in lobster, shrimp, pork and mussels. Bring to a boil, then reduce heat and simmer for 10 minutes. Garnish with pimientos. Serve hot. Divide evenly. Makes 6 evening meal servings.

Each serving is equivalent to: 2 oz Poultry; 4 oz Limited Vegetable; ⅓ serving Vegetables; 1 serving Choice Group; ⅓ serving Bonus (⅔ oz tomato purée); 3 oz Fish; 1 oz 'Beef' Group

Note: This recipe must be counted as a 'Beef' Group meal.

Swiss-Style Pot-au-Feu

2 lbs boned pork cut into 1-inch cubes
2 lbs boned veal shoulder, cut into 1-inch cubes
1 pint 12 fl oz Chicken Stock (see page 135)
1½ lbs peeled potatoes, cut into 1-inch cubes
12 oz carrots, cut into 2-inch thick slices
8 oz cabbage, shredded
4 oz peeled white turnips, cut into 2-inch thick slices
4 oz onion, diced
bouquet garni (2 cloves, 2 sprigs thyme, 1 bay leaf, tied in muslin) (optional)
¼ teaspoon pepper
salt to taste

Grill pork and veal on rack until well browned on all sides. Transfer to heavy saucepan. Add remaining ingredients. Bring to a boil; reduce heat. Cover and simmer for 1½ to 2 hours, or until meat is very tender. Remove cover for the last hour if desired, to reduce liquid. Discard bouquet garni if used. Divide evenly. Makes 8 evening meal servings.

Each serving is equivalent to: 3 oz 'Beef' Group; 3 oz Veal; ⅔ serving Something Extra (4 fl oz stock); 1 serving Choice Group; 1 serving Vegetables; ½ oz Limited Vegetable

Baked Fresh Ham

To bake, place fresh ham on rack in roasting tin. Insert meat thermometer into centre, not touching bone. Bake at 325°F, Gas Mark 3, for 18 to 24 minutes per lb or until thermometer registers 170°F. Slice and weigh portions.

Barbecue Ham on Rolls

2 oz onion, finely diced
1 teaspoon beef stock powder
1 garlic clove, crushed
8 oz cooked ham, cut into ¼-inch dice
2 oz tomato purée
2 fl oz water
3 tablespoons plus 1 teaspoon chilli sauce
2 tablespoons cider vinegar
1 tablespoon prepared mustard
2 teaspoons lemon juice
½ teaspoon barbecue spice
salt to taste
2 hamburger baps, split

In nonstick frying pan combine onion, stock powder and garlic; cook for 2 minutes. Add remaining ingredients except baps and stir to combine. Simmer for 10 minutes. Divide evenly. Serve each portion on 1 hamburger bap. Makes 2 evening meal servings.

Each serving is equivalent to: 1 oz Limited Vegetable; 3 servings Something Extra (½ teaspoon stock powder and 1 tablespoon plus 2 teaspoons chilli sauce); 4 oz 'Beef' Group (smoked); ½ serving Bonus (1 oz tomato purée); 2 servings Bread (once-a-week selection)

Bologna Cornucopia Salad

6 oz bologna or boiled ham, sliced
6 oz peeled cooked potato, diced
4 oz cooked peas
2 oz cooked beetroot, diced
2 tablespoons mayonnaise

2 tablespoons water
pinch prepared horseradish
2 dill pickled cucumbers, 3 oz each
parsley sprigs to garnish

Roll each slice of meat into cone-shaped cornucopia. In bowl combine all remaining ingredients except pickles and parsley; fill each cornucopia with equal amount of mixture. Divide evenly into 2 portions. Serve each portion with 1 dill pickled cucumber and parsley to garnish. Makes 2 midday meal servings.

Each serving is equivalent to: 3 oz 'Beef' Group (smoked); 1 serving Choice Group; 3 oz Limited Vegetable; 3 servings Fat; 1 serving Vegetables

Barbecued Frankfurters

4 fl oz cold water
3 oz onion, chopped, or 2
    tablespoons dried onion flakes
6 tablespoons tomato ketchup
3 tablespoons cider vinegar

¾ teaspoon dry mustard
¾ teaspoon paprika
freshly ground pepper to taste
12 oz frankfurters, cut in half,
    lengthwise

In saucepan combine water, onion, tomato ketchup, vinegar, dry mustard, paprika and pepper; bring to boil. Reduce heat; simmer for 5 minutes. Arrange frankfurters side by side in shallow 9 × 9-

inch baking tin. Cover with onion–tomato ketchup mixture and bake at 350°F, Gas Mark 4, for 30 to 40 minutes. Divide evenly. Makes 3 evening meal servings.

Each serving is equivalent to: 1 oz Limited Vegetable (optional); 3 servings Something Extra (2 tablespoons tomato ketchup); 4 oz Frankfurters

Quick-and-Easy Cassoulet

A modern-day version of a famous French stew that originally required long preparation. Done our way it's still delicious, and it's also economical and fast. Serve it with a tossed salad and fresh fruit for dessert.

1 lb drained canned dried kidney or white beans, plus 4 fl oz liquid	9 oz cooked carrots, sliced
	4 oz tomato purée
	4 fl oz water
8 oz frankfurters, cut into 1-inch thick slices	2 teaspoons chopped fresh parsley
	1 small garlic clove, crushed

Combine all ingredients in large saucepan. Cover; bring to a boil. Reduce heat and simmer for 15 minutes. Remove cover and continue cooking until thickened, stirring occasionally. Divide evenly. Makes 4 evening meal servings.

Each serving is equivalent to: 4 oz Dried Beans; 2 oz Frankfurters; ¾ serving Vegetables; ½ serving Bonus (1 oz tomato purée)

Offal

Offal includes hearts, kidneys, sweetbreads and tripe. Tongue also comes into this category but may be eaten more frequently than the above meats. (See 'Rules for Using "Beef" Group', page 155).

Offal is usually a good buy because it is a good source of nutrients and often in less demand than other cuts. Since hearts, kidneys, etc. are more perishable than other meats, they should be cooked and served as soon after purchase as possible.

Sweetbreads

Sweetbreads, the two lobes of the thymus gland, are a tender and delicately flavoured meat. They should be used immediately after purchase or precooked and used within a day or two.

Soak sweetbreads for 1 hour in cold water to cover. Drain. Then place in saucepan and cover with water. Add 1 teaspoon salt and 1 tablespoon lemon juice or vinegar for each quart of water used. Simmer, uncovered, for 15 to 20 minutes. Drain and plunge sweetbreads in cold water to firm. When cool, trim to remove sinews, tubes, membranes and connective tissue. Weigh portions.

Suggestions for serving sweetbreads
For each serving:

1. Place 6 oz cooked sweetbreads in shallow pan. Cover with 1 serving (¼ recipe) hot Basic White Sauce (see page 278) seasoned with lemon juice and parsley. Heat and serve in 2 Toast Cups I (see page 80) with 4 oz cooked peas. Makes 1 evening meal serving.

Each serving is equivalent to: 6 oz Sweetbreads; Basic White Sauce (see page 278); Toast Cups I (see page 80); 4 oz Limited Vegetable

2. In shallow pan combine 3 oz diced cooked sweetbreads and 2 oz cooked ham. Top with 1 serving (¼ recipe) Tomato Sauce (see page 288). Season with cayenne pepper and Worcester sauce. Heat and serve. Makes 1 evening meal serving.

Each serving is equivalent to: 3 oz Sweetbreads; 2 oz 'Beef' Group (smoked); Tomato Sauce (see page 288)

3. In nonstick pan scramble 1 standard egg with 2 oz diced cooked sweetbreads. Serve topped with 2½ fl oz natural unsweetened yogurt and 1½ oz tomato, sliced. Makes 1 midday meal serving.

Each serving is equivalent to: 1 Egg; 2 oz Sweetbreads; ½ serving Milk (2½ fl oz yogurt); ½ serving Vegetables

TRIPE

Tripe is usually partially cooked before it is sold. However, further preparation is necessary.

Put tripe in saucepan and cover with water. Allow 1 teaspoon salt for each quart of water used. Simmer in covered pan 1½ hours or until tender. Drain and dry between paper towels. Weigh servings.

Suggestions for serving tripe
1. Place 6 oz cooked tripe in shallow baking tin and cover with 1 serving (¼ recipe) Tomato Sauce (see page 288). Bake at 350°F, Gas Mark 4, until bubbling. Makes 1 evening meal serving.
   Each serving is equivalent to: 6 oz Tripe; Tomato Sauce (see page 288).
2. Place 6 oz cooked tripe in shallow tin, brush with 1 teaspoon margarine, and grill 1 minute. Makes 1 evening meal serving.
   Each serving is equivalent to: 6 oz Tripe; 1 serving Fat
3. Shred 6 oz cooked tripe and combine in saucepan with 6 fl oz Beef Stock (see page 157), 1 oz each diced celery, carrot and green pepper, 2 oz diced onion and 3 oz diced peeled potato. Cover and simmer until vegetables are tender. Add ¼ oz nonfat dry milk mixed with 2 tablespoons water. Makes 1 evening meal serving.
   Each serving is equivalent to: 6 oz Tripe; 1 serving Something Extra (6 fl oz stock); 1 serving Vegetables; 2 oz Limited Vegetable; 1 serving Choice Group; ¼ serving Milk (2½ fl oz skim milk)

Heart and Wheat Pilaf

Before cooking hearts, wash thoroughly; remove fat, arteries and veins. Weigh.

3 lbs veal or beef heart, cut into ½-inch thick slices
1 pint 4 fl oz beef bouillon (made with 2 stock cubes)
6 oz dry cracked wheat (Bulgur)
6 oz onion, chopped

12 oz green peppers, seeded and chopped
½ teaspoon cinnamon
½ teaspoon salt, or to taste
¼ teaspoon pepper, or to taste

In saucepan simmer heart in water to cover for 1 hour. Drain. Add remaining ingredients and cook for 1 hour or until heart is tender, adding water if necessary. Divide evenly. Makes 6 evening meal servings.

Each serving is equivalent to: 6 oz Heart; $^1/_3$ serving Something Extra ($^1/_3$ stock cube); 1 serving Choice Group; 1 oz Limited Vegetable; $^2/_3$ serving Vegetables

Kidneys in Parsley 'Butter'

2 teaspoons margarine
1 lb trimmed, cooked veal or lamb
  kidneys, cut into ¼-inch thick
  slices
1 teaspoon lemon juice

salt and freshly ground pepper to
  taste
1 tablespoon chopped fresh parsley
2 slices white bread, toasted

Melt margarine in top of double boiler over boiling water. Add kidneys, lemon juice, salt and pepper. Simmer for 10 minutes or until heated through. Stir in parsley and serve on toast. Divide evenly. Makes 2 evening meal servings.

Each serving is equivalent to: 6 oz Kidneys; 1 serving Fat; 1 serving Bread

Boiled Fresh Beef Tongue

2½ lbs to 3 lbs fresh beef or calf
  tongue
4 oz carrots, sliced
2 oz celery with leaves, sliced
4 parsley sprigs

1 lemon slice
8 peppercorns
2 cloves
1 teaspoon salt for each quart
  water

Rinse tongue and place in large pot with remaining ingredients except salt. Cover with boiling water; add salt. Bring to a boil, then reduce heat and simmer until tongue is tender, for 2 to 3 hours. Add more water as needed. Drain. Cool by immersing tongue in cold water. When it is easy to handle, remove skin, roots, small bones, and gristle. Slice the tongue on a slight diagonal. Serve hot or cold. Weigh portions. Makes about 4 midday or evening meal servings.

Each serving is equivalent to: 4 to 6 oz 'Beef' Group

When using smoked or pickled tongue—These tend to be salty. First blanch tongue for 10 minutes. Immerse in cold water, drain and proceed as above, omitting salt. When weighing portions, use

the low end of the range (see 'The Food Programme', page 6).
Each serving is equivalent to: 3 to 4 oz 'Beef' Group (smoked)

Tongue and Potato Salad

12 oz peeled cooked potatoes, diced	1½ oz dill pickled cucumber, chopped
8 oz cooked peas	
6 oz cooked smoked beef tongue, diced	2½ fl oz natural unsweetened yogurt
9½ oz cooked cut green beans	2 tablespoons mayonnaise
3 oz celery, diced	1 tablespoon lemon juice

In bowl combine first 6 ingredients. In separate bowl combine remaining ingredients; pour over potato mixture and toss to combine. Chill. Divide evenly. Makes 4 midday meal servings. Supplement as required.

Each serving is equivalent to: 1 serving Choice Group; 2 oz Limited Vegetable; 1½ oz 'Beef' Group (smoked); 1⅙ servings Vegetables; ⅛ serving Milk (⅝ fl oz yogurt); 1½ servings Fat

Sweet-and-Sour Tongue with Water Chestnuts

1 slice currant bread, torn into pieces	artificial sweetener to equal ½ teaspoon sugar, or to taste (optional)
4 fl oz chicken bouillon (made with ½ stock cube)	8 oz Boiled Fresh Beef Tongue, sliced (see page 178)
2 oz onion, diced	
2 tablespoons cider vinegar	4 oz drained canned water chestnuts, sliced
1 slice fresh ginger root	

In a small saucepan combine first 6 ingredients. Simmer, stirring occasionally, until bread falls apart and mixture thickens. Add tongue and water chestnuts. Cook until thoroughly heated. Divide evenly. Makes 2 midday meal servings.

Each serving is equivalent to: ½ serving Bread; ¼ serving Something Extra (¼ stock cube); 3 oz Limited Vegetable; 4 oz 'Beef' Group

LIVER

If you've had only grilled or baked liver, or liver paté we think you're in for a treat once you discover liver in all its versatile flavours and cooking styles.

Try marinating liver or cooking it Polynesian Style. Flavour liver recipes with ginger, soy sauce or our Basic White Sauce. There's really no end to the interesting variety you can get from a few kinds of liver. Try them all.

Rules for Using Liver

1. Amounts (net cooked weight):
   Women, Men and Teenagers: 3 to 4 oz at the midday meal
   Women and Teenagers: 4 to 6 oz at the evening meal
   Men: 6 to 8 oz at the evening meal
2. The range of 3 to 4 oz of liver at the midday meal, and 4 to 6 oz for Women and Teenagers (6 to 8 oz for Men) at the evening meal, provides flexibility. It is a way to individualise the Programme to meet your specific needs.
3. Select liver only once a week.
4. As a 'rule of thumb', for each serving of liver allow 2 oz for shrinkage in cooking.
5. All liver is 'legal'. Do not split a liver meal. Do not take it as a breakfast selection.
6. **Cooking procedures:** May be boiled, poached, grilled, dry-fried or baked. Cooked or uncooked liver may be used with added ingredients (e.g. casseroles, stews, etc). Liquid and added ingredients may be consumed.

How to Cook Liver

For grilling, have liver sliced ½ to ¾ inch thick. Grill according to directions on page 157 ('How to Cook Meat') just long enough to brown lightly. Allow about 3 minutes on each side. To dry-fry, cook liver in a nonstick frying pan, at moderate temperature, until done. Turn occasionally.

Beef Liver Oriental

4 oz spring onions, sliced
2 oz celery, chopped
1 garlic clove, crushed
1½ lbs beef liver, cut into 1-inch cubes

1 tablespoon flour
⅛ teaspoon ginger
⅛ teaspoon pepper
6 fl oz water
3 tablespoons soy sauce

Sauté spring onions, celery and garlic in nonstick pan for 3 minutes; remove from pan and set aside. Add liver to pan and brown on all sides over high heat. Sprinkle with flour, ginger and pepper. Stir in water and soy sauce, and simmer for 3 minutes. Add vegetables and cook to heat vegetables. Divide evenly. Makes 4 midday meal servings.

Each serving is equivalent to: 1 oz Limited Vegetable; ¹⁄₆ serving Vegetables; 4 oz Liver; ¾ serving Something Extra (¾ teaspoon flour)

Liver and Cucumber Soup

12 oz beef liver, cut into 1-inch cubes
6 oz cucumber, peeled
12 fl oz beef bouillon (made with 2 stock cubes)

1 small piece dried tangerine peel (optional)*
salt and pepper to taste
6 oz cooked rice (optional)

*Available in Chinese grocery store.

Blanch the liver in boiling water to cover for 3 minutes; drain and dry. Cut cucumber in half, lengthwise; remove and discard seeds. Cut into ¼-inch slices. In saucepan combine liver, cucumber, bouillon and tangerine peel, if desired. Bring to boil, reduce heat, and simmer for 20 minutes. Season with salt and pepper. Stir in rice if desired. Divide evenly. Makes 2 midday meal servings.

Each serving is equivalent to: 4 oz Liver; 1 serving Vegetables; 1 serving Something Extra (1 stock cube); 1 serving Choice Group (optional)

Liver and Vegetables in One Pot

3 oz peeled potato, diced
3 oz courgettes, sliced
2 oz onion, diced
1½ oz aubergine, peeled and diced
1½ oz mushrooms, sliced
4 fl oz water
½ garlic clove, crushed

1 teaspoon salt
pinch cayenne pepper
8 oz beef liver, cut into ½-inch
    thick slices
2 oz peas
1 tablespoon chopped fresh parsley

Combine all ingredients except liver, peas and parsley in saucepan. Bring to a boil, then reduce heat, cover and simmer for 15 minutes. In bowl cover liver with boiling water and let stand for 3 minutes; drain and dry with paper towels. Add liver and peas to vegetables and simmer for 5 minutes, or until liver slices are done. Sprinkle with parsley and serve. Makes 1 evening meal serving.

Each serving is equivalent to: 1 serving Choice Group; 2 servings Vegetables; 4 oz Limited Vegetable; 6 oz Liver

Liver Chop Suey

½ oz dried mushrooms
1½ lbs beef liver, cut into ¼-inch
    thick slices
6 fl oz chicken bouillon (made with
    1 stock cube)
1 tablespoon cornflour
1 teaspoon soy sauce

6 oz green pepper, seeded and
    sliced
3 oz canned bamboo shoots, sliced
1½ oz celery, finely sliced
1 garlic clove, crushed
4 oz Chinese pea pods (mange tout)
4 oz tomato, cut into 8 wedges

In small bowl cover mushrooms with boiling water and let soak for 20 minutes or until soft. Drain. Cut stems from mushrooms. Discard stems; slice and reserve caps. Cut sliced liver into ½-inch long strips and place in medium bowl. Cover with boiling water. Drain and dry. Combine bouillon, cornflour and soy sauce in bowl. Mix well to dissolve cornflour. Set aside. Brown liver in preheated nonstick frying pan or wok over high heat. Lower heat and add green pepper, bamboo shoots, celery, garlic, mushrooms, and bouillon-cornflour-soy sauce mixture; sauté stirring frequently, until slightly thickened. Add Chinese pea pods (mange tout) and tomato. Sauté for 3 minutes. Divide evenly. Makes 4 midday meal servings.

Each serving is equivalent to: 1¼ servings Vegetables; 4 oz Liver; 1 serving Something Extra (¼ stock cube and ¾ teaspoon cornflour); 1 oz Limited Vegetable.

Variation: If Chinese pea pods (mange tout) are not available, 6 oz cooked green beans may be substituted. Add 1 oz finely diced spring onions before serving.

Each serving is equivalent to: 1¾ servings Vegetables; 4 oz Liver; 1 serving Something Extra (1½ fl oz bouillon and ¾ teaspoon cornflour); ¼ oz Limited Vegetable

Liver Pudding

A Scandinavian dish.

12 oz beef liver
2 oz onion
6 oz cooked rice, chilled

4 dried medium prunes, stoned
and chopped
salt and pepper to taste

In bowl pour boiling water over liver and let stand for a few minutes. Drain and dry. Put liver and onion through mincer. Combine minced liver mixture, rice, prunes, salt and pepper. Pour into nonstick baking tin. Bake at 350°F, Gas Mark 4, for 45 minutes or until pudding is hot and bubbling. Divide evenly. Makes 2 midday meal servings.

Each serving is equivalent to: 4 oz Liver; 1 oz Limited Vegetable; 1 serving Choice Group; ½ serving Fruit

Grilled Liver and Onions

6 oz onion, sliced
4 fl oz chicken bouillon (made with
  ½ stock cube)
¼ teaspoon Worcester sauce

pinch nutmeg
salt and pepper to taste
1½ lbs calf or beef liver, sliced

In saucepan combine all ingredients except liver. Cook until onions are tender and most of the liquid is evaporated. Place liver on rack; grill 4 inches from source of heat, turning once, until done to taste. Serve onion mixture over liver. Divide evenly. Makes 4 midday meal servings.

Each serving is equivalent to: 1½ oz Limited Vegetable; ⅛ serving Something Extra (⅛ stock cube); 4 oz Liver

Liver Casserole

1½ lbs calf or beef liver
9 oz carrots, thinly sliced
12 oz peeled potatoes, thinly sliced
8 oz onion, sliced
16 fl oz beef bouillon (made with 2
  stock cubes)

3 oz canned tomatoes, chopped
1½ teaspoons basil
1 bay leaf
salt and pepper to taste

Cut liver into thin strips; place in bowl and cover with boiling water; let stand for 3 minutes. Drain and dry with paper towels. In saucepan add carrots to boiling water, boil for 5 minutes; add potatoes, boil for 5 minutes longer. Drain. Layer liver, carrots, potatoes and onion in a large casserole. Combine remaining ingredients and add to casserole. Bake at 350°F, Gas Mark 4, for 1 hour or until vegetables are tender. Divide evenly. Makes 4 midday meal servings.

Each serving is equivalent to: 4 oz Liver; 1 serving Vegetables; 1 serving Choice Group; 2 oz Limited Vegetable; ½ serving Something Extra (½ stock cube)

Liver Mexican Style

2 lbs calf or beef liver
½ teaspoon garlic powder
salt and pepper to taste
2 oz chilli peppers, cut into strips
2 tablespoons plus 2 teaspoons
  vegetable oil

2 tablespoons lemon juice
2 tablespoons chopped fresh
  parsley
8 toasted tortillas (6 inches each)

Cut liver into thin strips; season with garlic powder, salt and pepper. Brown in nonstick frying pan over moderately high heat for 6 minutes or until done to taste. Transfer to serving bowl and toss immediately with chilli peppers, oil, lemon juice and parsley. Divide evenly onto toasted tortillas. Makes 4 evening meal servings.

Each serving is equivalent to: 6 oz Liver; $\frac{1}{6}$ serving Vegetables; 2 servings Fat; 2 servings Bread (once-a-week selection)

Liver 'n' Noodle Casserole

12 oz calf or beef liver, cut into ½-
  inch cubes
4 oz onion, sliced
3 oz green pepper, seeded and
  diced
4 oz tomato purée

4 fl oz water
¼ teaspoon thyme
¼ teaspoon gravy browning
salt and pepper to taste
6 oz cooked wide noodles
3 oz cooked carrots, sliced

Brown liver, onion and green pepper in a preheated nonstick frying pan over moderately high heat. Add tomato purée, water, thyme, gravy browning, salt and pepper. Sauté over medium heat until pepper is tender. Stir in noodles and carrots and heat thoroughly. Divide evenly. Makes 2 midday meal servings.

Each serving is equivalent to: 4 oz Liver; 2 oz Limited Vegetable; 1 serving Vegetables; 1 serving Bonus (2 oz tomato purée); 1 serving Choice Group

Baked Whole Calf Liver

2 lbs calf liver
1 teaspoon salt
¼ teaspoon pepper
6 oz mushrooms, sliced

4 oz onion, sliced
2 oz celery, diced
6 fl oz beef bouillon (made with 1
   stock cube)

Sprinkle liver with salt and pepper. Place in 2-pint baking dish. Surround with mushrooms, onion and celery. Add bouillon. Cover and bake at 350°F, Gas Mark 4, for 1½ hours or until liver is done to taste. Divide evenly. Makes 4 evening meal servings.

Each serving is equivalent to: 6 oz Liver; ²/₃ serving Vegetables; 1 oz Limited Vegetable; ¼ serving Something Extra (¼ stock cube)

Calf Liver with Grapes

1 lb calf liver, cut into ½-inch
   thick slices
salt and freshly ground pepper to
   taste

2 teaspoons lemon juice
40 small seedless green grapes
2 teaspoons margarine
2 teaspoons chopped fresh parsley

In medium bowl pour boiling water over liver; drain and dry with paper towels. Season with salt and pepper. Brown liver in preheated nonstick frying pan over high heat, remove from pan and keep hot. Reduce heat to medium level. Add lemon juice and grapes to pan, mashing a few of the grapes to release their juices and to heat fruit. Remove pan from heat and stir in margarine. Serve sauce over liver. Garnish with parsley. Divide evenly. Makes 2 evening meal servings.

Each serving is equivalent to: 6 oz Liver; 1 serving Fruit; 1 serving Fat

'Creamed' Calf Liver

12 oz calf liver, cut into ¼-inch
   thick slices

½ recipe Basic White Sauce (2
   servings, see page 278)
2 teaspoons chopped fresh parsley

Grill liver on a rack 4 inches from source of heat, turning once until done to taste. Cut into 1-inch long pieces and combine with remaining ingredients in top of double boiler over boiling water. Heat thoroughly. Divide evenly. Makes 2 midday meal servings.

Each serving is equivalent to: 4 oz Liver; Basic White Sauce (see page 278)

Variation:
Liver Tetrazzini—Serve 'Creamed' Calf Liver on a bed of 6 oz cooked spaghetti surrounded with 6 oz drained canned artichoke hearts. Add 1 serving Choice Group and 3 oz Limited Vegetable to equivalent listing.

Lemony Calf Liver

1½ lbs calf liver
salt and freshly ground pepper to
taste
2 tablespoons vegetable oil

1 tablespoon lemon juice
1 teaspoon finely chopped fresh
parsley

Dry liver with paper towel; season with salt and pepper. Place in flameproof casserole and grill 4 inches from source of heat, turning once, until done. Brush with oil and lemon juice. Place under grill for 1 minute; sprinkle with parsley and serve. Divide evenly. Makes 4 midday meal servings.

Each serving is equivalent to: 4 oz Liver; 1½ servings Fat

Mustard Grilled Liver

1 lb calf liver, cut into ½-inch
thick slices
salt and pepper to taste
1 slice white bread, made into
crumbs
1 tablespoon chopped fresh parsley

1 tablespoon Dijon mustard
1 teaspoon dried onion flakes,
reconstituted in 1 teaspoon
water
1 garlic clove, crushed
1 tablespoon margarine

Sprinkle liver with salt and pepper; grill 3 inches from source of heat, turning once. In bowl combine crumbs, parsley, mustard, onion flakes and garlic. Place liver in heatproof shallow casserole. Top with crumb mixture. Dot with margarine. Place under grill for 1 minute. Divide evenly. Makes 2 evening meal servings.

Each serving is equivalent to: 6 oz Liver; ½ serving Bread; 1½ servings Fat

Poached Liver

1½ lbs calf liver
3 oz celery with leaves, cut into
   2-inch pieces
10 parsley sprigs

1 tablespoon dried onion flakes
6 black peppercorns, crushed
½ teaspoon salt
1 bay leaf

Place liver, celery, parsley, onion flakes, peppercorns, salt and bay leaf in 8-pint saucepan. Add enough water to barely cover meat. Bring to a boil; cover and lower heat; simmer for 45 minutes or until liver is no longer pink in centre when slashed. Remove from liquid and serve hot, or cool in liquid, cover, and refrigerate. Remove from liquid and serve cold. Divide evenly. Makes 4 midday meal servings.

Each serving is equivalent to: 4 oz Liver

Brown Rice, Vermicelli and Liver Pilaf

1½ lbs chicken livers, halved
4 oz onion, finely diced
3 oz mushrooms, sliced
3 oz green pepper, seeded and
   finely diced
6 oz cooked toasted vermicelli (see
   page 114)

6 oz cooked toasted brown rice (see
   page 114)
4 oz tomato purée
4 fl oz water
4 fl oz chicken bouillon (made with
   ½ stock cube)
salt and pepper to taste

Place livers in grill pan and grill 4 inches from source of heat for 3 to 4 minutes, turning until all sides are browned. Transfer to saucepan and add vegetables. Cook 3 minutes. Add remaining ingredients and simmer for 10 minutes. Divide evenly. Makes 4 midday meal servings.

Each serving is equivalent to: 4 oz Liver; 1 oz Limited Vegetable; ½ serving Vegetables; 1 serving Choice Group; ½ serving Bonus (1 oz tomato purée); ⅛ serving Something Extra (⅛ stock cube)

Chicken Liver and Celery Sandwich

4 oz cooked chicken livers
2 oz celery, chopped
¼ recipe Basic French Dressing (1 serving, see page 283)

1 slice rye bread
1 oz red onion, sliced

Mash liver in a small bowl. Stir in celery and French Dressing. Cut bread horizontally to make two thin slices. Spread liver on one thin slice, top with onion and remaining slice of bread. Makes 1 midday meal serving.

Each serving is equivalent to: 4 oz Liver; ⅔ serving Vegetables; Basic French Dressing (see page 283); 1 serving Bread; 1 oz Limited Vegetable

Chicken Livers in Orange Sauce

2 lbs chicken livers
salt and pepper to taste
8 oz orange sections, no sugar added

8 fl oz orange juice
1 oz onion, chopped
1 teaspoon soy sauce

Cut each liver in half, sprinkle with salt and pepper, and place in grill pan. Grill 3 inches from source of heat for 1 minute on each side. Do not overcook; inside should be pink. Combine remaining ingredients in 4-pint flameproof casserole. Bring to a boil; reduce heat. Simmer for 7 minutes or until mixture is reduced by about ⅓. Add grilled livers, cook just long enough to heat livers. Divide evenly. Makes 4 evening meal servings.

Each serving is equivalent to: 6 oz Liver; 1 serving Fruit; ¼ oz Limited Vegetable

Chicken Liver Rolls

4 oz poached chicken livers
1 tablespoon mayonnaise
1 oz onion, grated
salt and pepper to taste
4 lettuce leaves

3 oz tomato, sliced
3 oz cucumber, peeled and sliced
1½ oz radishes, sliced
1½ oz canned pimiento, sliced

In small bowl, mash livers while still warm. Stir in mayonnaise, onion, salt and pepper. Chill. Spoon ¼ of mixture onto each lettuce leaf. Roll, folding sides in; secure with toothpicks if necessary. Serve with tomato and cucumber. Garnish with radishes and pimiento. Makes 1 midday meal serving.

Each serving is equivalent to: 4 oz Liver; 3 servings Fat; 1 oz Limited Vegetable; 3 servings Vegetables

Liver with Croutons

2 oz onion, sliced
12 oz chicken livers, halved
2 fl oz chicken bouillon (made with
   ¼ stock cube)
3 tablespoons red wine vinegar
1 teaspoon capers

1 garlic clove, crushed
¼ teaspoon salt
⅛ teaspoon pepper
6 oz cooked cauliflower florets
2 slices white bread, toasted and
   cut into ½-inch cubes

In nonstick frying pan, cook onions over medium heat until lightly browned. Add liver; cook for 10 minutes. Add bouillon, vinegar, capers, garlic, salt and pepper. Simmer for 10 minutes. Spoon chicken liver mixture onto serving dish. Surround with cauliflower florets and top with bread cubes. Divide evenly. Makes 2 midday meal servings.

Each serving is equivalent to: 1 oz Limited Vegetable; 4 oz Liver; ⅛ serving Something Extra (⅛ stock cube); 1 serving Vegetables; 1 serving Bread

Polynesian Livers with Bean Sprouts

1½ pints water
1 lb chicken livers
12 oz green peppers, seeded and
  sliced
3 oz bean sprouts
6 fl oz chicken bouillon (made with
  1 stock cube)
2 oz onion, diced
1 teaspoon salt
¼ teaspoon ginger

pepper to taste
8 oz canned pineapple chunks, no
  sugar added
½ oz dried mushrooms,
  reconstituted in warm water and
  diced
2 tablespoons cider vinegar
1 tablespoon cornflour, dissolved in
  3 tablespoons water

Bring water to a boil in large frying pan; add livers and boil for one minute. Drain and discard liquid. Add peppers, bean sprouts, bouillon, onion, salt, ginger and pepper. Cover and simmer for 10 minutes. Add pineapple and mushrooms to frying pan. Stir in vinegar and cornflour; simmer, stirring constantly, until mixture is thickened. Divide evenly. Makes 2 evening meal servings.

Each serving is equivalent to: 6 oz Liver; 2½ servings Vegetables; 2 servings Something Extra (½ stock cube and 1½ teaspoons cornflour); 1 oz Limited Vegetable; 1 serving Fruit

Quick-and-Easy Chicken Livers and Mushrooms

3 oz green pepper, seeded and
  diced
1½ oz mushrooms, diced
1 oz onion, diced
6 oz chicken livers, quartered
2 teaspoons flour

½ teaspoon salt
⅛ teaspoon paprika
4 fl oz Chicken Stock (see page
  135)
1 slice white bread, toasted, or
  3 oz cooked rice

In nonstick frying pan brown green pepper, mushrooms and onion. Add livers and sprinkle with flour, salt and paprika. Sauté over moderate heat, stirring frequently, until liver loses pink colour. Add stock and bring to a boil. Reduce heat and simmer, stirring often, until thickened. Serve on toast or over rice. Makes 1 midday meal serving.

Each serving is equivalent to: 1½ servings Vegetables; 1 oz Limited Vegetable; 4 oz Liver; 2 ²/₃ servings Something Extra (2 teaspoons flour and 4 fl oz stock); 1 serving Bread or 1 serving Choice Group

Variation: Add 3 oz drained canned or frozen peas to preceding recipe. Add 3 oz Limited Vegetable to equivalent listing.

Spiced Chinese Livers

1 lb chicken livers, halved	1 tablespoon lemon juice
1 oz spring onions, sliced	½ teaspoon fresh ginger root,
3 tablespoons soy sauce	sliced
artificial sweetener to equal ½	⅛ teaspoon anise seed
teaspoon sugar, or to taste	1 teaspoon sesame oil

In saucepan pour boiling water over livers; drain, dry, and return to pan. Add all remaining ingredients except oil. Cover pan and sauté for 10 minutes or until livers are done. Transfer to bowl; stir in oil. Cover and chill for several hours or overnight. Remove livers from marinade; slice. Serve cold with marinade. Divide evenly. Makes 2 evening meal servings.

Each serving is equivalent to: 6 oz Liver; ½ oz Limited Vegetable; ½ serving Fat

FISH

*

Cast your fishing line in any ocean, lake, or stream around the world . . . and anything you hook that's edible is also 'legal'. You can be quite creative with fish, too. Use it in soups, stews, salads or pies, in fish cakes and loaves, or even stuffed with vegetables.

Rules for Using Fish

1. Amounts (net cooked weight):
   Women, Men and Teenagers: 2 oz at the morning meal
                                          3 to 4 oz at the midday meal
   Women and Teenagers: 4 to 6 oz at the evening meal
   Men: 6 to 8 oz at the evening meal
2. The range of 3 to 4 oz of fish at the midday meal, and 4 to 6 oz for Women and Teenagers (6 to 8 oz for Men) at the evening meal, provides flexibility. It is a way to individualise the Programme to meet your specific needs.
3. If smoked fish is selected, use the *lower* end of the serving range.
4. Select any fish in the marketplace at least 3 to 5 times weekly. Vary selections. Use fresh, frozen, canned or smoked fish. Do not use fish packed in olive oil. All canned fish must be well drained.
5. It is strongly recommended that 5 fish meals be eaten weekly. However, if fish is selected 3 or 4 times a week, chicken must be substituted for the 1 or 2 fish meals which have been omitted.
6. As a 'rule of thumb', for each serving of fish allow 2 oz for shrinkage in cooking and 2 oz for bone. When splitting an item from the fish category, for each half-serving allow 1 oz for

193

shrinkage in cooking and 1 oz for bone. Weigh the serving after cooking, whenever possible.
7. As a 'rule of thumb', count 5 small scallops, or 4 scampi or 6 prawns as equal to 1 oz of fish.
8. When fish is selected at the morning meal or in combination with poultry, meat, egg, cheese, or dried peas/beans at the midday meal or evening meal, it may not be counted as a fish meal.
9. *Cooking Procedures:* May be boiled, poached, grilled, dry-fried or baked. Cooked or uncooked fish may be used with added ingredients (e.g. casseroles, stews, etc.) Liquid and added ingredients may be consumed.

Fish Tips

Fresh and Frozen Fish

Fresh and frozen fish are available in the following forms:
1. *Whole*—Fish as it comes from the water. Before cooking, it must be scaled, gutted, and the head, tail, and fins removed.
2. *Cleaned*—Whole fish with only scales and entrails removed. May be cooked as is or cut into fillets, steaks, or chunks.
3. *Steaks*—Cross-section slices from large cleaned fish. A cross-section of the backbone is the only bone in a steak.
4. *Fillets*—Sides of the fish cut lengthwise away from the backbone.

Purchasing tips for fish
1. *Fresh Fish*—Flesh should be firm and elastic. Steaks and fillets should have a fresh-cut appearance. There should be no unpleasant odour—really fresh fish has, in fact, hardly any smell. Eyes should be bright, clear and transparent; they should not appear sunken. Gills should be red and free from slime. Skin should be shiny and bright in colour.
2. *Frozen Fish*—Flesh should be solidly frozen, with no brown tinge or white cottony appearance. There should be little or no smell. Wrapping should be of moistureproof, vapourproof material, such as aluminium foil or freezer paper. There should be

little or no air space between the fish and the wrapping, and the package should appear undamaged.

Shellfish

Shellfish are available in a wide variety of forms:
1. *Live in the Shell*—Crabs, lobsters, mussels and oysters must be kept alive until cooked.
2. *Cooked in the Shell*—Crabs, lobsters and shrimps, chilled or frozen.
3. *Headless*—Lobster tails and shrimps ready to cook.
4. *Shucked or Fresh Meat*—Fresh or frozen mussels, oysters, scallops and shrimps.
5. *Cooked Meat*—Cooked crabs, lobsters, mussels, oysters and shrimps; meat picked from the shell. Available fresh, frozen or canned.

Shopping hints for shellfish:
Mussels and oysters in the shell should close tightly when tapped. If shell remains open, the shellfish is dead and not edible. Shucked oysters are plump, with a mild smell, creamy colour and a clear liquid. Cooked crabs and lobsters are bright red with no disagreeable smell. Fresh shrimps should be firm in texture with a mild smell. Scallops should have a mild, sweet smell and no excess liquid when purchased in packages.

Storage Tips for Fish and Shellfish

Fresh fish and shellfish should be rewrapped in foil or plastic wrap before refrigeration. Refrigerate as soon as possible after purchasing. Do not hold longer than a day or two before cooking. Fresh shellfish should be stored at approximately 32°F. It is best if eaten on the day of purchase.

Frozen fish and shellfish should be cooked immediately after thawing. Never refreeze it. Do not keep uncooked frozen fish in the freezer longer than six months.

Cooked fish and seafood should be stored either in the refrigerator or freezer; in the refrigerator, for no longer than 3 or 4 days; in the freezer, no more than 3 months. Store in the refrigerator, in a covered container; in the freezer, in moistureproof, vapourproof wrapping materials intended for freezers, such as aluminium foil or freezer paper.

Cooking Fish

The following directions apply chiefly to wet fish, but the same methods may be adapted to shellfish.

Never overcook. Fish cooked at too high a temperature or for too long a time becomes tough, dry, and loses its delicate flavour. When cooked, fish should be opaque, flake easily, and fall away from the bones. Handle gently. Fish flesh is delicate. Frozen fillets and steaks do not have to be thawed before cooking if cooking time is increased to allow for thawing during the cooking process.

Baking—Baking is cooking with dry heat. This is one of the easiest methods of cooking fish. It should usually be baked in an uncovered baking dish at a moderate temperature, 350°F, Gas Mark 4, for a relatively short time. This retains the moistness and flavour, prevents drying, and keeps fish tender and palatable.

Grilling—Grilling, like baking, is cooking with dry heat. In grilling, however, the heat is direct, intense and comes from only one source. Place fish in a single layer in grill pan. The surface of the fish should be 3 to 4 inches from the source of heat. Cooking time should range from 10 to 15 minutes. As a rule, fish fillets do not need to be turned because the heat of the pan cooks the underside adequately. Turn thicker pieces halfway through the cooking time. Always serve grilled fish sizzling hot.

Poaching—Poaching is cooking in a simmering liquid. Use a shallow frying pan wide enough to hold fish in a single layer. Barely cover with liquid, such as lightly salted water, fish stock or water seasoned with spices and herbs. Simmer in covered pan until fish flakes easily, usually 5 to 10 minutes. The poaching liquid may be reduced and thickened to make a tasty sauce for the fish. Poached fish may be served as it is, with a sauce, in a casserole, or chilled and flaked in cold dishes.

Steaming—Steaming is cooking by means of the steam generated from boiling water. Use a steam cooker or a deep pan with a tight cover and steaming rack, to keep the fish from touching the water. Use plain water or water seasoned with spices or herbs. Heat the water to a boil; then place the fish on the rack and cover the pan. Steam 5 to 10 minutes or until fish flakes easily when tested with a fork. Steamed fish may be served in the same manner as poached fish.

Court Bouillon for Poaching Fish

Enough for about 2 lbs of fish. If necessary, add more water to cover fish.

3½ pints water	2 teaspoons salt
4 oz celery, diced	4 parsley sprigs
4 oz carrots, sliced	3 peppercorns
¼ lemon, sliced	2 cloves
1 tablespoon chives	1 garlic clove, crushed
1 tablespoon lemon juice	1 bay leaf

Combine all ingredients in saucepan. Bring to a boil, simmer for 20 minutes. Drain and discard solids. Use court bouillon as poaching liquid for fish.

Fish Stock or Fumet

This broth can be the beginning of a hearty soup. It costs nothing if you ask for the trimming when you buy a filleted fish. Stock the trimmings in your freezer until you have enough to use, then just add vegetables and cook as below. You can vary seasonings: thyme and marjoram one time, a sprig of basil and oregano the next. The cooked, strained broth can be frozen too.

2 lbs fish bones and heads, gills removed	1 tablespoon lemon juice
2 pints water	2 garlic cloves, crushed
2 oz carrots, sliced	2 parsley sprigs
2 oz celery with leaves, chopped	1 bay leaf
2 oz onion, sliced	5 peppercorns
	salt to taste

Rinse the fish bones and heads thoroughly under running water. Combine with remaining ingredients in large saucepan. Simmer for 30 to 40 minutes, skimming off scum. Strain, pressing out juices. Adjust seasonings, if desired. Use in recipes calling for fish stock.

Basting Fish

Lean fish should be basted before it is baked or grilled. Other fish may be basted for additional flavour, if desired. Here are some suggestions:

1. A mixture of vegetable oil or melted margarine and lemon juice can be used for fish if it is to be baked. Use individual casseroles. Allow 1 serving of fat for each serving of fish. Pan juices must be consumed.
2. Fish to be grilled can be basted with low-calorie salad dressings (see 'Speciality Foods' page 294). *Do not baste* with a mixture of vegetable oil or melted margarine and lemon juice.
3. *After* fish is grilled, it *may* be basted with a mixture of melted margarine or vegetable oil and lemon juice, provided the grill pan has sides that will contain the pan juices. The grilled fish, topped with this base, may be put under the grill for no more than 1 minute (see 'Cooking Procedures', page 276). Serve fish with pan juices. Allow 1 serving of Fat for each serving of fish.
4. Slices of tomato put on fish before baking or grilling will keep it moist.
5. Nonfat dry milk (¼ oz) mixed with 3 tablespoons Fish Stock (see page 197) or water can be used to baste each serving of fish to be either baked or grilled. All pan juices must be consumed. Each serving of this basting liquid is equivalent to ¼ serving Milk (2½ fl oz skim milk)

Fish—a First Course

Anchovy Roll—Wrap 1 oz flat anchovies round 1 oz small radishes; secure with toothpicks. Garnish with capers speared on ends of toothpicks. Makes 1 serving. Serve at mealtime only. Supplement as required.

Each serving is equivalent to: 1 oz Fish; $^1/_3$ serving Vegetables

Mashed Tuna—Combine 2 oz drained tuna, flaked, and 1 teaspoon mayonnaise. Stuff into 1 whole roasted pepper and sprinkle with 1 teaspoon vinegar. Serve on lettuce leaves. Makes 1 serving. Serve at mealtime only. Supplement as required.

Each serving is equivalent to: 2 oz Fish; 1 serving Fat; 2 servings Vegetables

Sardine Canapés—In bowl mash 2 oz drained canned sardines with ½ oz chopped canned pimiento, 1 teaspoon tomato ketchup, 1 teaspoon dried onion flakes, dash Worcester sauce, salt and pepper to taste. Stir in 1 teaspoon mayonnaise or 1 tablespoon natural unsweetened yogurt. Spread sardine mixture on 1 serving Melba Toast (see page 80) and cut as desired. Makes 1 serving. Serve at mealtime only. Supplement as required.

Each serving is equivalent to: 2 oz Fish; $^1/_6$ serving Vegetables; ½ serving Something Extra (1 teaspoon tomato ketchup); 1 serving Fat or $^1/_{10}$ serving Milk (½ fl oz yogurt); Melba Toast (see page 80)

Seafood Cocktail—Chill 3 oz cooked crab, shrimp, or lobster meat. Serve on 1 oz shredded lettuce with 1 serving (¼ recipe) Cocktail Sauce (see page 286). Makes 1 evening meal serving. Supplement as required.

Each serving is equivalent to: 3 oz Fish; $^1/_3$ serving Vegetables; Cocktail Sauce (see page 286)

Smoked Salmon Canapés—Arrange ½ oz onion, thinly sliced, 1 oz tomato, sliced, and 1½ oz smoked salmon on 1 slice pumpernickel bread. Cut into quarters. Makes 1 midday meal serving. Supplement as required.

Each serving is equivalent to: ½ oz Limited Vegetable; $^1/_3$ serving Vegetables; 1½ oz Smoked Fish; 1 serving Bread

Baked Fish

For easy clean-up, line pan with aluminum foil.

1 lb fish fillets   **4 fl oz Fish Stock (see page 197)**
salt, pepper and paprika to taste

Place fish in nonstick pan and season. Add fish stock; bake at 350°F, Gas Mark 4, for 20 minutes or until fish flakes readily. Divide evenly and serve. Makes 2 evening meal servings.

Each serving is equivalent to: 6 oz Fish

Baked Mullet with Grapes

4 × 8 oz cleaned mullet   **6 fl oz chicken bouillon (made with**
¼ teaspoon thyme   **1 stock cube)**
salt and pepper to taste   **2 tablespoons lemon juice**
4 oz onion, sliced   **40 small seedless grapes**
1 bay leaf   **1 tablespoon chopped fresh parsley**

Place fish in shallow ovenproof dish. Sprinkle with thyme, salt and pepper. Top with onion and bay leaf and add bouillon and lemon juice to dish. Cover and bake at 400°F, Gas Mark 6, for 15 minutes. Add grapes and continue baking for 10 minutes or until fish flakes at the touch of a fork. Sprinkle with parsley. Divide evenly. Makes 4 midday meal servings.

Each serving is equivalent to: 4 oz Fish; 1 oz Limited Vegetable; ¼ serving Something Extra (¼ stock cube); ½ serving Fruit

Baked Fish Creole

Serve this delicious dish with cooked hominy grits, a traditional accompaniment to Fish Creole.

Arrange 1 lb fish fillets in shallow baking dish. Prepare ½ recipe Creole Sauce (2 servings, see page 285) Pour over fish. Bake, uncovered at 350°F, Gas Mark 4, for 30 to 35 minutes or until fish flakes easily at the touch of a fork. Divide evenly. Makes 2 evening meal servings.

Each serving is equivalent to: 6 oz Fish; Creole Sauce (see page 285)

Bouillabaisse for One

Any fish may be used, or a mixture of several types.

2 oz onion or leeks, diced
1 garlic clove, crushed
1 parsley sprig
1 small bay leaf
pinch saffron or turmeric
pinch thyme

pinch paprika
salt and pepper to taste
16 fl oz water
3 oz tomato, diced
3 oz peeled potato, diced
8 oz boned fish

In small nonstick saucepan sauté onion and garlic for 2 minutes. Add parsley and seasonings; cook for 1 minute longer. Add all remaining ingredients except fish. Cover; simmer for 5 minutes. Add fish, simmer for about 7 minutes or until fish flakes easily at touch of a fork. Serve in soup bowl. Makes 1 evening meal serving.

Each serving is equivalent to: 2 oz Limited Vegetable; 1 serving Vegetables; 1 serving Choice Group; 6 oz Fish

Variation: Omit potato. Place 1 slice French Bread (approximately 2 oz) in soup bowl. Pour Bouillabaisse over bread. Eliminate 1 serving Choice Group and add 2 servings Bread (once-a-week selection) to equivalent listing.

Fish Baked with Vegetables

6 oz green pepper, seeded and
  sliced
4 oz tomato, sliced
4 oz onion, sliced
1 lb fish fillets

¼ teaspoon salt
⅛ teaspoon pepper
2 fl oz water
1 tablespoon margarine
⅛ teaspoon paprika

Place half the vegetables in baking dish. Season fish with salt and pepper and arrange on top of vegetables. Cover with remaining vegetables. Add water, dot with margarine, and sprinkle with paprika. Bake at 350°F, Gas Mark 4, for 20 to 25 minutes or until fish is cooked. Divide evenly. Makes 2 evening meal servings.

Each serving is equivalent to: $1^2/_3$ servings Vegetables; 2 oz Limited Vegetable; 6 oz Fish; 1½ servings Fat

Fish Pie

12 oz peeled cooked potatoes	2 standard eggs
5 fl oz skim milk	1 oz tomato purée
1 tablespoon plus 1 teaspoon	2 tablespoons water
margarine	1 tablespoon chopped fresh parsley
2 standard eggs, hard-boiled	1 teaspoon Worcester sauce
8 oz cooked fish, flaked	salt and pepper to taste
4 oz boiled onion, diced	

In medium bowl mash potatoes with milk and margarine until blended. Set aside. Chop hard-boiled eggs and place in separate bowl; add fish, onion, 1 egg, tomato purée mixed with water, parsley, Worcester sauce, salt, pepper and about a quarter of the potato mixture; mix well. Spoon into 8 × 8 × 2-inch baking dish. Spread with remaining potato mixture. Beat remaining egg and pour over potato. Bake at 400°F, Gas Mark 6, for 20 to 30 minutes or until top is golden brown. Divide evenly. Makes 4 midday meal servings.

Each serving is equivalent to: 1 serving Choice Group; ⅛ serving Milk (1¼ fl oz skim milk); 1 serving Fat: 1 Egg; 2 oz Fish; 1 oz Limited Vegetable; ⅛ serving Bonus (¼ oz tomato purée)

Fish Stew in Green Sauce

1 lb fish fillets, cut into 1-inch long pieces	4 oz onion or shallots, finely chopped
2 fl oz lime or lemon juice	4 oz peas
1 teaspoon salt	1 teaspoon chopped fresh parsley
12 oz green peppers, seeded and finely chopped	1 teaspoon red wine vinegar
	1 garlic clove, chopped
8 oz green tomatoes, peeled and chopped	¼ teaspoon pepper
	2 teaspoons vegetable oil (optional)

Place fish in medium bowl. Add enough water to cover. Add lime or lemon juice and ½ teaspoon salt. In another bowl combine all remaining ingredients except oil. Spread half the mixture in shallow saucepan. Drain fish; place over vegetable mixture. Top with remaining vegetable mixture. Cover and simmer on low heat for 15 minutes or until liquid is almost evaporated. Remove from heat. Sprinkle with oil, if desired, and serve hot. Divide evenly. Makes 2 evening meal servings.

Each serving is equivalent to: 6 oz Fish; $3^1/_3$ servings Vegetables; 4 oz Limited Vegetable; 1 serving Fat (optional)

Halibut Ring

4 standard eggs, separated
12 oz halibut fillets, minced
½ oz nonfat dry milk
2 fl oz water
½ teaspoon salt

¼ teaspoon pepper
9 oz cooked whole green beans
4 oz tomato purée, mixed with 4 fl
oz water, heated

Preheat oven to 375°F, Gas Mark 5. In large bowl beat egg yolks slightly. Add fish, milk, water, salt and pepper; mix thoroughly. In separate bowl, beat egg whites until stiff and fold into fish mixture. Pour into 2-pint nonstick cake ring tin; set in pan containing 1 inch water; bake for 30 to 40 minutes. Turn out onto serving dish. Garnish with green beans and serve with tomato purée. Divide evenly. Makes 4 midday meal servings.

Each serving is equivalent to: 1 Egg; 2 oz Fish; ⅛ serving Milk (1¼ fl oz skim milk); ¾ serving Vegetables; ½ serving Bonus (1 oz tomato purée)

Variation: Mince 2 oz onion with the fish. Make 2 slices white bread into crumbs; soak crumbs in 2 fl oz skim milk and stir into fish mixture before folding in egg white. Add ½ oz Limited Vegetable, ½ serving Bread, and $^1/_{20}$ serving Milk (½ fl oz skim milk); to equivalent listing.

Lemon-Grilled Trout

1 cleaned trout, 10 oz
2 fl oz lemon juice
1 teaspoon margarine

2 teaspoons chopped fresh parsley
lemon wedges to garnish

Cut trout in half lengthwise. Place skin side up on foil-lined grill pan. Sprinkle with 2 tablespoons lemon juice. Grill 4 inches from source of heat for 3 minutes. Turn trout over and sprinkle with remaining lemon juice; grill for 3 to 5 minutes till fish flakes easily at the touch of a fork. Dot trout with margarine and grill 1 minute longer. Garnish with parsley and lemon wedges. Makes 1 evening meal serving.

Each serving is equivalent to: 6 oz Fish; 1 serving Fat

Mackerel in Mustard Sauce

4 × 10 oz cleaned mackerel
2 fl oz lemon juice
1½ teaspoons salt
1 tablespoon plus 2 teaspoons
  Dijon mustard

2 teaspoons chopped fresh parsley
2 garlic cloves, crushed
freshly ground pepper to taste

Cover fish with water in bowl. Add 2 tablespoons lemon juice and 1 teaspoon salt; let stand for 15 minutes. Drain and dry fish. In small bowl, combine remaining ingredients. Spread over fish. Loosely wrap fish in foil; place on baking sheet. Bake at 350°F, Gas Mark 4, for about 30 minutes or until fish flakes easily at the touch of a fork. Divide evenly. Makes 4 evening meal servings.

Each serving is equivalent to: 6 oz Fish

Smoked Salmon and Potato Pudding

1 lb 2 oz peeled cooked potatoes,
  sliced
6 oz onion, diced
9 oz smoked salmon, diced
1 pint skim milk

3 standard eggs, slightly beaten
½ teaspoon salt
½ teaspoon pepper
3 standard eggs, hard-boiled and
  sliced

Line bottom of 3-pint casserole with half the potatoes. Add a layer of half the onion and half the smoked salmon. Repeat layers. In a bowl combine milk, beaten eggs, salt and pepper. Pour into casserole. Bake at 375°F, Gas Mark 5, for 1¼ hours or until eggs are set. Arrange slices of hard-boiled eggs on top. Divide evenly. Makes 6 midday meal servings.

Each serving is equivalent to: 1 serving Choice Group; 1 oz Limited Vegetable; 1½ oz Smoked Fish; ⅓ serving Milk (3 ⅓ fl oz skim milk); 1 Egg

Steamed Fish Chinese Style

This is a simple and good way to prepare almost every kind of fish.

8 oz fish fillets or 10 oz fish steak   **½ teaspoon shredded fresh ginger**
½ oz spring onions, sliced   **root**
2 teaspoons soy sauce

Wash fish and pat dry with paper towels. Place fish on a heat-resistant plate. Top with spring onions, soy sauce and ginger root. For easy removal, tie the plate in a piece of muslin. Pour boiling water into a steamer below the level of the steaming rack. Put the plate holding the fish on the rack. You can raise the level of the rack, if necessary, to prevent fish from touching water, by setting it on two coffee cups. Place cover over fish and steamer, bring water to boiling point, and steam fish for 5 to 10 minutes for thin fillets and up to 10 to 15 minutes for thick steaks. Serve fish hot on the plate in which it was steamed, or flake and chill for use in salads. Makes 1 evening meal serving. You can do this for 1 serving or for many, depending on the size of your steamer. It must be large enough to accommodate the fish in a single layer.

Each serving is equivalent to: 6 oz Fish; ½ oz Limited Vegetable

Baked Shrimp Thermidor

4 tablespoons margarine
3 oz mushrooms, sliced
4 tablespoons flour
1 teaspoon salt
½ teaspoon dry mustard
pinch cayenne pepper
10 fl oz skim milk

8 oz cooked shrimps
2 slices white bread, made into
   crumbs
2 oz Parmesan cheese, grated
2 oz Cheddar cheese, finely diced
½ teaspoon paprika

Melt margarine in top of double boiler over boiling water; add mushrooms. Cook for 5 minutes. Blend in flour, salt, mustard and cayenne. Slowly add milk, stirring constantly; cook until thick. Add shrimps; stir to combine. Transfer mixture to 3-pint casserole. In a medium bowl combine breadcrumbs, Parmesan cheese, Cheddar cheese and paprika. Sprinkle over shrimp mixture. Bake at 400°F, Gas Mark 6, for 20 minutes or until top is brown and bubbly. Divide evenly. Makes 4 midday meal servings.

Each serving is equivalent to: 3 servings Fat; ¼ serving Vegetables; 3 servings Something Extra (1 tablespoon flour); ¼ serving Milk (2½ fl oz skim milk); 2 oz Fish; ½ serving Bread; 1 oz Hard Cheese

Cornish Crab Cakes

1 lb cooked crab meat, flaked
4 slices white bread, made into
   crumbs
4 tablespoons chopped fresh
   parsley

4 tablespoons mayonnaise
2 tablespoons prepared mustard
¼ teaspoon salt
⅛ teaspoon pepper
few drops hot sauce

Combine all ingredients in large bowl. Divide mixture evenly into 8 portions and shape into patties. Place on baking sheet. Bake at 350°F, Gas Mark 4, for 15 minutes; turn patties over and bake for 10 minutes longer or until crispy. Makes 4 midday meal servings, 2 patties each.

Each serving is equivalent to: 4 oz Fish; 1 serving Bread; 3 servings Fat

Baked Scampi

1½ lbs large peeled scampi
2 tablespoons lemon juice
4 tablespoons margarine, melted
4 tablespoons finely chopped fresh
  parsley

2 garlic cloves, crushed
2 slices white bread, made into
  crumbs
1 teaspoon paprika
4 lemon wedges

Make scampi butterflies by cutting lengthwise along the back, being careful not to cut all the way through; spread and flatten to form the butterfly shape. Place 6 oz scampi in each of 4 individual baking dishes. Sprinkle each with 1½ teaspoons lemon juice. In small bowl, combine margarine, 3 tablespoons parsley and garlic; dot each portion of scampi with ¼ of margarine mixture. In another bowl, combine breadcrumbs, remaining parsley and paprika. Sprinkle ¼ breadcrumb mixture over each serving. Bake at 400°F, Gas Mark 6, for 15 minutes or until scampi are pink and crumbs golden brown. Garnish each serving with 1 lemon wedge. Makes 4 midday meal servings.

Each serving is equivalent to: 4 oz Fish; 3 servings Fat; ½ serving Bread

Crab or Mussel Chowder

4 oz onion, diced
2 oz celery, diced
1 pint chicken or beef bouillon
  (made with 3 stock cubes)
6 oz peeled potatoes, diced

8 oz cooked fresh or drained
  canned seafood (see note)
½ oz nonfat dry milk
2 fl oz water

Cook onion and celery in covered medium saucepan, stirring occasionally, until transparent. Add bouillon and bring to a boil. Add potatoes; cover and simmer for 15 to 20 minutes or until vegetables are almost tender. Stir in seafood and non-fat dry milk mixed with water; heat but do not boil. Divide evenly into bowls. Makes 2 midday meal servings.

Each serving is equivalent to: 2 oz Limited Vegetable; ⅓ serving Vegetables; 1½ servings Something Extra (1½ stock cubes); 1

serving Choice Group; 4 oz Fish; ¼ serving Milk (2½ fl oz skim milk)

Note: Select one of the following:

Crab—Use 8 oz drained canned crab meat, flaked. If desired, add 4 oz cooked peas with the fish. Add 2 oz Limited Vegetable to equivalent listing, if peas are used.

Mussels—Steam mussels until shells open. Cool. Remove from shells and discard rubberlike band that surrounds each mussel. Weigh 8 oz. If desired, add 3 oz green pepper, diced, with potato. For seasoning, add Worcester sauce to taste. Add ½ serving Vegetables to equivalent listing if green pepper is used.

Smoked Fish Dip

Here's a dip for vegetables or spread for pumpernickel bread.

10 oz cottage cheese	**2 to 4 tablespoons water**
8 oz drained canned mussels,	**¼ teaspoon dill weed**
minced or 6 oz smoked fish,	**¼ teaspoon Worcester sauce**
minced	**pinch white pepper**

Purée cottage cheese in food mill or blender. Stir in remaining ingredients, adjusting the amount of water until desired consistency is obtained. Divide evenly. Makes 4 midday meal servings.

Each serving is equivalent to: 2½ oz Soft Cheese; 2 oz Fish or 1½ oz Smoked Fish

How to Prepare Frozen Lobster Tails

To grill: Thaw lobster tails. Cut under-shell round edges and remove. Grasp tail in both hands and bend backwards towards shell side to crack and prevent curling; or insert skewer to keep tail flat. Arrange shell side up on rack of grill pan. Place 5 inches from source of heat; grill for 5 minutes. Turn flesh side up; sprinkle with lemon juice and grill according to the following timetable. To serve, loosen meat by inserting fork between meat and shell. Weigh portions. Serve with measured amount of melted margarine and lemon wedges.

To boil: Place lobster tails, either thawed or frozen, into large kettle of boiling salted water to cover. (Use 1 teaspoon salt for each quart of water.) When water returns to the boiling point, lower heat and begin counting the time, following timetable below. To remove meat easily, drain lobster tails and rinse with cold water. Cut through under-shell with kitchen scissors. Insert finger between shell and meat, and pull firmly. Weigh portions. Serve hot with measured amount of melted margarine and lemon wedges; or chill and serve on a bed of shredded lettuce with Cocktail Sauce (see page 286).

Timetable for Preparing Lobster Tails (in minutes)

Weight	3 oz	4 oz	5 oz	6 oz	7 oz	8 oz	9 oz
Grilling:							
Shell Side	5	5	5	5	5	5	5
Flesh Side	6	6	6	6	7	7	7
*Boiling:							
Thawed	4	5	6	7	8	9	10
Frozen	6	7	8	9	10	11	12

*As a general rule, thawed lobster tails should be boiled one minute longer than their individual weight in oz. Add two minutes to all boiling times, if tails are cooked frozen. The above table is based on weights of individual tails. When two or more tails of the same weight are cooked at the same time, use time indicated for a single tail.

Lobster Rarebit

In the top of double boiler over boiling water prepare Enriched White Sauce (see page 278). Stir in 8 oz cooked diced lobster, 4 oz diced sharp Cheddar cheese, 1 tablespoon plus 1 teaspoon tomato ketchup and a few drops Worcester sauce. Heat to melt cheese. Divide evenly into 4 portions. Serve each portion over 1 slice white bread, toasted. Sprinkle with chopped fresh parsley. Makes 4 mid-day meal servings.

Each serving is equivalent to: Enriched White Sauce (see page 278); 2 oz Fish; 1 oz Hard Cheese; ½ serving Something Extra (1 teaspoon tomato ketchup); 1 serving Bread

Cornish Mussel Chowder

8 fl oz Fish Stock (see page 197)
4 fl oz water
3 oz peeled potato, diced
2 oz celery, finely diced
1 oz canned tomatoes, chopped
1 oz onion, diced

1 chicken stock cube, crumbled
½ bay leaf
¼ teaspoon garlic powder
¼ teaspoon thyme
4 oz drained canned mussels, minced

Combine all ingredients except mussels in medium saucepan. Bring to a boil; reduce heat and simmer for 15 minutes or until potato and celery are tender. Add mussels and heat thoroughly. Remove bay leaf before serving. Makes 1 midday meal serving.

Each serving is equivalent to: 1 serving Choice Group; 1 serving Vegetables; 1 oz Limited Vegetable; 1 serving Something Extra (1 stock cube); 4 oz Fish

Mussels Vinaigrette

12 oz drained canned mussels
Basic French Dressing (see page 283)

2 oz onion, sliced
6 oz lettuce, shredded

Combine all ingredients except lettuce in bowl and refrigerate for 1 hour. Serve on lettuce. Divide evenly. Makes 4 evening meal servings. Supplement as required.

Each serving is equivalent to: 3 oz Fish; Basic French Dressing (see page 283); ½ oz Limited Vegetable; ½ serving Vegetables

Oysters Creole Maryland

Serve over hot rice.

1 lb drained, canned oysters or   **Creole Sauce (see page 285)**
   1½ lbs shucked fresh oysters

In saucepan combine oysters and Creole Sauce. Simmer for 10 minutes or until thoroughly heated. If using fresh oysters, cook until edges of oysters curl. Divide evenly. Makes 4 midday meal servings.

Each serving is equivalent to: 4 oz Fish; Creole Sauce (see page 285)

Oyster Stew

2 tablespoons plus 2 teaspoons   **1 teaspoon Worcester sauce**
   margarine   **dash hot sauce**
2 tablespoons plus 2 teaspoons   **10 fl oz skim milk**
   flour   **1½ lbs shucked oysters**
1 teaspoon salt

Melt margarine in top of double boiler over boiling water. Stir in flour, salt, Worcester sauce and hot sauce. Slowly add milk, stirring constantly, and cook until thickened. Add oysters and cook for 4 minutes or until edges of oysters curl. Divide evenly. Makes 4 midday meal servings.

Each serving is equivalent to: 2 servings Fat; 2 servings Something Extra (2 teaspoons flour); ¼ serving Milk (2½ fl oz skim milk); 4 oz Fish

Peppery Shrimps

Try as a first course.

1½ lbs peeled and deveined
  shrimps
12 fl oz Double-Strength Chicken
  Stock (see page 135)
4 fl oz red wine vinegar
4 oz onion, sliced

2 teaspoons dry mustard
1 teaspoon hot sauce
½ teaspoon thyme
lemon slices to garnish
parsley sprigs to garnish

In saucepan combine all ingredients except lemon and parsley. Bring to a boil; reduce heat and simmer for about 4 minutes or until shrimps turn pink. Remove from heat. Allow to cool. Chill shrimps in liquid. Drain and discard liquid. Garnish shrimps and onions with lemon slices and parsley sprigs. Divide evenly. Makes 8 midday or evening meal servings. Supplement as required.

Each serving is equivalent to: 2 oz Fish; ½ serving Something Extra (1½ fl oz Double-Strength Stock); ½ oz Limited Vegetable

Portuguese Mussel Soup

1¼ pints water
6 oz peeled potato, sliced
4 oz onion, sliced
3 teaspoons chicken stock powder

1 garlic clove, crushed
pinch thyme
1½ lbs cleaned shucked mussels
6 oz cooked rice
1 teaspoon chopped fresh parsley

In large saucepan combine water, potato, onion, stock powder, garlic and thyme. Bring to a boil; reduce heat and cover. Simmer for 15 minutes or until potato is tender. Add mussels and rice; cook for 5 minutes or until mussels are tender. Sprinkle with parsley. Divide evenly. Makes 4 midday meal servings.

Each serving is equivalent to: 1 serving Choice Group; 1 oz Limited Vegetable; ¾ serving Something Extra (¾ teaspoon stock powder); 4 oz Fish

Riverboat Shrimps

4 fl oz chicken bouillon (made with
  ½ stock cube)
6 oz green pepper, seeded and
  chopped
4 oz onion, chopped
12 oz tomatoes, chopped
1 teaspoon oregano

1 teaspoon salt
½ teaspoon rosemary
½ teaspoon pepper
dash hot sauce
1½ lbs cooked shrimps
12 oz cooked rice

In medium saucepan, combine chicken bouillon, green pepper and onion. Simmer until tender, for 5 minutes. Add tomatoes and seasonings; simmer gently for 10 minutes. Add shrimps and heat thoroughly. Divide evenly into 4 portions and serve each over 3 oz hot rice. Makes 4 evening meal servings.

Each serving is equivalent to: ⅛ serving Something Extra (⅛ stock cube); 1½ servings Vegetables; 1 oz Limited Vegetable; 6 oz Fish; 1 serving Choice Group

Poached Scallops

In frying pan combine scallops with a bay leaf and a few sprigs of fresh parsley. Cover with water and poach 3 to 5 minutes (see directions for poaching fish, page 196). Weigh portions and serve.

Grilled Scallops

If scallops are very large cut them into even-size pieces. Dip them in lemon juice or chicken bouillon and grill until firm (see directions for grilling fish, page 196). Weigh portions and serve.

Baked Scallops

3 oz scallops, diced
½ recipe Creamy Cheese Sauce (1
  serving, see page 64)

dash Worcester sauce
½ slice white bread, made into
  crumbs

Combine all ingredients except breadcrumbs in bowl and spoon into large shell or individual casserole. Top with breadcrumbs. Baked at 425°F, Gas Mark 7, for 15 to 20 minutes or until top is browned. Makes 1 midday meal serving.

Each serving is equivalent to: 2 oz Fish; Creamy Cheese Sauce (see page 64); ½ serving Bread

Seafood Chef's Salad

3 oz cooked macaroni twists
2 oz cooked seafood, cut into 1-inch cubes
1½ oz green pepper, seeded and diced
1 oz celery, diced
½ oz spring onion, chopped

1 tablespoon mayonnaise
1 tablespoon water
1 tablespoon chilli sauce
salt and pepper to taste
lettuce leaves
1 standard egg, hard-boiled and quartered

In bowl combine macaroni, seafood, green pepper, celery and spring onion. In separate bowl combine mayonnaise, water and chilli sauce; pour over salad; toss to combine. Season with salt and pepper. Serve on lettuce leaves surrounded with egg quarters. Makes 1 midday meal serving.

Each serving is equivalent to: 1 serving Choice Group; 2 oz Fish; ¾ serving Vegetables; ½ oz Limited Vegetable; 3 servings Fat; 1½ servings Something Extra (1 tablespoon chilli sauce); 1 Egg

Seafood Salad

½ medium red apple, cored and diced
1 tablespoon lemon juice
4 oz cooked seafood, cut into 1-inch cubes
2 oz pickled cucumber, chopped

1½ oz cucumber, peeled and diced
1 tablespoon mayonnaise, mixed with 1 tablespoon water
½ oz drained canned pimiento, chopped
lettuce leaves

Place apple in medium bowl; sprinkle with lemon juice and toss. Add all remaining ingredients except lettuce. Chill. Serve on bed of lettuce leaves. Makes 1 midday meal serving.

Each serving is equivalent to: ½ serving Fruit; 4 oz Fish; 1 serving Vegetables; 3 servings Fat

Cantonese Shrimps with Rice

8 oz celery, diagonally cut into thin slices
4 oz onion, sliced
1 lb cooked shrimps
6 oz spinach leaves, chopped
4 oz Chinese pea pods (mangetout)
4 oz drained canned water chestnuts, sliced
3 oz drained canned bamboo shoots, sliced
12 fl oz Chicken Stock (see page 135)
2 fl oz soy sauce
2 tablespoons cornflour, dissolved in 2 tablespoons water
¼ teaspoon pepper
12 oz cooked rice

Brown celery and onion in large nonstick frying pan. Add shrimps, spinach, Chinese pea pods (mange tout), water chestnuts and bamboo shoots. Cover and cook for 1 minute. In small bowl combine stock, soy sauce, cornflour and pepper. Stir into shrimp-vegetable mixture. Cook, stirring, for 2 minutes or until sauce is thickened. Serve over hot rice. Divide evenly. Makes 4 midday meal servings.

Each serving is equivalent to: $1\frac{1}{3}$ servings Vegetables; 3 oz Limited Vegetable; 4 oz Fish; 2 servings Something Extra (3 fl oz stock and 1½ teaspoons cornflour); 1 serving Choice Group

Variation:
Cantonese Shrimps and Pork—Follow basic recipe but use 8 oz cooked shrimps and 8 oz shredded cooked pork. Change equivalent listing from 4 oz Fish to 2 oz Fish and 2 oz 'Beef' Group

Red Mussel Sauce

Serve this tempting sauce over cooked spaghetti.

6 oz green pepper, seeded and
  chopped
2 oz onion, finely chopped
1 garlic clove, crushed
4 fl oz Fish Stock (see page 197)
4 oz canned tomatoes, crushed
½ teaspoon oregano

¼ teaspoon salt
⅛ teaspoon pepper
8 oz drained canned mussels,
  minced
2 tablespoons chopped fresh
  parsley

In nonstick saucepan combine green pepper, onion and garlic. Sauté for 3 minutes. Add fish stock, tomatoes, oregano, salt and pepper. Bring to a boil; reduce heat and simmer for 5 minutes. Add mussels and parsley. Simmer for 3 minutes longer. Divide evenly. Makes 4 midday or evening meal servings. Supplement as required.

Each serving is equivalent to: ¾ serving Vegetables; ½ oz Limited Vegetable; 2 oz Fish

White Mussel Sauce (for Pasta)

8 fl oz Fish Stock (see page 197)
4 fl oz chicken bouillon (made with
  ½ stock cube)
2 tablespoons chopped fresh
  parsley
1 garlic clove, crushed

1 bay leaf
¼ teaspoon salt
⅛ teaspoon white pepper
8 oz drained canned mussels,
  minced

Combine all ingredients except mussels in small saucepan. Bring to a boil; reduce heat and simmer for 5 minutes. Add mussels; heat thoroughly. Remove bay leaf. Divide evenly. Makes 4 midday or evening meal servings. Supplement as required.

Each serving is equivalent to: ⅛ serving Something Extra (⅛ stock cube); 2 oz Fish

Anchovies, Capers and Chicory Salad

2 oz chicory
1 oz drained canned anchovy
fillets, chopped
¼ recipe Basic French Dressing (1
serving, see page 283)

¼ teaspoon Dijon mustard
1 garlic clove, crushed
½ teaspoon drained capers

Place chicory in shallow saucepan and cover with boiling water. Simmer until tender. Drain and chill. Combine all remaining ingredients and serve over chicory. Makes 1 serving. Serve at mealtime only. Supplement as required.

Each serving is equivalent to: ²/₃ serving Vegetables; 1 oz Fish; Basic French Dressing (see page 283)

Salmon Loaf

3 slices white bread, made into
crumbs
1 oz nonfat dry milk, mixed with 8
fl oz water
12 oz drained canned salmon,
flaked
1 tablespoon margarine, melted

1 tablespoon dried onion flakes,
reconstituted in 1 tablespoon
water
1 teaspoon lemon juice
2 standard eggs, beaten
4 standard eggs, hard-boiled

In large bowl, combine breadcrumbs and dissolved milk. Let stand for 10 minutes. In medium bowl combine salmon, margarine, onion flakes, lemon juice and beaten eggs. Add to bread mixture; mix thoroughly. Spoon half the mixture into a 9 × 5 × 3-inch nonstick loaf tin. Shell the hard-boiled eggs and arrange in a row through the centre of the salmon mixture. Cover with remaining salmon mixture. Bake at 350°F, Gas Mark 4, for 45 to 50 minutes or until loaf is firm and browned. Divide evenly. Makes 6 midday meal servings.

Each serving is equivalent to: ½ serving Bread; ¹/₆ serving Milk (1²/₃ fl oz skim milk); 2 oz Fish; 1 Egg; ½ serving Fat

Salmon Salad

Garlic French Dressing (see page
  284)
5 fl oz natural unsweetened yogurt
1 tablespoon prepared mustard
1 teaspoon seasoned salt

1 lb drained canned salmon, flaked
8 oz cooked peas
4 oz celery, thinly sliced
2 oz pickled cucumber, diced
lettuce leaves

In a bowl combine Garlic French Dressing, yogurt, mustard and seasoned salt. Add salmon, peas, celery and pickle. Toss to combine. Chill. Divide evenly and serve on lettuce leaves. Makes 4 midday meal servings.

    Each serving is equivalent to: Garlic French Dressing (see page 284); ¼ serving Milk (1¼ fl oz yogurt); 4 oz Fish; 2 oz Limited Vegetable; ½ serving Vegetables

Sardine Luncheon Platter

2 oz canned button mushrooms
2 oz cooked cauliflower florets
2 oz small tomatoes
2 oz drained canned sardines
1 oz celery, diagonally cut into thin
  slices

1 oz cooked beets, sliced
1 standard egg, hard-boiled and
  cut into quarters
¼ recipe Garlic French Dressing
  (1 serving, see page 284)
2 oz canned pimiento, sliced

Arrange the first 7 ingredients on large plate. Top with dressing. Garnish with pimientos. Makes 1 midday meal serving.

    Each serving is equivalent to: 3 servings Vegetables; 1 oz Limited Vegetable; 2 oz Fish; 1 Egg; Garlic French Dressing (see page 284)

Scalloped Salmon or Herring

1 lb drained canned salmon or
  herring
½ teaspoon dill weed
freshly ground black pepper to
  taste
4 slices white bread, toasted and
  made into crumbs

1 tablespoon lemon juice
2 oz nonfat dry milk
12 fl oz water
2 tablespoons margarine
lemon wedges to garnish

Red Mary Mix (page 300)

Fines Herbes Spread (page 279)

Chicken Liver Paté (page 308)

Artichokes in Tomato Jelly (page 324)

Spiced Beetroot (page 324)

Asparagus Guacamole (page 242)

Layer half the salmon in 2-pint baking dish. Sprinkle with dill weed and pepper. Top with half the crumbs. Add remaining salmon; sprinkle with lemon juice and cover with remaining crumbs. Combine dry milk and water and pour over fish. Dot evenly with margarine. Bake at 350°F, Gas Mark 4, for 35 minutes or until top is golden brown. Garnish with lemon wedges. Divide evenly. Makes 4 midday meal servings.

Each serving is equivalent to: 4 oz Fish; 1 serving Bread; ½ serving Milk (5 fl oz skim milk); 1½ servings Fat

Tuna Sandwich Spread

4 oz drained canned tuna, flaked
1 tablespoon mayonnaise
1 teaspoon dried onion flakes, reconstituted in 1 teaspoon water

1 teaspoon prepared mustard
½ oz celery, diced
1 bap, about 2 oz, toasted

In small bowl combine tuna, mayonnaise, onion flakes and mustard. Mash together to form a spread. Fold in celery. Serve on toasted bap. Makes 1 midday meal serving.

Each serving is equivalent to: 4 oz Fish; 3 servings Fat; $^1/_6$ serving Vegetables; 2 servings Bread (once-a-week selection)

Tuna Tetrazzini on Broccoli

¼ recipe Mushroom White Sauce (1 serving, see page 279)
1 oz Cheddar cheese, grated

2 oz drained canned tuna, flaked
3 oz cooked broad noodles
3 oz cooked broccoli, chopped

In top of double boiler, over boiling water, combine Mushroom White Sauce and cheese. Simmer, stirring constantly, until cheese melts. Remove from heat. Stir in tuna. Make a layer of hot noodles on a serving dish. Top with hot broccoli. Spoon tuna mixture over broccoli and noodles. Makes 1 midday meal serving.

Each serving is equivalent to: Mushroom White Sauce (see page 279); 1 oz Hard Cheese; 2 oz Fish; 1 serving Choice Group; 1 serving Vegetables

Tuna-Vegetable Pie

1 lb 2 oz peeled cooked potatoes
1½ lbs drained canned tuna,
  flaked

1½ recipes 'Ravigote' Sauce (6
  servings, see page 279)
1 teaspoon paprika
12 oz cooked carrot, diced
6 oz cooked peas

Mash the potatoes in a bowl, add tuna, 'Ravigote' Sauce and paprika. Spread half the mixture in 3-pint shallow, nonstick casserole. In separate bowl combine carrots and peas; arrange over tuna mixture in casserole. Spread remaining tuna mixture over vegetable layer. Bake at 350°F, Gas Mark 4, for 30 minutes or until piping hot. Divide evenly. Makes 6 midday meal servings.

Each serving is equivalent to: 1 serving Choice Group; 4 oz Fish; 'Ravigote' Sauce (see page 279); $^2/_3$ serving Vegetables; 1 oz Limited Vegetable

DRIED PEAS/BEANS

*

Dried peas and beans are an economical, efficient and low-cost source of protein. We've provided general tips on cooking them, along with the best of our recipes. Try our soups: Black Bean, fragrant with cumin and coriander; hearty Split Pea Minestrone, and Bean and Potato Soup. Our stews include beans, rice and vegetables. Other favourites include a Pilaf of Chick Peas and Kasha, and Lentils Creole with a diced raw onion. Our salads are made with beans and tuna, kidney beans with eggs and cauliflower, even garliky chick peas. Family favourites include Soybean Vegetable Loaf and Soyburgers.

Rules for Using Dried Peas/Beans

1. Amounts (net drained, cooked weight):
   Women, Men and Teenagers: 6 oz at the midday meal
   Women and Teenagers: 8 oz at the evening meal
   Men: 12 oz at the evening meal
2. Select up to 3 times weekly, if desired:
   beans
     kidney, lima, pink, soy or white beans
     (dried or canned dried)
   lentils
     (dried or canned dried)
   peas
     black eyed (cowpeas), chick (garbanzos) or split
     (dried or canned dried)
3. Canned dried peas/beans packed with sugar are 'illegal'.

4. A half-serving of dried peas/beans combined with chicken, veal, fish, egg or cheese must be considered a dried peas/beans meal. A half-serving of dried peas/beans combined with a selection from the 'Beef' Group category must be counted as a 'Beef' Group meal.

5. *Cooking Procedures:*
Follow package directions. Cook until tender; drain, reserving liquid if desired; weigh portions. Cooked dried peas/beans may be combined with other ingredients. Cooking liquid and added ingredients may be consumed.

Unless package states otherwise, all dried peas/beans should be washed and picked through to remove any dirt or grit.

Overnight Soaking Method—Soak dried peas/beans for 6 to 8 hours or overnight in cold unsalted water. Allow plenty of water as they can double their bulk in soaking. Discard any which float to the surface. To cook, drain the peas or beans, rinse well, then cook in lightly salted water to cover plus 1 inch. Add more salt at the end of cooking time if needed. Split peas and lentils may be cooked without soaking, but soaking does reduce the cooking time.

One-Hour Hot Soak Method—In saucepan, cover beans with hot water and bring to a boil. Cook for 2 minutes; then set aside for one hour. Drain. Add enough water to cover plus 1 inch. Bring to a boil and cook until tender, adding more water if necessary. Cooking time depends on type and age of bean and place of origin. Drain, weigh and use as recipe directs.

Bean, Rice and Vegetable Stew

8 fl oz chicken bouillon (made with 1 stock cube)
2 oz carrots, sliced
2 oz onion, chopped
1 bay leaf
1 garlic clove, crushed
12 oz cooked dried chick peas (garbanzos)
8 oz canned tomatoes, chopped
6 oz frozen broccoli, chopped
¼ teaspoon seasoned salt
⅛ teaspoon pepper
6 oz cooked brown rice

In saucepan combine bouillon, carrots, onion, bay leaf and garlic. Simmer for 10 minutes. Add chick peas, tomatoes, broccoli, seasoned salt and pepper. Simmer for 15 minutes. Add rice. Cook over low heat for 4 minutes or until thoroughly heated. Divide evenly. Makes 2 midday meal servings.

Each serving is equivalent to: ½ serving Something Extra (½ stock cube); 2⅔ servings Vegetables; 1 oz Limited Vegetable; 6 oz Dried Beans; 1 serving Choice Group

Chick Peas and Kasha Pilaf

1 oz dry buckwheat groats (kasha)
3 oz drained canned dried chick
  peas (garbanzos) (reserve 2 fl oz
  liquid)

1 teaspoon chicken stock powder
1½ oz canned pimiento, chopped
2½ fl oz natural unsweetened
  yogurt

In small saucepan cover kasha with boiling salted water. Cover saucepan and cook over low heat for 15 minutes or until kasha is tender. Drain any excess liquid. Set kasha aside. In saucepan, heat liquid from chick peas. Add stock powder and stir to dissolve. Add kasha and pimiento; heat thoroughly. Remove from heat; stir in yogurt. Makes 1 midday meal serving. Supplement as required.

Each serving is equivalent to: 1 serving Choice Group; 3 oz Dried Peas/Beans; 1 serving Something Extra (1 teaspoon stock powder); ½ serving Vegetables; ½ serving Milk (2½ fl oz yogurt)

Chick Peas (Garbanzo Beans) in Pita

Pita, a round Middle Eastern Bread, is available at many supermarkets.

6 pita breads (2 oz each)
1 lb 2 oz drained canned chick
  peas (garbanzos), lightly mashed
2 tablespoons chopped fresh
  parsley
1 tablespoon lemon juice
1 small garlic clove, mashed
¼ teaspoon cayenne pepper

¼ teaspoon cumin
¼ teaspoon ground coriander
4 oz lettuce, shredded
9 oz tomatoes, chopped
6 oz cucumber, peeled and diced
6 oz onion, diced
3 fl oz natural unsweetened yogurt

Cut a small piece of each pita bread off and reserve. Open breads to form a pouch. Set aside. In bowl combine chick peas, parsley, lemon juice, garlic, cayenne, cumin and coriander. In separate bowl combine remaining ingredients. Divide each mixture into 6 portions. Stuff each pita bread with one portion of chick pea mixture and top each with one portion of vegetable-yogurt mixture. Serve each with reserved end used as a garnish. Makes 6 midday meal servings. Supplement as required.

Each serving is equivalent to: 2 servings Bread (once-a-week selection); 3 oz Dried Peas/Beans; 1 serving Vegetables; 1 oz Limited Vegetable; $1/10$ serving Milk ($1/2$ fl oz yogurt)

Garbanzo Dip

Combine 12 oz drained canned dried chick peas (garbanzos), 1 teaspoon sesame oil, 1 small garlic clove and as much water as necessary to moisten in blender container. Blend until smooth. Season with salt, freshly ground pepper and curry powder. Serve dip surrounded by 9 oz crisp raw vegetables. Divide evenly. Makes 2 midday meal servings.

Each serving is equivalent to: 6 oz Dried Peas/Beans; $1/2$ serving Fat; $1\frac{1}{2}$ servings Vegetables

Variation: Follow above recipe and stir in 2 teaspoons mayonnaise. Add 2 servings fat to equivalent listing.

Black Bean Soup

2¼ lbs cooked dried black beans
16 fl oz water
8 oz carrots, diced
8 oz tomatoes, diced
6 oz onion, diced
2 oz celery, diced
2 garlic cloves, crushed

1 tablespoon chopped fresh parsley
1½ teaspoons salt
1 teaspoon cumin seed
½ teaspoon ground coriander
1 lb 2 oz cooked brown rice
6 lemon slices

In large saucepan combine all ingredients except rice and lemon. Cover and simmer for 1 hour or until beans are very soft; add more water to adjust consistency if desired. Divide evenly into deep bowls, each containing 3 oz hot brown rice. Float a lemon slice on each serving. Makes 6 midday meal servings.

Each serving is equivalent to: 6 oz Dried Peas/Beans; 1 serving Vegetables; 1 oz Limited Vegetable; 1 serving Choice Group

Bean and Meat Stew

12 oz cooked lamb, diced
4 oz onion, chopped
2 garlic cloves, crushed
16 fl oz Beef Stock (see page 157)
1 oz tomato purée

1 lb cooked dried beans (such as
  haricot beans, field beans etc.)
3 tablespoons chopped fresh
  parsley
pinch thyme

In nonstick saucepan, combine lamb, onion and garlic; sauté until onion is browned. Stir in stock and tomato purée. Add beans, parsley and thyme; cook until most of the liquid has evaporated. Divide evenly. Makes 4 evening meal servings.

Each serving is equivalent to: 3 oz 'Beef' Group; 1 oz Limited Vegetable; $^2/_3$ serving Something Extra (4 fl oz stock); $^1/_8$ serving Bonus (¼ oz tomato purée); 4 oz Dried Peas/Beans

Kidney Bean and Egg Salad

4 tablespoons mayonnaise
2 teaspoons prepared mustard
4 oz onion, finely diced
4 oz celery, diced
12 oz drained canned dried red
  kidney beans

6 oz cucumber, peeled and diced
4 lettuce leaves
4 standard eggs, hard-boiled and
  quartered
6 oz cucumber, peeled and sliced
1 teaspoon capers

In bowl combine first 4 ingredients in order given. Add kidney beans and diced cucumber; chill. Divide evenly onto lettuce leaves; surround each with one egg and a quarter of the cucumber slices. Garnish with capers. Makes 4 midday meal servings.

Each serving is equivalent to: 3 servings Fat; 1 oz Limited Vegetable; $1^1/_3$ servings Vegetables; 3 oz Dried Peas/Beans; 1 Egg

Variation:
Soybean and Egg Salad—Omit mustard and substitute 1 table-spoon lemon juice. Replace kidney beans with 12 oz cooked dried soybeans.

Mexicali Bean Dip

Serve this with vegetable 'dippers'.

12 oz drained canned dried red kidney beans (reserve 2 tablespoons liquid)
¼ teaspoon garlic powder

¼ teaspoon cumin seed, crushed
4 oz Cheddar cheese, grated
4 tablespoons vegetable oil

In saucepan, heat beans, mashing with a wooden spoon. Stir in garlic powder and cumin. Add reserved bean liquid. Stir in cheese until melted. Remove from heat; stir in oil. Divide evenly. Makes 4 midday meal servings.

Each serving is equivalent to: 3 oz Dried Peas/Beans; 1 oz Hard Cheese; 3 servings Fat

Quick-and-Easy Bean Salad with Yogurt

12 oz drained canned dried red kidney beans
6 oz green pepper, seeded and diced
2 oz celery, diced
2 oz onion, diced
1 garlic clove, crushed
2½ fl oz natural unsweetened yogurt

2 tablespoons vegetable oil
1 tablespoon lemon juice
6 oz mixed salad greens (endive, coss and round lettuce)
4 oz tomato, sliced
2 tablespoons chopped fresh chives
2 tablespoons chopped fresh parsley
salt and pepper to taste

In bowl combine beans, green pepper, celery, onion and garlic. In small cup combine yogurt, oil and lemon juice; pour over bean mixture. Chill until ready to use. Arrange greens on serving dish; top with bean mixture and surround with tomato slices. Sprinkle with chives, parsley, salt and pepper; serve at once. Divide evenly.

Makes 4 midday meal servings. Supplement as required.

Each serving is equivalent to: 3 oz Dried Peas/Beans; 1½ servings Vegetables; ½ oz Limited Vegetable; ⅛ serving Milk (⅝ oz yogurt); 1½ servings Fat

Lentils and Rice

Delicious with salad and yogurt dressing (see 'Sauces and Salad Dressings' page 276). If red lentils are not available, green ones may be used.

4 oz onion, finely chopped
½ teaspoon cumin
2 fl oz Chicken Stock (see page 135)
12 oz cooked dried red lentils (see note)

12 oz cooked brown rice (see note)
½ teaspoon salt
1 tablespoon plus 1 teaspoon vegetable oil (optional)

In saucepan simmer onion and cumin in stock until liquid is evaporated. Add lentils, rice and salt. Cook until thoroughly heated. Remove from heat. Stir in oil, if desired. Serve hot or cold. Divide evenly. Makes 4 midday meal servings. Supplement as required.

Each serving is equivalent to: 1 oz Limited Vegetable; $\frac{1}{12}$ serving Something Extra (½ fl oz stock); 3 oz Dried Peas/Beans; 1 serving Choice Group; 1 serving Fat (optional)

Note: Cook lentils with 2 crushed garlic cloves. Discard garlic; drain and reserve liquid. Weigh lentils. Use reserved liquid for cooking the rice, adding more water if necessary. Measure rice.

Lentil and Courgette Curry

5 oz courgettes, sliced
4 oz onion, diced
3 oz mushrooms, sliced
¼ teaspoon curry powder
1 lb cooked dried lentils
8 fl oz chicken bouillon (made with 1 stock cube)

1 tablespoon chopped fresh parsley
¾ teaspoon salt
½ teaspoon lemon juice
freshly ground pepper to taste
1 tablespoon plus 1 teaspoon vegetable oil (optional)

In saucepan combine courgettes, onion, mushrooms and curry powder. Cook for 4 minutes. Add all remaining ingredients except oil. Cover and simmer for 15 minutes or until vegetables are tender. Remove from heat; stir in oil, if desired. Divide evenly. Makes 4 evening meal servings. Supplement as required.

Each serving is equivalent to: $^2/_3$ serving Vegetables; 1 oz Limited Vegetable; 4 oz Dried Peas/Beans; ¼ serving Something Extra (¼ stock cube); 1 serving Fat (optional)

Lentils Creole Style

4 oz onion, finely diced (reserve 2 tablespoons)
4 oz tomato, finely chopped
3 oz green pepper, seeded and chopped

2 oz canned pimiento, chopped
8 oz cooked dried lentils
1 teaspoon chicken stock powder
½ teaspoon Worcester sauce
salt and pepper to taste

Combine onion, tomato, green pepper and pimiento in nonstick frying pan. Sauté until tender-crisp. Add lentils, stock powder, Worcester sauce, salt and pepper. Cook, stirring occasionally, until thoroughly heated. Divide evenly; top each with 1 tablespoon reserved onion. Makes 2 evening meal servings. Supplement as required.

Each serving is equivalent to: 2 oz Limited Vegetable; 1½ servings Vegetables; 4 oz Dried Peas/Beans; ½ serving Something Extra (½ teaspoon stock powder)

Lentils with Prunes

In saucepan combine 3 oz cooked dried lentils, 2 dried medium prunes and 2 tablespoons water. Cook at medium heat, stirring often, until liquid is evaporated. Makes 1 midday meal serving. Supplement as required.

Each serving is equivalent to: 3 oz Dried Peas/Beans, ½ serving Fruit.

Lentil Soup

16 fl oz water
6 oz cooked dried lentils
3 oz tomato, chopped
1½ oz carrots, diced
1½ oz green pepper, seeded and
    diced

1 oz celery, diced
1 oz parsnips, diced
1 chicken stock cube, crumbled
1 teaspoon chopped fresh parsley
½ teaspoon dill weed
salt and pepper to taste

Combine all ingredients in saucepan and simmer until vegetables are tender. Add more water to adjust consistency if desired. Divide evenly. Makes 2 midday meal servings. Supplement as required.

Each serving is equivalent to: 3 oz Dried Peas/Beans; 1¹⁄₆ servings Vegetables; ½ oz Limited Vegetable; ½ serving Something Extra (½ stock cube)

Variation: Add 1 oz spinach with other vegetables. Cook as directed. Add ¹⁄₁₂ serving Vegetables to equivalent listing.

Lima Bean and Carrot Soup

1 lb cooked dried lima or butter
    beans
9 oz carrots, sliced
6 oz onion, sliced
2 tablespoons chopped fresh
    parsley

1 tablespoon Worcester sauce
1 teaspoon salt
white pepper to taste
2 oz nonfat dry milk
8 fl oz water
chopped watercress to garnish

In large saucepan, combine first 7 ingredients. Add water to cover. Bring to a boil; reduce heat and simmer for 20 minutes or until vegetables are tender. Pour bean mixture into blender container in two batches, if necessary; blend until puréed. Return to saucepan. Mix dry milk with water and stir in. Heat, but do not boil. Divide evenly and serve garnished with watercress. Makes 4 evening meal servings. Supplement as required.

Each serving is equivalent to: 4 oz Dried Peas/Beans; ¾ serving Vegetables; 1½ oz Limited Vegetable; ½ serving Milk (5 fl oz skim milk)

Three-Bean Soup

1½ lbs cooked dried red kidney
   beans (reserve cooking liquid)
8 oz cut green beans
1 to 2 garlic cloves, crushed
½ teaspoon basil

salt and pepper to taste
1½ lbs cooked dried butter beans
12 oz courgettes, diced
4 oz canned tomatoes, chopped
1½ lbs cooked noodles

In large saucepan combine reserved cooking liquid and enough water to make 3½ pints liquid. Add red kidney and green beans, garlic, basil, salt and pepper; bring to a boil, reduce heat and simmer for 45 minutes. Add butter beans, courgettes and tomatoes. Simmer for 30 minutes longer. Divide evenly into 8 soup bowls, each containing 3 oz hot noodles. Makes 8 midday meal servings.

Each serving is equivalent to: 6 oz Dried Peas/Beans; 1 serving Vegetables; 1 serving Choice Group

Pinto Beans Texas Style

4 oz onion, chopped
12 oz cooked dried pinto beans
4 oz canned tomatoes, crushed
2 tablespoons chilli sauce
1 teaspoon prepared mustard
   (optional)

½ teaspoon Worcester sauce
salt and cayenne pepper to taste
6 oz cooked brown rice

Brown onion in nonstick frying pan. Add all remaining ingredients except rice. Simmer, stirring occasionally, until hot. Serve over hot rice. Divide evenly. Makes 2 midday meal servings.

Each serving is equivalent to: 2 oz Limited Vegetable; 6 oz Dried Peas/Beans; ⅔ serving Vegetables; 1½ servings Something Extra (1 tablespoon chilli sauce); 1 serving Choice Group

Portuguese-Style Bean Soup

1 lb cooked dried haricot beans
  (reserve cooking liquid)
2 pints cooking liquid (or cooking
  liquid plus water to equal 2
  pints)
12 oz peeled potatoes, diced

6 oz tomato purée
4 oz onion, diced
1 garlic clove, crushed
½ teaspoon allspice
salt and freshly ground pepper to
  taste

In a large saucepan, combine all ingredients except salt and pepper. Bring to a boil. Reduce heat; cover and simmer for 30 minutes or until vegetables are tender. Season with salt and pepper. Divide evenly. Makes 4 evening meal servings. Supplement as required.

Each serving is equivalent to: 4 oz Dried Peas/Beans; 1 serving Choice Group; 1 oz Limited Vegetable; ¾ serving Bonus (1½ oz tomato purée)

Variation: To make 4 delicious complete evening meal servings, add 8 oz diced cooked ham during the last 15 minutes of cooking. Add 2 oz 'Beef' Group (smoked) to equivalent listing.

Soybean Casserole

8 oz celery, chopped
2 oz onion, chopped
2 oz green pepper, seeded and
  chopped
½ chicken stock cube, dissolved in
  2 fl oz hot water
2 tablespoons plus 2 teaspoons
  flour

1 pint skim milk
1½ lbs cooked dried soybeans
1 teaspoon salt
2 slices white bread, made into
  crumbs
1 tablespoon plus 1 teaspoon
  margarine

In saucepan sauté celery, onion and green pepper for 3 minutes. Add dissolved stock cube; cook for 5 minutes. Blend in flour. Slowly add milk and cook, stirring constantly until mixture thickens. Add beans and salt. Mix well. Pour into 2-pint nonstick baking dish. Sprinkle evenly with breadcrumbs. Dot evenly with margarine. Bake at 350°F, Gas Mark 4, for 30 minutes or until golden brown. Divide evenly. Makes 4 midday meal servings.

Each serving is equivalent to: ¾ serving Vegetables; ½ oz Limited Vegetable; 2⅛ serving Something Extra (⅛ stock cube and 2 teaspoons flour); ½ serving Milk (5 fl oz skim milk); 6 oz Dried Peas/Beans; ½ serving Bread; 1 serving Fat

Soybean Cheese Casserole

8 fl oz chicken bouillon (made with
  1 stock cube)
6 oz green pepper, seeded and
  chopped
4 oz onion, chopped
1 garlic clove, crushed
4 oz canned tomatoes, crushed
1 oz tomato purée

1 teaspoon basil
¼ teaspoon oregano
salt and pepper to taste
12 oz cooked, dried soybeans
4 oz sharp Cheddar cheese, grated
2 slices white bread, made into
  crumbs

In nonstick saucepan combine stock, green pepper, onion and garlic. Sauté until vegetables are tender. Add tomatoes, tomato purée and seasonings. Simmer until slightly thickened; add soybeans. Transfer mixture to 3-pint casserole. In small bowl, combine cheese and crumbs. Sprinkle over tomato-bean mixture. Bake at 350°F, Gas Mark 4, for 40 minutes or until golden. Divide evenly. Makes 4 midday meal servings.

Each serving is equivalent to: ¼ serving Something Extra (¼ stock cube); 1 oz Limited Vegetable; ¾ serving Vegetables; ⅛ serving Bonus (¼ oz tomato purée); 3 oz Dried Peas/Beans; 1 oz Hard Cheese; ½ serving Bread

Soybean Stuffed Peppers

4 medium green peppers, 6 oz
  each, halved and seeded
1 lb cooked dried soybeans,
  mashed
8 oz tomatoes, diced
4 oz celery, diced
1 tablespoon water

1 teaspoon dried onion flakes
pinch garlic powder
salt and pepper to taste
2 slices white bread, made into
  crumbs
1 tablespoon plus 1 teaspoon low-
  fat spread, melted

In large saucepan cook pepper halves in boiling, salted water for 3 minutes or until tender-crisp. Drain; set aside to cool. In medium bowl combine next 8 ingredients; divide evenly into 8 portions and fill each pepper half. In small bowl combine breadcrumbs and low-fat spread. Sprinkle an equal amount of crumb mixture over each pepper half. Place peppers in large nonstick baking tin. Bake at 350°F, Gas Mark 4, for 25 to 30 minutes or until peppers are soft. Makes 4 evening meal servings, 2 halves each. Supplement as required.

Each serving is equivalent to: 3 servings Vegetables; 4 oz Dried Peas/Beans; ½ serving Bread; ½ serving Fat

Soybean and Vegetable Loaf

12 fl oz chicken bouillon (made with 2 stock cubes)
6 oz green pepper, seeded and finely chopped
4 oz celery, finely chopped
3 oz mushrooms, sliced
3 oz onion, finely chopped
1 garlic clove, crushed
1 lb 2 oz cooked, dried soybeans
8 oz carrots, grated

4 tablespoons flour
4 tablespoons chopped fresh parsley
½ teaspoon oregano
½ teaspoon thyme
pinch ground cloves
6 standard eggs, slightly beaten
3 slices wholemeal bread, made into crumbs

In saucepan combine bouillon, green pepper, celery, mushrooms, onion and garlic. Cook for 5 minutes. Cool slightly. Stir in remaining ingredients in order given until well combined. Press mixture into large nonstick loaf tin. Bake at 350°F, Gas Mark 4, for 40 minutes or until golden. Divide evenly. Makes 6 midday meal servings.

Each serving is equivalent to: 2 $^1/_3$ servings Something Extra ($^1/_3$ stock cube and 2 teaspoons flour); 1$^1/_6$ servings Vegetables; ½ oz Limited Vegetable; 3 oz Dried Peas/Beans; 1 Egg; ½ serving Bread

Soyburgers

12 oz minced beef
12 oz cooked dried soybeans,
   mashed

1 tablespoon dried onion flakes
½ teaspoon salt
⅛ teaspoon pepper

Combine all ingredients in bowl. Divide into 4 equal patties. Place on rack and bake at 375°F, Gas Mark 5, for 25 minutes or until done to taste. Serve hot. Makes 4 midday meal servings, 1 patty each.

Each serving is equivalent to: 2 oz 'Beef' Group; 3 oz Dried Peas/Beans

Split Pea Minestone

Generally 8 oz of split peas will make about 1 lb cooked. Cook peas according to package directions, drain and reserve liquid; weigh peas.

10 oz courgettes, sliced
6 oz onion, chopped
5 oz mushrooms, sliced
2 oz celery, diced
1 pint 4 fl oz Ham or Chicken
   Stock (see page 157 or 135)

1 lb cooked dried split peas
½ teaspoon salt
½ teaspoon basil
black pepper to taste
12 oz peeled cooked potatoes, diced
   (optional)

In large nonstick saucepan combine courgettes, onion, mushrooms and celery. Sauté for 5 minutes. Add all remaining ingredients except potatoes. Simmer, stirring occasionally, for 45 minutes or until soup thickens. Add water to adjust consistency, if necessary. Add potatoes, if desired. Cook for 10 minutes. Divide evenly. Makes 4 evening meal servings. Supplement as required.

Each serving is equivalent to: $1^1/_3$ servings Vegetables; 1½ oz Limited Vegetable; 1 serving Something Extra (6 fl oz stock); 4 oz Dried Peas/Beans; 1 serving Choice Group (optional)

Split Pea Soup

4 oz carrots, diced
3 oz cooked onion, diced
12 oz cooked dried split peas

16 fl oz water
2 chicken stock cubes, crumbled
½ bay leaf

In nonstick saucepan sauté carrots and onion for 3 minutes. Add remaining ingredients. Cover and simmer, stirring often, for 25 to 30 minutes or until desired consistency. Divide evenly. Makes 2 midday meal servings.

Each serving is equivalent to: ²/₃ serving Vegetables; 1½ oz Limited Vegetable; 6 oz Dried Peas/Beans; 1 serving Something Extra (1 stock cube)

Baked Beans with Frankfurters

12 oz cooked dried white beans
1 medium apple or small pear, cored, peeled and diced
6 oz green pepper, seeded and diced
1 oz onion or spring onions, finely diced

2 tablespoons tomato ketchup
1 teaspoon prepared mustard
few drops hot sauce
12 oz canned tomatoes, crushed
6 oz frankfurters, sliced

In shallow 4-pint casserole combine first 7 ingredients. Top with tomatoes and frankfurters. Bake at 350°F, Gas Mark 4, for 30 minutes. Divide evenly. Makes 4 midday meal servings.

Each serving is equivalent to: 3 oz Dried Peas/Beans; ¼ serving Fruit; 1½ servings Vegetables; ¼ oz Limited Vegetables; ¾ serving Something Extra (1½ teaspoons tomato ketchup); 1½ oz Frankfurters

Variation: Substitute 6 oz sliced cooked ham for frankfurters. Substitute 1½ oz 'Beef' Group (smoked) for Frankfurters in equivalent listing.

Bean Salad Turkish Style

6 oz peeled cooked potatoes, diced	½ oz chopped fresh parsley
6 oz cooked carrots, diced	salt and freshly ground pepper to
6 oz tomatoes, diced	taste
1 garlic clove, crushed	2 teaspoons vegetable oil (optional)
8 oz cooked dried white beans	6 oz shredded lettuce
2 fl oz water	

In nonstick saucepan combine potatoes, carrots, tomatoes and garlic. Sauté for 3 minutes. Add beans and water. Simmer until most of the water is evaporated and beans are hot. Stir in parsley and season with salt and pepper. Remove from heat. Stir in oil if desired. Serve on lettuce. Divide evenly. Makes 2 evening meal servings. Supplement as required.

Each serving is equivalent to: 1 serving Choice Group; 3 servings Vegetables; 4 oz Dried Peas/Beans; 1 serving Fat (optional)

Bean and Potato Soup

1½ lbs cooked, dried white beans	8 oz celery, chopped
(reserve cooking liquid)	4 oz onion, diced
3½ pints cooking liquid (or	2 small garlic cloves, crushed
cooking liquid plus water to	salt and white pepper to taste
equal 3½ pints)	12 oz cooked brown rice
12 oz peeled potatoes, diced	chopped fresh parsley to garnish

In a large saucepan combine beans, liquid, potatoes, celery, onion, garlic, salt and pepper. Bring to a boil. Reduce heat, cover and simmer for 30 minutes or until vegetables are tender. If desired, remove cover and cook until thickened, stirring occasionally. Adjust seasonings. Divide evenly into 8 soup bowls, each containing 1½ oz hot rice. Garnish each serving with chopped parsley. Makes 8 midday meal servings. Supplement as required.

Each serving is equivalent to: 3 oz Dried Peas/Beans; 1 serving Choice Group; ⅓ serving Vegetables; ½ oz Limited Vegetable

White Bean and Tuna Salad

Tomato wedges and cooked green beans are fine additions to this salad plate.

2 tablespoons vegetable oil
2 teaspoons lemon juice or red wine vinegar
6 oz cooked dried white beans
4 tablespoons chopped fresh parsley

½ oz spring onions, chopped
salt and pepper to taste
4 oz drained canned tuna
2 large lettuce leaves

In bowl combine oil and lemon juice or vinegar. Add beans, parsley, spring onions, salt and pepper. Toss to combine. Chill. Break tuna into chunks. Divide bean mixture evenly onto lettuce leaves. Top each with half the tuna. Makes 2 midday meal servings.

Each serving is equivalent to: 3 servings Fat; 3 oz Dried Peas/Beans; ¼ oz Limited Vegetable; 2 oz Fish; ⅓ serving Vegetables

VEGETABLES

*

Hundreds of thousands of edible plants flourish around the world, but only a relatively few kinds are ordinarily used as food. Our chapter on vegetables includes most of the popular vegetables, and a lively sprinkling of those less well-known. Please do try the strange and exotic vegetables you might be lucky enough to find at your greengrocers. They will perk up your menu. For the same reason, cook some of the vegetables which you usually eat raw—celery, cucumber and tomato, for instance. And, in reverse, try eating raw, some vegetables which you normally cook, such as broccoli, cauliflower or courgettes.

Rules for Using Vegetables

1. Use vegetables raw or cooked, fresh, frozen (without sauce) or canned.
2. Select at least 2 servings daily.
   Serving size: 3 oz
3. Vegetables must be eaten at the midday and evening meals. They may also be eaten at any other time. Vary selections. Select a reasonable number of servings of raw or cooked vegetables.
4. Limited Vegetables
   Serving size: 4 oz
   The following vegetables are optional and must be weighed. Do not exceed a combined total of 4 oz, drained weight, daily.
   artichoke, globe
   artichoke, hearts

artichoke, Jerusalem
beetroot
broad beans
Brussels sprouts
Chinese pea pods (mange tout)
leeks
mange tout (Chinese Pea Pods)
okra
onions
parsnips
peas
pumpkin
salsify
shallots
spring onions
swede
water chestnuts

5. Vegetables are 'illegal' if they contain. added sugar (with the exception of canned peas).

Crudités

For party-goers or party-givers who want taste without waste, these raw crisp vegetables, called crudités in France, are a favourite hors d'oeuvre. Prepare them ahead and refrigerate until party time.

Beans, French or Runner—Use uncooked whole, or parboil and cut on diagonal.

Bean Sprouts—Prepare as Vinaigrette (see page 245).

Broccoli—Rinse tiny raw florets in ice water containing 1 teaspoon lemon juice or vinegar. Drain and dry.

Carrots—Cut off slivers or strips using a vegetable knife. To make curls, roll up strips, secure with toothpick, and put in ice water to set the curl.

Cauliflower—Dip tiny raw florets in ice water containing 1 teaspoon lemon juice or vinegar. Drain and dry.

Celeriac (celery root)—Peel and cut in long strips, blanch 1 or 2 minutes in water containing lemon juice, drain and serve.

Celery—Cut sticks into long, slim fingers. Use raw or poach lightly in chicken bouillon. Celery sticks look pretty served with the green leaves left on.

Chinese Cabbage—Use halved stalks or rolled-up leaf sections.

Chinese Pea Pods (mange tout)—Serve them whole and crisp. (Limited Vegetable)

Courgettes—Use young thin-skinned courgettes. Cut into fingers or slices, and serve.

Cucumbers—Peel or, if young, rinse and use. With tines of a fork, make parallel gashes from top to bottom round the whole cucumber, then slice in rounds or cut in long, thin strips. Sprinkle with chopped fresh dill or chives, if desired.

Fennel—Cut into slices and serve raw.

Kale—Serve this curly-leaved member of the cabbage family raw. Cut off and discard root ends. Rinse and dry leaves.

Kohlrabi—Peel it just as you would turnip, then slice and serve.

Lettuce—Rinse crisp firm leaves of lettuce, endive and an assortment of other available greens.

Mushrooms—Dip whole mushroom caps in lemon juice or cut through cap and stem in slices and dip in lemon juice. Serve raw.

Parsley—Use crisp sprigs, rinsed and dried.

Peppers—Use both red and green for colour contrast. Seed and cut into strips or rings.

Radishes—Prepare radish roses or accordions (see page 265).

Spring Onions—Trim off root end, but leave plenty of green leaf. Cut the thick ones in half, lengthwise. (Limited Vegetable)

Spinach—Rinse several times to remove sand. Drain well and serve raw. Cut out tough ribs with scissors, if necessary.

Tomatoes—Use whole small tomatoes, or serve medium tomatoes, cut in quarters and sprinkled with basil, fresh dill or chopped fresh garlic.

Watercress—Use fresh sprigs, rinsed and dried.

Suggested plate of crudités for 1 serving:
1½ oz raw broccoli florets
2 oz carrot strips or curls
1½ oz raw cauliflower florets
1½ oz barely cooked crisp green beans
1½ oz small tomatoes
1 oz red pepper, cut into strips
1 oz spring onions
½ oz celery

½ oz radishes, made into radish roses
sprigs of watercress and parsley
Suggested dips for individual servings:
  1 serving Pimiento Dressing (see page 313)
    or
  1 serving Basic French Dressing (see page 283)
    or
  1 serving 'Hollandaise' (see page 281)

Vegetable Stock

9 oz celery sticks and leaves, diced	Bouquet Garni (see page 297)
4 oz onion, studded with cloves	½ teaspoon salt
2 oz lettuce, shredded	pinch each white and cayenne
1 oz each carrots, turnips and	pepper
parsnips	

In large saucepan combine all ingredients and add enough water to
cover. Bring to a boil. Reduce heat and cover partially with a lid.
Simmer for 1½ hours or until vegetables are tender. Strain and
chill. Use liquid as base for soup with cooked leftover vegetables.

Artichokes

When buying artichokes look for compact green leaves. Loose or
discoloured leaves are signs of overmaturity or poor quality. When
preparing artichokes, wash, drain and cut off stem. Remove any
tough, dry outer leaves. Using kitchen scissors or a knife, remove
the thorny tip of each leaf. To avoid discolouration before cooking,
place artichokes in water to cover with 3 tablespoons lemon juice
or vinegar added to each quart of water.

Use a stainless steel or enamelled saucepan to keep artichokes
from discolouring during cooking. Adding lemon juice to the cooking liquid will also keep them from discolouring, but this can cause
a loss in flavour. Therefore, salted water is preferable for home
preparation. Cook artichokes in boiling liquid to cover or in a
steamer until tender.

Asparagus

Buy asparagus that have straight stalks, with tightly closed tips. When preparing asparagus, gently rinse several times. Remove the bottom part of the stalk where it snaps easily. Using a vegetable peeler, remove outer scales from each stalk. Using string, tie asparagus into serving-size bundles. Use only a few inches of water to cook. Stand asparagus upright in a steamer and cover, or in the bottom part of a double boiler, inverting the top of a double boiler over the asparagus tips. The steam will cook the upper part of the stalk and tips. Cook approximately 12 to 15 minutes or until stalks are tender. You may also place stalks flat in a wide shallow pan and add ½ inch of boiling salted water; cover pan and simmer 10 to 12 minutes, or until tender. Regardless of cooking method, asparagus should be removed from water immediately when tender, untied and served or allowed to cool for later use.

Asparagus Guacamole

A pretty salad when served as a dip with orange sections and sliced vegetables.

24 medium asparagus spears, cooked and chopped	1 teaspoon lemon juice
6 oz tomatoes, chopped	1 garlic clove, crushed
2 oz onion, chopped	½ teaspoon salt
2 oz green chilli peppers	¼ teaspoon freshly ground pepper
1 tablespoon plus 1 teaspoon vegetable oil	4 slices bread, sliced horizontally to make 8 thin slices

Combine all ingredients, except bread, in blender container; blend until smooth. Chill. Place bread on baking sheet; bake at 425°F, Gas Mark 7, until bread is crisp and golden. Serve with Guacamole. Divide evenly. Makes 4 servings. Serve at mealtime only.

Each serving is equivalent to: $1^2/_3$ servings Vegetables; ½ oz Limited Vegetable; 1 serving Fat; 1 serving Bread

Asparagus Vinaigrette

6 oz cooked asparagus spears   **¼ recipe Basic French Dressing (1 serving, see page 283)**

Arrange asparagus spears on plate and top with Basic French Dressing. Chill. Makes 1 serving. Serve at mealtime only.

Each serving is equivalent to: 1 serving Vegetables; Basic French Dressing (see page 283)

Sprouting Beans

The best-known and most commonly used bean sprout is the mung bean, but any dried bean or seed can be sprouted. Some examples are: alfalfa, aduki, chick peas and lentils.

1 lb of beans for sprouting will make 5 to 7 lbs of this fresh vegetable. Buy dried mung beans for sprouting. Discard split or discoloured beans. Soak 1½ oz rinsed beans overnight in water to cover. Drain, rinse, place in 2-pint jar, and tie muslin over the opening. To grow white tender sprouts, store bottle on its side in a dark place or cover with papers to exclude light. Rinse and drain beans several times a day to keep them moist, for about 4 days, or until sprouts are 1 to 2 inches long; they are ready for use at this stage. 1½ oz of mung beans will yield about ¾ lb of sprouts.

Treat sprouted beans like any fresh vegetable. Store in refrigerator as soon as they are ready for eating and use as soon as possible. Sprouted beans may be eaten raw or cooked. To cook, place sprouts in a pan with a small amount of boiling salted water. Cover and cook to desired degree of tenderness. They can also be served blanched. Place in a strainer and pour boiling water over them. Drain and serve. To freshen canned bean sprouts, transfer them to a strainer and rinse several times under running water. Then soak in ice water, using lots of ice cubes. This should crisp them in about an hour.

Bean sprouts add a crunchy texture to sandwich fillings and are delicious in tossed salads.

Bean Sprout Casserole

12 oz drained canned whole kernel corn
9 oz blanched or canned bean sprouts, rinsed
3 oz green pepper, seeded and diced

2 oz canned pimiento, diced
salt and pepper to taste
Basic White Sauce (see page 278)
paprika to garnish

In medium bowl combine corn, bean sprouts, green pepper, pimiento, salt and pepper. Transfer to 2-pint ovenproof casserole. Top with Basic White Sauce; sprinkle with paprika. Bake at 350°F, Gas Mark 4, for 25 minutes or until piping hot. Divide evenly. Makes 4 servings. Serve at mealtime only.

Each serving is equivalent to: 1 serving Choice Group; $1^1/_6$ servings Vegetables; Basic White Sauce (see page 278)

Bean Sprout Curry

1 medium apple, peeled and diced
4 oz celery, diced
4 oz onion, finely diced
2 teaspoons chicken stock powder
2 teaspoons curry powder
12 fl oz water

8 dried medium prunes, stoned and diced
2 tablespoons cornflour, dissolved in 2 tablespoons water
9 oz canned bean sprouts, rinsed

In medium non-stick saucepan combine apple, celery, onion, stock powder and curry powder. Sauté over medium heat, stirring frequently until onions are transparent. Add water and prunes. Bring to boil; reduce heat and simmer for 15 to 20 minutes or until celery is tender-crisp. Stir in cornflour; simmer until thickened. Add bean sprouts; toss to combine. Heat for about 1 minute. Divide evenly. Makes 4 servings.

Each serving is equivalent to: ¾ serving Fruit; 1 serving Vegetables; 1 oz Limited Vegetable; 2 servings Something Extra (½ teaspoon stock powder and 1½ teaspoons cornflour)

Bean Sprout Vinaigrette

In bowl combine 4 oz bean sprouts, 1 oz diced celery, 1½ oz cucumber, peeled and diced, and ½ oz sliced radishes. In separate bowl or measuring jug, combine 1½ teaspoons soy sauce, 1 teaspoon sesame oil, 1 teaspoon lemon juice, and ½ teaspoon chopped chives. Pour over salad, and toss. Makes 1 serving. Serve at mealtime only.

Each serving is equivalent to: $2^1/_3$ servings Vegetables; 1 serving Fat

Banana, Beetroot and Water Chestnut Salad

1 medium banana, sliced
2 tablespoons lemon juice
8 oz drained canned sliced beetroot
4 oz drained canned water
  hestnuts, sliced
9 oz lettuce, shredded

2 tablespoons vegetable oil
1 tablespoon red wine vinegar
1 tablespoon prepared mustard
¼ teaspoon salt
⅛ teaspoon pepper

Place banana in medium bowl. Sprinkle with lemon juice. Add beetroot and water chestnuts; toss lightly to combine. Arrange lettuce on large serving dish; top with banana mixture. Place remaining ingredients in small jar with tight-fitting cover; shake well to combine. Pour over banana mixture. Divide evenly. Makes 4 servings. Serve at mealtime only.

Each serving is equivalent to: ½ serving Fruit; 3 oz Limited Vegetable; $^2/_3$ serving Vegetables; 1½ servings Fat

Iced Borscht

8 oz drained canned beetroot, with
  2 fl oz liquid
12 fl oz beef or chicken bouillon
  (made with 2 stock cubes)
1 teaspoon lemon juice

10 fl oz natural unsweetened
  yogurt
3 oz cucumber, peeled and diced
2 lemon wedges

Combine beetroot with liquid, bouillon and lemon juice in blender container; blend until smooth. Chill. Before serving, stir in 5 fl oz yogurt and cucumber. Serve with additional yogurt on the side and garnish with lemon wedges. Divide evenly. Makes 2 servings.

Each serving is equivalent to: 4 oz Limited Vegetable; 1 serving Something Extra (1 stock cube); 1 serving Milk (5 fl oz yogurt); ½ serving Vegetables

Variations:
1. Add 3 oz tomato, peeled and diced, to blender container. Continue as above. Add ½ serving Vegetables to equivalent listing.
2. Add 6 oz peeled cooked potato, diced, just before serving. Add 1 serving Choice Group to equivalent listing.

Stir-Cooked Broccoli and Water Chestnuts

To brighten up your Chinese meal.

1½ lbs broccoli
2 fl oz chicken bouillon (made with
    ¼ stock cube)
2 tablespoons soy sauce
1 garlic clove, crushed

4 oz drained canned water
    chestnuts, sliced
1 tablespoon plus 1 teaspoon
    vegetable oil (optional)

Cut broccoli into florets and cut stems into pieces about the same size as the florets. Place in large saucepan; cover with water. Bring to a boil; reduce heat and simmer for about 3 minutes. Drain. In a wok or large nonstick frying pan combine chicken bouillon, soy sauce and garlic. Bring to a boil; add broccoli and water chestnuts. Cook, stirring constantly, for 3 to 4 minutes or until broccoli is tender-crisp. Remove from heat; stir in oil if desired. Divide evenly. Makes 4 servings. If oil is used, serve at mealtime only.

Each serving is equivalent to: 2 servings Vegetables; $^1/_{16}$ serving Something Extra ($^1/_{16}$ stock cube); 1 oz Limited Vegetable; 1 serving Fat (optional)

Brussels Sprouts

Wash fresh Brussels sprouts in salted water. Remove a thin slice from stem end and make a crosswise cut in each stem. Remove any loose or discoloured leaves. Brussels sprouts may be cooked in boiling salted water, steamed or cooked in a pressure cooker until tender. This is a limited vegetable and must be weighed.

Quick-and-Easy Brussels Sprouts

12 oz Brussels sprouts
1 tablespoon plus 1 teaspoon
  margarine

salt and freshly ground pepper to
  taste

Add Brussels sprouts to saucepan with boiling salted water to cover. Return water to a boil; reduce heat and simmer for 12 minutes or until tender. Drain. Toss with margarine; sprinkle with salt and pepper. Divide evenly. Makes 4 servings. Serve at mealtime only.

Each serving is equivalent to: 3 oz Limited Vegetable; 1 serving Fat

Cabbage

Choose firm green or red cabbage heads. Cabbage may be eaten raw or cooked. Allow 1 lb fresh cabbage for 12 oz cooked. Quarter or shred cabbage and cook in boiling salted water until just tender.

Chinese Cabbage

A staple of the Oriental diet, Chinese cabbage is also known as 'Chinese Leaves'. It has long, wide, white stalks with a crinkly, leafy, light green edge. Eat raw or cook in boiling salted water until tender. Serve as a vegetable.

Creamy Cole Slaw

1 lb shredded cabbage
8 oz carrots, grated
5 fl oz natural unsweetened yogurt
4 tablespoons mayonnaise
artificial sweetener to equal 1
  teaspoon sugar, or to taste

½ teaspoon salt
¼ teaspoon onion powder
¼ teaspoon dried onion flakes
⅛ teaspoon celery seed
pinch white pepper

In large bowl combine cabbage and carrots. In small bowl combine remaining ingredients. Pour over cabbage mixture. Toss lightly. Chill. Divide evenly. Makes 6 servings. Serve at mealtime only.

Each serving is equivalent to: 1 serving Vegetables; ⅙ Serving Milk (⅚ fl oz yogurt); 2 servings Fat

Carrot and Pineapple Mould

1 tablespoon unflavoured gelatine
4 fl oz water
4 oz carrots, coarsely grated
8 fl oz low-calorie orange-flavoured
  carbonated beverage
4 oz canned crushed pineapple, no
  sugar added

artificial sweetener to equal 1
  teaspoon sugar, or to taste
⅛ teaspoon peppermint extract or
  1 teaspoon chopped fresh mint

In medium saucepan soften gelatine in water. Simmer over low heat, stirring constantly, until gelatine is dissolved. Remove from heat. Add remaining ingredients and stir to combine. Pour into 1-pint mould and chill until firm. Turn out. Divide evenly. Makes 2 servings.

Each serving is equivalent to: 1 serving Something Extra (1½ teaspoons gelatine); ⅔ serving Vegetables; ½ serving Fruit

Cauliflower

Buy cauliflower with white, tightly formed florets. Avoid discoloured or spreading florets, as these are signs of age. Cut away outer leaves and stem. Separate the florets, rinse, drain and dry on paper towels. Raw cauliflower is delicious served with a dip. (See Yogurt Onion Dressing, page 292).

Celeriac

Whether your greengrocer calls it 'celery root' or 'celeriac' do try this delicious root vegetable. It may be eaten cold in salads or hot, as a side dish, with beef or poultry, or as flavouring in soups or stews. The small size celeriac usually has more flavour than the large size, which tends to be woody. To cook: wash, peel and slice the root. Cook in a small amount of boiling salted water for 20 minutes or until tender.

Cooked Celery

12 oz celery   salt and pepper to taste

Cut up celery as desired. Cook until tender in boiling salted water to cover. Drain and season with salt and pepper. Divide evenly. Makes 4 servings.

Each serving is equivalent to: 1 serving Vegetables

Celery and Broad Beans in 'Creamy' Chive Sauce

4 oz cooked celery, sliced   ¼ oz nonfat dry milk, mixed with
2 oz cooked fresh broad beans   2 tablespoons water
                                       ½ teaspoon chives

Combine all ingredients in small saucepan. Cook gently until thoroughly heated; DO NOT BOIL. Makes 1 serving.

Each serving is equivalent to: 1⅓ servings Vegetables; 2 oz Limited Vegetable; ¼ serving Milk (2½ fl oz skim milk)

Celery in Mushroom Sauce

12 oz cooked celery, sliced
3 oz cooked mushrooms, sliced

¼ recipe Basic White Sauce (1
serving, see page 278)

Combine all ingredients in baking dish. Bake at 375°F, Gas Mark 5, for 15 minutes or until hot and bubbly. Makes 1 serving. Serve at mealtime only.

Each serving is equivalent to: 5 servings Vegetables; Basic White Sauce (see page 000)

Creamy Cucumber Soup

This summer soup is a perfect beginning for a fish dinner.

1 lb 2 oz cucumbers
salt to taste
4 tablespoons margarine
2 tablespoons flour
1 pint hot skim milk

¼ teaspoon dill weed
18 fl oz Chicken Stock (see page
135)
¼ teaspoon white pepper
chopped fresh chives to garnish

Cut ½ of 1 cucumber into 6 even slices. Reserve for garnish. Peel, seed and grate remaining cucumbers. Sprinkle with salt and let stand for 20 minutes. Drain and set aside. In top of double boiler over hot water melt margarine, stir in flour and simmer for 5 minutes. Add milk, dill and grated cucumber. Simmer for 30 more minutes. Remove from heat and blend until smooth. Transfer to bowl and add stock, salt and pepper. Refrigerate for 3 hours or until well chilled. Stir; divide evenly into 6 bowls; garnish each with chives and one cucumber slice. Makes 6 servings. Serve at mealtime only.

Each serving is equivalent to: 1 serving Vegetables; 2 servings Fat; 1½ servings Something Extra (1 teaspoon flour and 3 fl oz stock); ⅓ serving Milk (3⅓ fl oz skim milk)

Mushroom Stuffed Fish (page 326)

Frankfurters in Tomato Sauce (page 325)

Cheese Latkes with Blackberry Topping
(page 302)

Blackberry Muffins (page 84) and Chocolate
Currant Cake with Apricot Sauce (page 86)

Spinach Cocktail (page 323)

Apricot Almandine Mousse (page 23)
and Jellied Orange Cups (page 316)

Peach Drink (page 120),
Chocolate Milk Shake (page 119)
and Tangy Strawberry Shake (page 120)

Minty Hot Cucumber

Serve as a side dish for salmon or lamb.

6 oz cucumber, peeled, seeded and   **1 teaspoon chopped fresh mint**
  cut into 1-inch long slices   **½ teaspoon salt**
1 teaspoon lemon juice

Place cucumber in small saucepan with enough water to cover. Bring to boil, reduce heat, and simmer for 5 minutes or until soft. Drain. In bowl toss cucumber with remaining ingredients. Divide evenly. Makes 2 servings.
    Each serving is equivalent to: 1 serving Vegetables

Baked Aubergine Casserole

The Turkish name for this dish is Patlijan.

2 lbs aubergines, peeled and cut   **1 lb 2 oz green peppers, seeded**
  into 1-inch thick slices   **and cut into ¼-inch thick slices**
2 tablespoons salt   **½ oz chopped fresh parsley**
6 oz onion, sliced   **2 garlic cloves, crushed**
1 lb tomatoes, peeled and sliced   **6 oz tomato purée, mixed with 6 fl**
    oz water

Sprinkle aubergines with salt and let stand for 20 minutes. Rinse, drain and dry with paper towels. In a large casserole make layers using half the ingredients, in order given, beginning with aubergines. Repeat layers using remaining ingredients. Bake at 425°F, Gas Mark 7, for 40 minutes or until vegetables are soft. Divide evenly. Makes 6 servings.
    Each serving is equivalent to: $3^2/_3$ servings Vegetables; 1 oz Limited Vegetable; ½ serving Bonus (1 oz tomato purée)

Baked Stuffed Aubergine

1 aubergine, about 1 lb, cut in half
  lengthwise, or 2 aubergines,
  about 8 oz each
4 oz tomato purée, mixed with 4 fl
  oz water
1½ teaspoons chopped fresh
  parsley

1 teaspoon dried onion flakes,
  reconstituted in 1 tablespoon
  water
½ garlic clove, crushed
¼ teaspoon basil
⅛ teaspoon fennel seeds
⅛ teaspoon pepper
4 oz Cheddar cheese, grated
6 oz cooked rice

Place aubergine halves, cut sides down, in a baking tin. Add ¼ inch water and bake at 350°F, Gas Mark 4, until soft. Remove and allow to cool slightly. Scoop out pulp leaving a ½-inch shell. Set aside. In saucepan combine next 7 ingredients and simmer for 10 minutes. In bowl combine pulp, cheese, rice and half the tomato mixture. Divide evenly and stuff into aubergine shells. Place in casserole, stuffed side up, and cover with remaining tomato mixture. Bake at 375°F, Gas Mark 5, for 25 minutes or until stuffing is hot and cheese is melted. Divide evenly. Makes 2 midday meal servings.

Each serving is equivalent to: 2⅔ servings Vegetables; 1 serving Bonus (2 oz tomato purée); 2 oz Hard Cheese; 1 serving Choice Group

Crisp Aubergine Slices, Italian Style

1 standard egg, slightly beaten
1 teaspoon mayonnaise
salt and pepper to taste
1 slice white bread, made into
  crumbs

1 oz Parmesan cheese, grated
¼ teaspoon oregano
4 oz aubergine, cut into ¼-inch
  thick slices

In small bowl combine egg, mayonnaise, salt and pepper. In separate bowl mix together breadcrumbs, cheese and oregano. Dip each slice of aubergine in egg mixture, then dip into crumb mixture to coat each side evenly. Place in shallow baking dish. Sprinkle with any extra egg and crumb mixture. Bake at 450°F, Gas Mark

8, for 15 minutes or until crispy, turning once. Makes 1 midday meal serving.

Each serving is equivalent to: 1 Egg; 1 serving Fat; 1 serving Bread; 1 oz Hard Cheese; $1^{1}/_{3}$ servings Vegetables

Aubergine Parmigiana

8 oz aubergine, peeled and cut into
** ¾-inch thick slices**
salt, pepper, and garlic powder to
** taste**

1½ oz Mozzarella cheese, grated
½ oz Parmesan cheese, grated
3 oz tomato purée, mixed with 3 fl
** oz water**

Sprinkle aubergine with salt, pepper and garlic powder. Place on baking sheet and grill 4 inches from source of heat for 8 minutes or until tender, turning once. Combine cheeses. In 2-pint casserole, layer half the aubergine, half the tomato purée mixed with water and half the cheese. Repeat layers. Cover and bake at 350°F, Gas Mark 4, for 15 minutes. Remove cover and bake 15 minutes longer. Divide evenly. Makes 2 midday meal servings. Supplement as required.

Each serving is equivalent to: $1^{1}/_{3}$ servings Vegetables; 1 oz Hard Cheese; ¾ serving Bonus (1½ oz tomato purée)

Fennel

This vegetable is also called 'anise' or 'fennocchi'. It has a liquorice flavour and is similar in appearance to celery but with feathery leaves and a large, bulbous root. Fennel is used raw in salads or cooked as a vegetable.

French Beans and Runner Beans

When shopping for green beans, look for firm pods. Snip off the ends and cut the pods into 1-inch pieces or long diagonal French beans slivers, or leave them whole. With runner beans, remove any tough 'strings' before cutting up the bean. Simmer in enough boiling salted water to cover for 10 minutes or until beans are tender-crisp; drain. Season with salt and pepper. Serve hot or cold.

Three-Bean Salad

4 tablespoons vegetable oil
2 fl oz cider vinegar
2 fl oz tomato juice
1 tablespoon chopped fresh parsley
1 tablespoon chopped chives
artificial sweetener to equal 1
   teaspoon sugar, or to taste

1 teaspoon tarragon
⅛ teaspoon garlic powder
8 oz cooked young broad beans
12 oz cooked cut French beans
12 oz cooked cut runner beans
salt and white pepper to taste

In large bowl combine oil, vinegar, tomato juice, parsley, chives, sweetener, tarragon and garlic powder. Add beans, salt and pepper; toss lightly. Chill lightly before serving. Divide evenly. Makes 4 servings. Serve at mealtime only.

Each serving is equivalent to: 3 servings Fat; $^1/_{16}$ serving Bonus (½ fl oz tomato juice); 2 oz Limited Vegetable; 2 servings Vegetables

Vine Leaves

The edible leaves of the grapevine are often used for wrapping fish, chicken, rice or mixtures. If you have access to a vine, you will find that fresh leaves gathered in June will be full grown but still tender. To prepare them for use, blanch for one minute; drain and dry. Vine leaves are also available canned and packed in brine. Remove the tough stem ends; rinse and dry leaves before filling.

Jerusalem Artichoke

The Jerusalem artichoke is a small, knobby, thin-skinned tuber of the sunflower species. It resembles a potato but has a sweeter, nutlike flavour and is more watery. It is used raw in salads, and cooked as a vegetable. Jerusalem artichoke is a limited vegetable and must be weighed.

It is best to cook the Jerusalem artichoke with the skin on, because it is bumpy and very difficult to peel and darkens quickly when the skin is removed.

Kale and Potato Stew

**12 fl oz chicken bouillon (made
  with 2 stock cubes)
2 oz kale**

**3 oz peeled potato, diced
1 oz onion, sliced**

Combine all ingredients in saucepan; cover and cook until potato is tender. Makes 1 serving. Serve at mealtime only.

Each serving is equivalent to: 2 servings Something Extra (2 stock cubes); $^2/_3$ serving Vegetables; 1 serving Choice Group; 1 oz Limited Vegetable

Kohlrabi

Only a few dozen vegetables are popular around the world, which still leaves hundreds of thousands of lesser known types. Kohlrabi looks like a turnip at its base and tastes like mild cabbage.

Here is an easy method of preparing it.

Peel and slice 6 oz kohlrabi. Put slices in steamer and steam for 25 minutes; or cover slices with boiling water in saucepan and cook for 20 minutes. Drain. Serve with a teaspoon of margarine, a pinch of nutmeg and chopped fresh parsley or chives, salt and pepper. Divide evenly. Makes 2 servings. Serve at mealtime only.

Each serving is equivalent to: 1 serving Vegetables; ½ serving Fat

Lettuce and Salad Greens

Lettuce, which has been cultivated for more than 2,500 years, was once known as the 'water plant' because it refreshed travellers. The most popular kinds are butterhead, chicory, cos, crisphead (iceberg), endive, escarole, loose leaf romaine and round. Raw spinach and watercress are also frequently used in salads.

All salad greens should be rinsed thoroughly, to restore lost moisture and to remove soil. Dry quickly. If greens are prepared in advance, wrap them in paper or cloth towelling and refrigerate until ready to use. Whenever possible, use more than one type in a salad.

Black Mushrooms

To prepare, pour boiling water over dried black mushrooms, then let them soak for 15 minutes or more. When the mushrooms are soft, squeeze to remove water and cut off tough stems. Mushrooms are now ready for slicing or cutting in wedges to use in recipes.

Baked Stuffed Mushrooms Florentine

8 oz large mushrooms
6 oz cooked spinach, chopped
2 teaspoons dried onion flakes, reconstituted in 1 tablespoon water

2 teaspoons vegetable oil
½ teaspoon chicken stock powder
½ teaspoon Worcester sauce
salt and pepper to taste

Wash mushrooms. Remove and finely chop stems; reserve caps. In bowl combine chopped stems and remaining ingredients. Stuff mushroom caps with spinach mixture. Place mushrooms, stuffed side up, in an 8 × 8-inch baking tin; cover. Bake at 375°F, Gas Mark 5, for 10 minutes. Remove cover, bake for 10 minutes longer or until mushrooms are tender. Divide evenly. Makes 4 servings.

Each serving is equivalent to: $1^1/_6$ servings Vegetables; ½ serving Fat, $^1/_8$ serving Something Extra (⅛ teaspoon stock powder)

Cooked Mushrooms

1 lb mushrooms
1 pint water

1 tablespoon lemon juice or red
   wine vinegar
¾ teaspoon salt

Wipe mushrooms with damp cloth and dry thoroughly. If ends are discoloured, trim a thin slice from the bottom. If the mushrooms are small, use them whole; otherwise, cut lengthwise in halves or slices. In saucepan bring water to a boil; add mushrooms, lemon juice or vinegar and salt. Cover and bring to quick boil; reduce heat and simmer for 10 minutes. Drain and reserve liquid. The mushroom liquid is good stock for soups or sauces. Divide evenly. Makes 4 servings.

Each serving is equivalent to: $1^{1}/_{3}$ servings Vegetables

Variation:

A Blanc—Use the mushrooms in salads, casseroles or in any dish calling for cooked white mushrooms. Small white mushrooms skewered with toothpicks make a nice hors d'oeuvre.

'Nuts'—Place 12 oz whole cooked mushrooms on a shallow pan. Grill for 25 minutes or until they become crisp. Salt and serve. Divide evenly. Makes 4 servings.

Each serving is equivalent to: 1 serving Vegetables

Caraway Mushroom Consommé

2 oz onion, finely diced
1 oz turnips, finely diced
1 oz carrots, finely diced
1 oz celery, finely diced
1 beef stock cube, crumbled

16 fl oz mushroom liquid (see
   Cooked Mushrooms, above)
8 fl oz water
2 teaspoons caraway seeds
1 teaspoon marjoram
1 bay leaf
salt to taste

In a medium saucepan combine onion, turnips, carrots, celery and stock cube; cook, stirring occasionally, until vegetables are tender; add mushroom liquid, water, caraway seeds, marjoram, bay leaf and salt. Bring to boil, reduce heat; simmer for 40 minutes. Strain and discard solids. Divide broth evenly into 4 bowls. Makes 4 servings.

Each serving is equivalent to: ¾ serving Something Extra (¼ stock cube and ½ teaspoon caraway seeds)

Mushroom Relish

3 tablespoons vegetable oil
2 tablespoons red wine vinegar
2 tablespoons Dijon mustard
1½ teaspoons chopped fresh
  parsley

1 garlic clove, crushed
artificial sweetener to equal ½
  teaspoon sugar, or to taste
1 teaspoon chopped chives
salt and pepper to taste
1 lb cooked mushrooms

In medium bowl combine oil, vinegar, mustard, parsley, garlic, sweetener, chives, salt and pepper. Mix well, add mushrooms, and let marinate overnight. Divide evenly. Makes 4 servings. Serve at mealtime only.

Each serving is equivalent to: 2¼ servings Fat; 1⅓ servings Vegetables

Mushroom Salad

4 oz tomato, diced
2½ oz cooked green beans
2½ oz cooked mushrooms
2 oz carrot sticks
1 tablespoon vegetable oil
1 tablespoon red wine vinegar

1 teaspoon tarragon
1 teaspoon Worcester sauce
1 teaspoon chopped fresh parsley
artificial sweetener to equal ½
  teaspoon sugar, or to taste
salt and pepper to taste

Arrange tomatoes, green beans, mushrooms and carrots on a serving plate. In a small bowl combine remaining ingredients. Pour over salad. Makes 1 serving. Serve at mealtime only.

Each serving is equivalent to: 3⅔ servings Vegetables; 3 servings Fat

Mushroom Sandwich Spread

6 oz cooked mushrooms, sliced
4 oz green pepper, seeded and
finely diced
2 oz canned pimiento, diced

2 tablespoons mayonnaise
1 teaspoon chopped chives
salt and pepper to taste
2 slices white bread, toasted

In medium bowl combine all ingredients except bread; mix thoroughly. Divide evenly and spread on toast slices. Makes 2 servings. Serve at mealtime only.

Each serving is equivalent to: 2 servings Vegetables; 3 servings Fat; 1 serving Bread

Okra

Look for young, tender, crisp pods. Scrub pods and slice, if desired. Cook in a small amount of boiling salted water for 10 to 15 minutes or until tender. Do not overcook. Okra has a gluey sap that helps thicken sauces. Okra is also available canned. This is a limited vegetable and must be weighed.

Okra Soup

Traditionally, this is served over cooked rice.

1 pint 4 fl oz Chicken Stock (see
page 135)
8 oz fresh or drained canned okra
½ oz celery, chopped
1 teaspoon dried onion flakes
1 teaspoon chopped fresh parsley

1 bay leaf
1 clove
salt, pepper and celery salt to taste
4 oz tomato purée, mixed with 4 fl
oz water

Combine all ingredients except tomato purée in saucepan and simmer for 25 minutes. Add tomato purée mixed with water. Heat and serve. Divide evenly. Makes 4 servings.

Each serving is equivalent to: 1 serving Something Extra (6 fl oz stock), 2 oz Limited Vegetable; ½ serving Bonus (1 oz tomato purée)

Onions

There are many kinds of onions, of various colours and sizes. They are part of the same family as shallots, leeks, spring onions, garlic and chives. Onions are used to flavour roasts, casseroles, salads, vegetables, soups and stews.

Onions can be peeled more easily if boiling water is poured over them and they are allowed to stand a few minutes. Onions are a limited vegetable and must be weighed.

Cooked Onions

Drop peeled onions into boiling salted water. Boil for 15 to 35 minutes depending on the size of the onion. Onions are cooked when they are transparent and can be pierced easily with a fork. Weigh and serve.

Sliced onions may be cooked the same way but require less time.

To brown onions, preheat a nonstick frying pan. Add onions and cook, stirring constantly with a wooden spoon to avoid scorching. Weigh and serve.

Garlic

Garlic in all forms is allowed on our Food Plan. Most of our recipes call for fresh garlic, but dried chopped garlic, garlic powder and garlic salt are all acceptable substitutes. To peel and crush the fresh clove, put it on a wooden board. Crush with the side of a cleaver or knife. Remove the skin.

Leeks

Leeks are closely related to spring onions and garlic. They are often used as a flavouring in soups, and their delicate flavour makes them a delicious vegetable, too. Wash in several changes of water to remove sand. Trim off the root end, discard any discoloured green stem. Cook in a small amount of boiling salted water for 15 minutes, or until tender. Drain and season to taste. Weigh and serve.

Spring Onions

Finely chopped spring onions are delicious in salads or as an additional seasoning ingredient in casseroles. Spring onions are a limited vegetable and must be weighed.

Shallots

The shallot is a mild-flavoured cousin of the onion, leek and garlic, and grows in clove form, similar to garlic. Fresh shallots are used raw in salads and as an additional seasoning ingredient cooked in dishes. Shallots are a limited vegetable and must be weighed.

Onion Soup

1 lb onions, thinly sliced
1 pint 16 fl oz Beef Stock (see page 157)
1 teaspoon steak sauce

pinch celery salt and pepper
4 slices white bread, toasted and cut into quarters
4 oz hard cheese, grated

Combine all ingredients except toast and cheese in large saucepan. Cover and bring to a boil; reduce heat. Simmer for 20 minutes or until onions are soft. Divide evenly into 4 ovenproof soup bowls. Top each with 4 toast quarters. Sprinkle each with 1 oz cheese. Bake at 350°F, Gas Mark 4, until cheese melts. Makes 4 midday meal servings. Supplement as required.

Each serving is equivalent to: 4 oz Limited Vegetable; 1½ servings Something Extra (9 fl oz stock); 1 serving Bread, 1 oz Hard Cheese

Stuffed Onions

1 lb small onions, cut in half
3 oz mushrooms, diced
1 teaspoon chicken stock powder
¼ teaspoon thyme
⅛ teaspoon salt

⅛ teaspoon pepper
2 slices white bread, made into
  crumbs
2 tablespoons vegetable oil

Remove centre of onions, dice inside portion and reserve pockets. In a nonstick frying pan combine diced onions, mushrooms, stock powder, thyme, salt and pepper; sauté until onions are brown. Transfer to a large bowl. Add breadcrumbs and oil; mix thoroughly. Divide mixture evenly and stuff into onion pockets. Place in a baking dish, add about ¼ inch water to dish. Bake at 350°F, Gas Mark 4, for 25 minutes. Divide evenly. Makes 8 servings. Serve at mealtime only.

Each serving is equivalent to: 2 oz Limited Vegetable; ⅛ Serving Vegetables, ⅛ serving Something Extra (⅛ teaspoon stock powder); ¼ serving Bread; ¾ serving Fat

Parsley

To store parsley, wash well in cold water. Drain leaves, dry in paper or cloth towels, and store in covered container in refrigerator.

Parsnips

An excellent vegetable! Scrape to clean; weigh, slice and drop into water containing vinegar or lemon juice, to prevent discolouration.

Drain and transfer to saucepan containing small amount of boiling water. Cover and cook until tender. Serve with a pinch of chopped fresh parsley.

Orange-Glazed Parsnips

1 lb parsnips, peeled and diced	½ teaspoon grated orange rind
2 tablespoons frozen orange juice concentrate	pinch ginger
2 tablespoons margarine	4 oz orange sections, no sugar added

In saucepan cook parsnips with water to cover until tender. Drain. In top of double boiler over boiling water combine orange juice concentrate, margarine, orange rind and ginger; cook until margarine is melted. Add parsnips and simmer for 10 minutes or until parsnips are glazed. Add orange sections and continue cooking for 5 minutes. Divide evenly. Makes 4 servings. Serve at mealtime only.

Each serving is equivalent to: 4 oz Limited Vegetable; ¾ serving Fruit; 1½ servings Fat

Chinese Pea Pods (Mange Tout)

The pea within the pod is extremely small, and both the peas and the pods are edible. They are most plentiful from May to September. To prepare them, break off tips and remove string on both sides. To retain the delicate flavour and colour, cook in a minimum of liquid just until tender-crisp. This is a limited vegetable and must be weighed.

Sweet, Green or Bell Peppers

To roast peppers: Wash and dry peppers and place on pan 5 inches from source of heat. Grill, turning with tongs, for 15 minutes or until skin is black and charred on all sides. Remove, place in paper bag, and let pepper steam 5 to 10 minutes or until cool enough to handle. Peel away charred skin and discard seeds and membranes. *To skin fresh peppers*: Bake peppers in oven at 350°F, Gas Mark 4, turning occasionally until the skin is scorched and can be removed easily.

To freeze peppers: Cut off stem ends, cut pepper in half, and discard seeds and membranes. Dice; spread on foil in baking pan and freeze. Remove from freezer, pack in freezer container, and label. You can easily remove a small amount from container for use in a recipe. Usually, no defrosting is necessary.

To prepare peppers for stuffing: Cut off the stem end and scoop out seeds and membranes. Drop peppers in a large pan of boiling water and parboil for 10 minutes or until nearly tender. Remove and turn upside down to drain. Fill peppers, bake in shallow tin or small basins at 350°F, Gas Mark 4, for 20 minutes or until filling is hot.

Pumpkin Fritters

2 oz canned pumpkin
1 standard egg
1 slice white bread, quartered
1 fl oz skim milk
1 tablespoon water

artificial sweetener to equal 1
    teaspoon sugar, or to taste
¼ teaspoon baking powder
⅛ teaspoon cinnamon

Combine all ingredients in blender container; blend until smooth. Drop by spoonfuls onto a preheated nonstick frying pan. When bottom is browned, turn to brown other side. Serve hot. Makes 1 morning or midday meal serving. Supplement as required.

Each serving is equivalent to: 2 oz Limited Vegetable; 1 Egg; 1 serving Bread, $^1/_{10}$ serving Milk (1 fl oz skim milk)

Quick-and-Easy Pumpkin Soup

1 lb canned pumpkin
1 pint 4 fl oz chicken bouillon
    (made with 4 stock cubes)
artificial sweetener to equal 1
    teaspoon sugar, or to taste

¼ teaspoon cinnamon
⅛ teaspoon nutmeg
⅛ teaspoon ginger

Combine all ingredients in large saucepan. Bring to a boil; reduce heat and simmer for 5 minutes. Divide evenly. Makes 4 servings.

Each serving is equivalent to: 4 oz Limited Vegetable; 1 serving Something Extra (1 stock cube)

Variation: For 'Cream' of Pumpkin Soup, follow preceding recipe. Stir in 2 oz nonfat dry milk mixed with 8 fl oz water; heat but do not boil. Add ½ serving Milk (5 fl oz skim milk) to equivalent listing.

Radishes

The red radish most frequently seen in the market is one of several varieties available. There are also white radishes and black radishes.
To cook radishes: Peel and slice, if desired. Cover with boiling water and cook until tender.
To make radish roses: Slice off the top. Make 4 or 5 cuts about ¼ inch deep all round radish to create petals. Place in bowl of ice water and refrigerate for an hour or two, or until 'rose' opens. Drain and use as garnish.
To make radish accordions: Trim a thin slice from each end, then make parallel slashes ⅛ inch apart along one side of radish, being careful not to cut through the opposite side. Refrigerate, as for radish roses.

Swede

Deep yellow flesh and strong flavour distinguish this cousin of the turnip. Cover peeled, diced swede with boiling salted water and cook for 20 to 30 minutes or until tender. Swede is delicious plain and is a special treat when combined with potato. This is a limited vegetable and must be weighed.

Swede and Potato Mash

4 oz peeled cooked swede, mashed   **1 teaspoon margarine**
3 oz peeled cooked potato, mashed

Combine swede and potato in saucepan; heat. Remove from heat, add margarine, and serve. Makes 1 serving. Serve at mealtime only.
  Each serving is equivalent to: 4 oz Limited Vegetable; 1 serving Choice Group; 1 serving Fat

Salsify

Salsify is shaped like a carrot or parsnip and can be white or black. The black variety is large and reputed to have a better flavour. Salsify is a limited vegetable and must be weighed.

To prepare, remove the tops and scrub the root. Peel and cover with acidulated water (2 pints water with 1 tablespoon lemon juice) to prevent discolouration until ready to use. Boil until tender; drain, season and serve.

Sauerkraut with Prunes
To garnish a roast.

12 oz canned sauerkraut, rinsed
6 fl oz chicken bouillon (made with
   1 stock cube)
2 oz onion, finely chipped

4 dried medium prunes, stoned
   and diced
pinch white pepper

Combine sauerkraut, bouillon and onion in a medium saucepan. Bring to a boil; reduce heat and simmer for 20 minutes or until onion is tender. Add prunes; cook about 10 minutes longer or until most of the liquid has evaporated. Season with pepper. Divide evenly. Makes 4 servings.

Each serving is equivalent to: 1 serving Vegetables; ¼ serving Something Extra (¼ stock cube); ½ oz Limited Vegetable; ¼ serving Fruit

Creamy Spinach

Wash fresh spinach several times to remove sand. Drain and dry on paper towels. Remove and discard tough stems.

12 oz spinach leaves
½ oz nonfat dry milk
2 fl oz water

1 tablespoon plus 1 teaspoon
   margarine
pinch nutmeg
salt and pepper to taste

Place spinach in boiling salted water to cover. Boil for 4 minutes or until tender. Drain well. Mix nonfat dry milk with water. In top of double boiler over boiling water combine milk, margarine and spinach. Cook until margarine is melted. Season with nutmeg, salt and pepper. Divide evenly. Makes 4 servings. Serve at mealtime only.

Each serving is equivalent to: 1 serving Vegetables; ⅛ serving Milk (1¼ fl oz skim milk); 1 serving Fat

Marrow, Courgettes and Squash

To cook marrow, courgettes or squash, cut in slices and steam until tender or cook in a small amount of boiling salted water. Drain well and serve with measured amounts of margarine. Small courgettes need not be peeled.

Courgette Boats

10 oz frozen chopped spinach
2 large courgettes, about 5 oz each
2 teaspoons chopped fresh parsley
1 teaspoon Italian seasoning, or ½ teaspoon oregano, ¼ teaspoon marjoram and ¼ teaspoon basil

½ teaspoon dried onion flakes
½ teaspoon salt
½ garlic clove
⅛ teaspoon pepper
8 oz cooked minced veal, chicken or turkey, crumbled

Cook spinach according to package directions; let cool. Squeeze out as much liquid as possible; transfer spinach to blender container. Place courgettes in medium saucepan with salted water to cover. Cook for 5 to 7 minutes. Remove courgettes from liquid and cut in half lengthwise. Gently scoop out seeds, leaving a firm shell; add seeds to blender container with spinach. Add seasonings and blend until mixture is puréed. Transfer to mixing bowl. Stir in crumbled veal, chicken or turkey. Divide mixture evenly and fill courgette shells. Bake at 350°F, Gas Mark 4, for 15 to 20 minutes or until thoroughly heated. Makes 2 midday meal servings, 2 courgette boats each.

Each serving is equivalent to: 3⅓ servings Vegetables; 4 oz Veal or Poultry

Courgette Salad

12 oz courgettes, thinly sliced
8 oz tomatoes, cut in wedges
3 oz mushrooms, thinly sliced
4 oz onion, thinly sliced

Basic French Dressing (see page 283)
5 oz lettuce leaves

In bowl combine all ingredients except lettuce. Arrange lettuce on serving dish. Top with salad. Divide evenly. Makes 4 servings. Serve at mealtime only.

Each serving is equivalent to: $2^1/_3$ serving Vegetables; 1 oz Limited Vegetable; Basic French Dressing (see page 283)

Swiss Chard

This often neglected but delicious vegetable is a type of beet which does not develop the fleshy root of the ordinary beet but is grown for the leaves and stalk. Wash carefully and remove the root ends. Cut the stalks in 2-inch thick slices; cut up the leaves if they are large. Cook in a small amount of boiling water for 5 to 10 minutes for the leaves and for 10 to 15 minutes for the stalks. Add a little crushed fresh garlic or lemon juice before serving.

Tomatoes

To skin fresh tomatoes, stroke each tomato with the dull edge of a knife until the skin wrinkles and can be removed. If the skin doesn't come off easily, immerse tomato in boiling water for a minute or two, then plunge it into cold water, drain and peel. Use canned tomatoes in the winter, when fresh ones are expensive. They make an excellent substitute in recipes calling for fresh tomatoes.

White Turnips

If you have never used raw white turnips, try washing them well and grating or slicing them into a salad. Cooked and browned turnips make a nice change from potatoes when serving a roast.

Water Chestnuts

The crunchiness of the water chestnut is welcome in many dishes. Stuff sliced water chestnuts into cooked prunes as an hors d'oeuvre or meat accompaniment dice them and use with apples in a salad; serve them with cooked green beans or other vegetables, and, of course, use them in Chinese dishes. Place unused water chestnuts in a small jar, cover with water, and refrigerate. They will keep a week or two if you remember to change the water daily. This is a limited vegetable and must be weighed.

Creamy Vegetable Soups

Purées of vegetables are just one step away from creamy soups. In saucepan heat 4 oz of a cooked puréed vegetable (asparagus, broccoli, carrot, cauliflower, celery, courgette, etc.) with 6 fl oz chicken bouillon (made with 1 stock cube). Stir in ¼ oz nonfat dry milk and reheat, but do not boil. Garnish with chopped fresh parsley, dill or watercress. Makes 1 serving.

Each serving is equivalent to: $1^1/_3$ serving Vegetables; 1 serving Something Extra (1 stock cube); ¼ serving Milk (2½ fl oz skim milk)

Variations:

1. Add 3 oz peeled cooked potatoes, diced. Serve at mealtime only. Add 1 serving Choice Group to equivalent listing.

2. Dissolve 1 teaspoon cornflour in 1 tablespoon water and stir in vegetable-bouillon mixture. Simmer, stirring often, for 2 minutes or until soup has thickened. Continue as above. Add 1 serving Something Extra (1 teaspoon cornflour) to equivalent listing.

3. Omit milk and heat as directed. Chill soup and stir in 2½ fl oz natural unsweetened yogurt. In equivalent listing change milk equivalent to ½ serving Milk (2½ fl oz yogurt)

Gazpacho

8 oz tomatoes, chopped
3 oz cucumber, peeled and
chopped
3 oz green pepper, seeded and
chopped
1 oz onion, diced
½ slice white bread, torn into
pieces (optional)
3 tablespoons water

3 tablespoons water
1 tablespoon vegetable oil
2 teaspoons red wine vinegar
½ teaspoon chilli powder, or to
taste
1 garlic clove
pinch artificial sweetener or to
taste (optional)
pinch cumin
salt and pepper to taste

Combine all ingredients in blender container; blend to desired consistency. Add more water to adjust consistency if necessary. Chill. Divide evenly. Makes 2 servings. Serve at mealtime only.

Each serving is equivalent to: 2⅓ servings Vegetables; ½ oz Limited Vegetable; ¼ serving Bread (optional); 1½ servings Fat

Mexican Cauliflower and Pepper Salad

To make a complete midday meal, for each serving slice 2 hard-boiled standard eggs and toss with the salad. Also good with shredded drained canned beetroot garnished with chopped fresh parsley.

6 oz cos lettuce
6 oz cauliflower florets, thinly
sliced
6 oz green pepper, seeded and
cubed
2 tablespoons vegetable oil
1 tablespoon plus 1 teaspoon chilli
sauce

1 tablespoon lemon juice or red
wine vinegar
1 tablespoon water
½ teaspoon prepared horseradish
pinch salt and cayenne pepper

Separate lettuce leaves, wash and dry well. Stack leaves and cut crosswise to make ¼ to ½-inch shreds. Place in large salad bowl; add cauliflower and green pepper. Combine all remaining ingredients in small jar with tightly fitting lid; cover and shake well. Pour over vegetables; toss to combine. Divide evenly. Makes 4 servings. Serve at mealtime only.

Each serving is equivalent to: 1½ servings Vegetables; 1½ servings Fat; ½ serving Something Extra (1 teaspoon chilli sauce)

Minestrone (Vegetable Soup Italian Style)

6 oz courgettes, sliced
4 oz celery, sliced
4 oz carrots, sliced
4 oz spring onions or onion, diced
3 oz cabbage, shredded, or
  cauliflower, coarsely chopped
4 teaspoons chicken stock powder
1 garlic clove, crushed

1¼ pints water
4 oz tomato purée, mixed with
  4 fl oz water
½ teaspoon basil
¼ teaspoon thyme
2 peppercorns, crushed
12 oz cooked elbow macaroni

In large saucepan combine courgettes, celery, carrots, spring onions, cabbage, stock powder and garlic. Simmer for 3 to 5 minutes over medium heat, stirring occasionally. Add all remaining ingredients except macaroni. Bring to a boil; cover. Reduce heat, simmer for 20 minutes or until vegetables are tender. Stir in macaroni; cook until thoroughly heated. Divide evenly. Makes 4 servings. Serve at mealtime only.

Each serving is equivalent to: 1⅓ servings Vegetables; 1 oz Limited Vegetable; 1 serving Something Extra (1 teaspoon stock powder); ½ serving Bonus (1 oz tomato purée); 1 serving Choice Group

Variations:

1. Omit macaroni and add 12 oz cooked barley, whole kernel corn or rice.

2. Omit macaroni and add 12 oz peeled diced potato to saucepan with water and remaining ingredients.

3. Omit macaroni and float 1 slice white bread, diced, on each serving. Change equivalent listing from 1 serving Choice Group to 1 serving Bread.

Oriental Vegetable Mix

8 oz bean sprouts
5 oz cabbage, shredded
4 oz celery, sliced diagonally
4 oz drained canned water
  chestnuts, sliced
2 oz spring onions, finely chopped

8 fl oz chicken bouillon (made with
  1 stock cube)
2 tablespoons soy sauce
½ teaspoon dry mustard, dissolved
  in 1 tablespoon water (optional)

Sauté first 5 ingredients for 3 minutes in large nonstick frying pan. Add bouillon and simmer, stirring often, until most of the liquid has evaporated. Stir in soy sauce and mustard if desired. Divide evenly. Makes 4 servings.

Each serving is equivalent to: $1^1/_3$ servings Vegetables; 1½ oz Limited Vegetable; ¼ serving Something Extra (¼ stock cube)

Ratatouille

Ratatouille may be folded into omelettes, or topped with hard cheese and baked until cheese melts and bubbles, or served with cottage cheese or scrambled eggs for the midday meal.

8 oz courgettes, cut into ¼-inch thick slices	8 oz canned tomatoes, coarsely chopped
6 oz onion, sliced	4 oz tomato purée, mixed with 4 fl oz water
6 oz green pepper, seeded and cut into ½-inch dice	1 teaspoon basil
4 oz aubergine, peeled and cut into ½-inch dice	1 teaspoon oregano
1 teaspoon chicken stock power	salt and freshly ground pepper to taste
1 garlic clove, crushed	

Combine first 6 ingredients in saucepan; cook for 5 minutes. Add all remaining ingredients and cook over medium heat, stirring often, for about 1¼ hours or until vegetables are tender. Divide evenly. Makes 4 servings.

Each serving is equivalent to: $2^1/_6$ servings Vegetables; 1½ oz Limited Vegetable; ¼ serving Something Extra (¼ teaspoon stock powder); ½ serving Bonus (1 oz tomato purée)

Vegetables à la Grecque

2 pints water
4 fl oz lemon juice
1 teaspoon salt
½ teaspoon thyme
½ teaspoon rosemary
½ teaspoon savory
10 peppercorns

2 garlic cloves, crushed
1 bay leaf
12 oz vegetables (cauliflower,
carrots, celery, green beans,
broccoli etc)
Basic French Dressing (see page
283)

In saucepan combine first 9 ingredients and simmer for 15 minutes. Add vegetables, return water to a boil, reduce heat and simmer until vegetables are tender-crisp. Allow vegetables to cool in liquid; drain.* Toss vegetables with Basic French Dressing. Chill. Divide evenly. Makes 4 servings. Serve at mealtime only.

Each serving is equivalent to: 1 serving Vegetables; Basic French Dressing (see page 283)

*Reserve liquid if desired; liquid may be used again for cooking additional vegetables.

Vegetable Purées

Bean and Pumpkin Purée

In blender container combine 4 oz cooked dried kidney or white beans and 4 oz cooked pumpkin. Blend until puréed, pushing mixture down with spatula if necessary. Transfer to small saucepan; cook over low heat, stirring constantly, until thoroughly heated. Makes 1 evening meal serving. Supplement as required.

Each serving is equivalent to: 4 oz Dried Peas/Beans; 4 oz Limited Vegetable

Puréed Broccoli and Cauliflower

In saucepan combine 6 oz each of chopped broccoli and cauliflower; cook in boiling salted water until tender. Drain; place in blender container, blend until pureéd, pushing mixture down with spatula if necessary. Season with salt, pepper, nutmeg and lemon juice. Serve hot. Divide evenly. Makes 4 servings.

Each serving is equivalent to: 1 serving Vegetables

Puréed Carrots

In blender container, combine 6 oz cooked carrots, 2 teaspoons nonfat dry milk mixed with 1 tablespoon water and 1 teaspoon margarine. Blend until pureéd, pushing mixture down with spatula if necessary. Transfer to small baking dish; bake at 350°F, Gas Mark 4, for 15 minutes or until thoroughly heated. Makes 1 serving. Serve at mealtime only.

Each serving is equivalent to: 2 servings Vegetables; ⅛ serving Milk (1¼ fl oz skim milk); 1 serving Fat

Puréed Potatoes and Turnips

If you or the children don't like green vegetables, turnips or parsnips and prefer potatoes, purée them together! You'll get the flavour of potatoes plus the food of the vegetable, and the potato taste survives almost any combination. In a medium saucepan combine 2 oz peeled, diced white turnip and 3 oz peeled, diced potato. Cover them with boiling salted water and cook for 25 minutes or until very soft. Drain. Mash, beat, or purée vegetables in food mixer of blender. Add 2 teaspoons nonfat dry milk mixed with 1 tablespoon water and 1 teaspoon margarine, if desired. Season to taste with salt and white pepper. Makes 1 serving. Serve at mealtime only.

Each serving is equivalent to: ⅔ serving Vegetables; 1 serving Choice Group; ⅛ serving Milk (1¼ fl oz skim milk); 1 serving Fat (optional)

Watercress Vegetable Purée

In blender container combine 2½ oz cooked green beans, 2½ oz cooked sliced courgettes, 1½ oz cooked sliced celery, ½ oz chopped watercress and 2 oz cooked sliced onion. Blend until puréed, pushing mixture down with spatula if necessary. Season to taste with salt and curry powder. Transfer to small saucepan; cook over low heat, stirring constantly, until thoroughly heated. Divide evenly. Makes 2 servings.

Each serving is equivalent to: 1¹/₆ servings Vegetables; 1 oz Limited Vegetable

SAUCES AND SALAD DRESSINGS

*

Sauces and salad dressings, some with fats and others without, are combined in this chapter for easy reference. Hot or cold, sweet, sour (or both at once), thick or thin, in all colours (white, red, yellow, brown), bland or nippy, bumpy or smooth – there's really something for everyone here. You must try our foolproof "Hollandaise" sauce. Enjoy, within your Menu Plan limits, of course.

Rules for Using Fats

1 Select 3 servings daily at mealtime only:
margarine, special (high in polyunsaturates), *1 level teaspoon,*
margarine, low-fat spread, *2 level teaspoons,*
mayonnaise, *1 level teaspoon,*
vegetable oil (corn, cottonseed, safflower, sesame, soybean, sunflower), *1 level teaspoon.*
2. You may mix-and-match fats; i.e., you may have 1 teaspoon margarine and 2 teaspoons mayonnaise daily, or 4 teaspoons low-fat spread and 1 teaspoon vegetable oil daily.
3. Any product labelled 'mayonnaise' and any oil labelled 'vegetable oil' may be used.
4. *Cooking Procedures:*
May be mixed with other ingredients and baked in a casserole.
May be melted over direct heat in a flameproof container, or in a double boiler.
After a food item has been grilled, pierce or cut slightly, if possible. Spread fat over food, and grill for no longer than one minute.
May never be used for sautéeing or frying.

Basic Brown Sauce

This sauce may be varied in many ways.

2 tablespoons plus 2 teaspoons
   margarine
2 tablespoons plus 2 teaspoons
   flour
1 oz tomato purée with 2
   tablespoons water
16 fl oz water
2 beef stock cubes, crumbled

2 teaspoons dried onion flakes,
   reconstituted in 2 teaspoons
   water
1½ teaspoons browning sauce
4 peppercorns
2 cloves
1 small bay leaf
pinch thyme
pinch garlic powder

Melt margarine in top of double boiler, over boiling water; using a wooden spoon or wire whisk, add flour, and cook for 7 minutes, stirring frequently. Stir in tomato purée mixed with water. Slowly add remaining water, stirring constantly. Add all remaining ingredients; cover and simmer for 30 minutes or until thickened, stirring often. Divide evenly. Makes 4 servings. Serve at mealtime only.

Each serving is equivalent to: 2 servings Fat; 2½ servings Something Extra (2 teaspoons flour and ½ stock cube); ⅛ serving Bonus (¼ oz tomato purée)

Variations:

Cherry Sauce—Prepare Basic Brown Sauce as above. Add 8 oz canned, stoned cherries, no sugar added. Divide evenly. Makes 4 servings. Serve at mealtime only. Add ½ serving Fruit to equivalent listing.

Mustard Sauce—Prepare Basic Brown Sauce as above. Dissolve 2½ teaspoons dry mustard in 1 oz nonfat dry milk, mixed with 4 fl oz water and add to Brown Sauce. Serve hot. Divide evenly. Makes 4 servings. Serve at mealtime only. Add ¼ serving Milk (2½ fl oz skim milk) to equivalent listing.

Basic White Sauce

A basic sauce you can perk up in many ways.

2 tablespoons margarine	**pinch white pepper**
2 tablespoons flour	**10 fl oz skim milk**
⅛ teaspoon salt	

Melt margarine in top of double boiler over hot water. Add flour, salt and pepper and cook over moderate heat for about 2 minutes, stirring constantly. Gradually add milk. Cook, stirring constantly with a wire whisk until mixture thickens. Keep warm in double boiler. Makes about 10 fl oz. Divide evenly into 4 servings. Serve at mealtime only.

Each serving is equivalent to: 1½ servings Fat; 1½ servings Something Extra (1½ teaspoons flour); ¼ serving Milk (2½ fl oz skim milk)

Variations:
Caper White Sauce—For boiled or poached fish. Stir in 1½ tablespoons capers and ½ teaspoon sherry flavouring.

Curry Sauce—Add 1 teaspoon curry powder, or to taste, with the flour.

Diavolo Sauce—To melted margarine in basic recipe, add 1 teaspoon dried onion flakes, reconstituted, before stirring in flour and seasonings. Use only 8 fl oz skim milk; add 1 oz tomato pureé mixed with 2 tablespoons water and ¼ to ½ teaspoon hot sauce. Reduce milk equivalent to ⅕ serving Milk and add ⅛ serving Bonus (¼ oz tomato purée) to equivalent listing.

Dill Sauce—Add ¾ teaspoon dill weed and pinch nutmeg with salt and pepper in the basic recipe. Substitute Fish Stock (see page 197) for half the skim milk. Delicious with poached fish. Reduce milk equivalent to ⅛ serving Milk (1¼ fl oz skim milk) in equivalent listing.

Enriched White Sauce—Use only 5 fl oz skim milk but mix with ½ oz nonfat dry milk; add 1 fl oz Double-Strength Chicken Stock (see page 135) and cook as directed in basic recipe. In equivalent listing add 1/12 serving Something Extra (¼ fl oz Double-Strength Stock).

Florentine Sauce—After adding milk, stir in 1 oz finely chopped spinach. Cook as directed in basic recipe. Add ¼ oz Vegetables to equivalent listing.

Herb Sauce—Add 1 teaspoon chopped fresh parsley, ½ teaspoon chopped fresh chives and ¼ teaspoon tarragon with the flour.

Horseradish White Sauce—To basic recipe add 1½ tablespoons prepared white horseradish and ½ teaspoon prepared mustard. Serve with chicken, beef or lamb.

Hot Tartare Sauce—Add 1 oz diced onion and 1½ oz green pepper, seeded and diced, to margarine before adding flour. After sauce has thickened, stir in 2 tablespoons mayonnaise, 1½ teaspoons lemon juice, 1 oz chopped pickled cucumber and 2 teaspoons chopped fresh parsley. Use for seafood, broccoli or asparagus. Add ¼ oz Limited Vegetable, ¼ oz Vegetables and 1½ servings Fat to equivalent listing.

Mushroom White Sauce—Add 1 oz diced onion and 1 oz sliced mushrooms to margarine before adding flour. When sauce thickens, add a dash of Worcester sauce. Add ¼ oz Limited Vegetable and ¼ oz Vegetables to equivalent listing.

'Ravigote' Sauce—Add 1 oz diced onion to margarine before adding flour. When sauce thickens, add 1 teaspoon each tarragon, chervil and chives. Add ¼ oz Limited Vegetable to equivalent listing.

Thin Basic White Sauce—Increase skim milk to 1 pint in basic recipe. Add ¼ serving Milk (2½ fl oz skim milk) to equivalent listing.

Fines Herbes Spread

Use as a sandwich spread or serve melted on hot cooked vegetables, fish, or grilled meat. This may be varied in many ways by using different combinations of herbs.

8 tablespoons margarine
1 teaspoon chives
1 teaspoon chopped fresh parsley
1 teaspoon tarragon
1 teaspoon marjoram

½ teaspoon grated lemon rind
pinch salt and pepper
chopped fresh parsley and chives
   to garnish

In small bowl combine all ingredients, except garnish; chill, form into a mound. Place in serving dish and garnish with parsley and chives. Divide evenly. Makes 8 servings. Serve at mealtime only.

Each serving is equivalent to: 3 servings Fat

Mustard Sauce for Vegetables

3 tablespoons low-fat spread   2 fl oz water
1 teaspoon prepared·mustard   salt and white pepper to taste
1 teaspoon flour

Combine margarine and mustard in top of double boiler and heat over boiling water to melt margarine. Stir in flour; cook for 1 minute. Add water; cook, stirring constantly until, mixture thickens. Season to taste. Divide evenly. Makes 3 servings. Serve at mealtime only.

Each serving is equivalent to: 1½ servings Fat; $^1/_3$ serving Something Extra ($^1/_3$ teaspoon flour)

Prune Sauce

Cornflour may be substituted for flour in many recipes which uses flour as a thickening agent. Generally you will need less cornflour than flour to thicken a sauce. It is an especially good thickener for clear fruit sauces and sauces to be served with Oriental foods. It is best to dissolve cornflour in a cold liquid before adding to other ingredients.

10 fl oz water   artificial sweetener to equal ½
12 dried large prunes, stoned and   teaspoon sugar, or to taste
  diced   ⅛ teaspoon ginger
1 tablespoon cornflour, dissolved in   pinch salt
  3 tablespoons water   1 tablespoon red wine vinegar
                                        2 teaspoons margarine

In small saucepan combine water and prunes. Bring to a boil; reduce heat and simmer for 10 minutes. Drain and measure liquid. Add more water if necessary to equal 10 fl oz liquid. Return to saucepan with prunes. In small bowl combine cornflour, sweetener, ginger and salt. Gradually stir into prune mixture. Cook over medium heat, stirring constantly until sauce comes to a boil. Remove from heat. Blend in vinegar and margarine. Serve over warm meat. If sauce thickens while standing, stir in water, a teaspoon at a time, until desired consistency. Divide evenly. Makes 4 servings. Serve at mealtime only.

Each serving is equivalent to: 1 serving Fruit; ¾ serving Something Extra (¾ teaspoon cornflour); ½ serving Fat

'Hollandaise'

Good over hot asparagus.

1 tablespoon cornflour	2 tablespoons mayonnaise
4 fl oz water	1 teaspoon lemon juice
1 chicken stock cube, crumbled	dash hot sauce
4 tablespoons low-fat spread	

In small saucepan, dissolve cornflour in water. Add crumbled stock cube. Stir over medium heat until thickened. Remove from heat. Stir in margarine until melted. Add mayonnaise; stir until blended. Add lemon juice and hot sauce; stir to combine. Divide evenly. Makes 6 servings. Serve at mealtime only.

Each serving is equivalent to: $^2/_3$ serving Something Extra (½ teaspoon cornflour and $^1/_6$ stock cube); 2 servings Fat

Lemony Mayonnaise

Delicious with vegetables or on a salad.

2 tablespoons mayonnaise	¼ teaspoon grated lemon rind
	pinch salt

Combine all ingredients in small bowl. Divide evenly. Makes 2 servings. Serve at mealtime only.

Each serving is equivalent to: 3 servings Fat

Rémoulade Sauce

Serve with crabmeat or sliced tomatoes.

2 tablespoons mayonnaise
¼ teaspoon finely chopped pickled
    cucumber
¼ teaspoon chopped capers

¼ teaspoon prepared mustard
pinch chopped fresh parsley
pinch tarragon

Combine all ingredients in small bowl. Divide evenly. Makes 2 servings. Serve at mealtime only.

Each serving is equivalent to: 3 servings Fat

Russian Mayonnaise

2 tablespoons mayonnaise
½ oz natural unsweetened yogurt
1 tablespoon chilli sauce
2 teaspoons tarragon vinegar

2 teaspoons lemon juice
¼ teaspoon prepared white
    horseradish
pinch salt and pepper

Combine all ingredients in small bowl. Divide evenly. Makes 2 servings. Serve at mealtime only.

Each serving is equivalent to: 3 servings Fat; $^1/_{20}$ serving Milk (¼ oz yogurt); ¾ serving Something Extra (1½ teaspoons chilli sauce)

Seafood Dressing—I

Delicious on cold lobster or shrimps.

4 tablespoons mayonnaise
4 tablespoons chilli sauce
¼ teaspoon chopped capers

pinch each basil, tarragon and
    savory

Combine all ingredients in small bowl. Chill before serving. Divide evenly. Makes 4 servings, about 2 tablespoons each. Serve at mealtime only.

Each serving is equivalent to 3 servings Fat; 1½ servings Something Extra (1 tablespoon chilli sauce)

Seafood Dressing—II

4 tablespoons mayonnaise	2 teaspoons lemon juice or
2½ fl oz natural unsweetened	tarragon vinegar
yogurt	2 teaspoons tomato ketchup
	(optional)

Combine all ingredients in small bowl. Chill before serving. Divide evenly. Makes 4 servings, about 2 tablespoons each. Serve at mealtime only.

Each serving is equivalent to: 3 servings Fat; ⅛ serving Milk (⅝ oz yogurt); ¼ serving Something Extra (½ teaspoon tomato ketchup) (optional)

Tartare Sauce

Serve with grilled, poached or baked fish.

2 tablespoons mayonnaise	dash each of Worcester sauce,
½ oz pickled cucumber, chopped	lemon juice and hot sauce
½ teaspoon chopped fresh parsley	pinch salt
½ teaspoon prepared mustard	

Combine all ingredients in small bowl. Divide evenly. Makes 2 servings. Serve at mealtime only.

Each serving is equivalent to: 3 servings Fat; ¼ oz Vegetables

Basic French or Vinaigrette Dressing

This dressing can be varied in dozens of ways with a change of seasoning, vinegar and herbs, and the addition of finely diced vegetables.

4 tablespoons vegetable oil	¼ teaspoon salt
2 fl oz red wine or tarragon	pinch white pepper
vinegar	

Combine all ingredients in a jar with tight-fitting cover. Shake vigorously before using. Divide evenly. Makes 4 servings. Serve at mealtime only.

Each serving is equivalent to: 3 servings Fat

Variations:

Garlic French Dressing—Prepare Basic French or Vinaigrette Dressing. Add 1 crushed garlic clove to the dressing; refrigerate. Remove garlic before serving.

Garlic Italian Dressing—Add 1 teaspoon Italian seasoning or ¼ teaspoon each of oregano, basil, thyme and rosemary to Garlic French Dressing. Two teaspoons prepared mustard may also be added.

Lemony Vinaigrette Dressing—Prepare Basic French or Vinaigrette Dressing. Add 2 tablespoons lemon juice and ¼ teaspoon grated lemon rind.

Lemony Vinaigrette Dressing with Sesame Seeds—Prepare Lemony Vinaigrette Dressing. Stir in 1 tablespoon toasted sesame seeds just before serving. Poppy seeds or caraway may be used instead of sesame seeds. These do not require toasting. Add ¾ serving Something Extra (¾ teaspoon seeds) to equivalent listing.

Lorenzo Dressing—Prepare Basic French or Vinaigrette Dressing. Blend 1 tablespoon plus 1 teaspoon chilli sauce or tomato ketchup into the dressing. Add ½ serving Something Extra (1 teaspoon chilli sauce) to equivalent listing.

Sweet-and-Sour Sauce

Delicious when served with roasted pork.

2 fl oz cider vinegar	artificial sweetener to equal 2
4 tablespoons tomato ketchup	teaspoons sugar, or to taste
2 fl oz water	1 tablespoon cornflour, dissolved in
2 to 3 tablespoons Worcester sauce	1 tablespoon water
1 tablespoon lemon juice	1 tablespoon vegetable oil
½ teaspoon salt	(optional)

In small saucepan combine vinegar, tomato ketchup, water, Worcester sauce, lemon juice, salt and sweetener. Bring to a boil; stir in cornflour. Cook, stirring constantly, until sauce thickens and clears. Remove from heat and stir in oil, if desired. Divide evenly. Makes 6 servings. If oil is used, serve at mealtime only.

Each serving is equivalent to: 1½ servings Something Extra (2 teaspoons tomato ketchup and ½ teaspoon cornflour); ½ serving Fat (optional)

Barbecue Fruit Sauce

Try this sauce when baking skinned and boned chicken breasts.

3 oz onion, finely chopped
3 tablespoons cider vinegar
1 tablespoon prepared mustard
2 teaspoons Worcester sauce

8 canned peach halves with 8 tablespoons juice, no sugar added
8 tablespoons tomato ketchup

In medium saucepan, cook onion over medium heat for 1 to 2 minutes, stirring frequently. Add vinegar, mustard and Worcester sauce; cook, stirring constantly for about 3 minutes. Add peach juice and tomato ketchup. Reduce heat and simmer, stirring occasionally, for 15 to 20 minutes or until mixture thickens. Place peaches in a small ovenproof casserole and heat. Serve sauce and peaches at the same meal. Divide evenly. Makes 4 servings.

Each serving is equivalent to: 1 oz Limited Vegetables; 1 serving Fruit; 3 servings Something Extra (2 tablespoons tomato ketchup)

Creole Sauce

Use over cooked vegetables, pasta, meat or fish. Also good as omelette filling.

6 oz green pepper, seeded and thinly sliced
4 oz onion, thinly sliced
2 oz celery, chopped
8 oz canned tomatoes, chopped (with liquid)
3 oz mushrooms, sliced

6 fl oz Beef Stock (see page 157)
½ oz canned pimiento, chopped
salt and pepper to taste
bouquet garni (1 bay leaf, 10 parsley springs, 2 cloves, 1 garlic clove, sliced, tied in muslin)

In medium saucepan cook green pepper, onion and celery over moderate heat for 5 minutes or until tender. Add tomatoes, mushrooms, stock, pimiento, salt and pepper. Add bouquet garni to sauce. Simmer, covered, for 25 minutes, stirring occasionally. Add water a little at a time, as necessary, to adjust consistency. Remove and discard bouquet garni. Serve hot. Divide evenly. Makes 4 servings.

Each serving is equivalent to: 1½ servings Vegetables; 1 oz Limited Vegetable; ¼ serving Something Extra (1½ fl oz stock)

Variation: Omit bouquet garni and add dash hot sauce, chilli powder or crushed red pepper.

Cocktail Sauce

2 tablespoons plus 2 teaspoons
  chilli sauce
4 tablespoons tomato ketchup

1 teaspoon lemon juice
½ teaspoon prepared horseradish
pinch salt

In small bowl combine all ingredients. Divide evenly. Makes 4 servings.

Each serving is equivalent to: 2½ servings Something Extra (2 teaspoons chilli sauce and 3 teaspoons tomato ketchup).

Fat-Free Salad Dressings

1. In small saucepan combine 8 fl oz red wine vinegar and ½ oz chopped fresh basil, dill, tarragon or thyme. Bring to a boil. Cool and pour into a jar with tight-fitting cover. Let stand at room temperature for 10 to 14 days. Strain and use as desired.
2. Omit herbs from preceding recipe and add 4 crushed garlic cloves. Allow to stand at room temperature for 3 to 5 days.
3. Serve freshly squeezed lemon juice over your salad.

Fat-Free White Sauce

1 pint skim milk
4 tablespoons flour, mixed with 2 fl
  oz water

dash lemon juice
salt and white pepper to taste

In medium saucepan combine milk and flour. Heat, stirring constantly until sauce is thickened. Season with remaining ingredients. Divide evenly. Makes 4 servings.

Each serving is equivalent to: ½ serving Milk (5 fl oz skim milk); 3 servings Something Extra (1 tablespoon flour)

Japanese Soy Sauce Dip

Serve hot as a dip for seafood and vegetables.
In saucepan combine 4 fl oz Beef Stock (see page 157), 2 tablespoons soy sauce and 1 teaspoon prepared white horseradish. Add 1 teaspoon sherry flavouring, if desired. Bring to a boil. Divide evenly. Makes 2 servings.

Each serving is equivalent to: $^1/_3$ serving Something Extra (2 fl oz stock)

Mustard Sauce

2 tablespoons plus 2 teaspoons
  flour
2 tablespoons dry mustard
4 fl oz water
1 teaspoon chicken stock powder
1½ oz shallots or spring onions,
  finely chopped

1 tablespoon lemon juice
1 tablespoon white wine vinegar
¼ teaspoon thyme
1 small bay leaf
15 fl oz skim milk
salt and white pepper to taste

In small bowl combine flour, mustard and 2 fl oz water to make a paste. Set aside. In medium saucepan combine remaining water and stock powder; add shallots or spring onions, lemon juice, vinegar, thyme and bay leaf. Simmer until most of liquid has evaporated. Remove and discard bay leaf. Add milk; heat gently. Using a wire whisk, beat mustard-flour mixture into milk mixture. Cook, stirring constantly, until thickened. Continue cooking for 5 minutes; DO NOT BOIL. Season with salt and pepper. Divide evenly. Makes 6 servings.

Each serving is equivalent to: 1½ servings Something Extra ($1^1/_3$ teaspoons flour and $^1/_6$ teaspoon stock powder); ¼ oz Limited Vegetable; ¼ serving Milk (2½ fl oz skim milk)

Tomato Sauce

3 oz green pepper, seeded and finely chopped
2 oz onion, chopped
1 garlic clove, crushed
1 lb 6 oz canned tomatoes, crushed
8 oz tomato purée mixed with 4 fl oz water

6 fl oz beef bouillon (made with 1 stock cube)
1½ teaspoons basil
¾ teaspoon salt
½ teaspoon chopped fresh parsley
½ teaspoon oregano
⅛ teaspoon pepper

In medium saucepan combine green pepper, onion and garlic. Cook for 2 to 3 minutes. Add remaining ingredients; simmer for about 35 minutes or until sauce reaches desired consistency, stirring often. Divide evenly. Makes 4 servings.

Each serving is equivalent to: 2 servings Vegetables; ½ oz Limited Vegetable; 1 serving Bonus (2 oz tomato purée); ¼ serving Something Extra (¼ stock cube)

Variations:
1. Prepare Tomato Sauce. Stir in 1 oz nonfat dry milk with 4 fl oz water. Heat, but do not boil. Add ¼ serving Milk (2½ fl oz skim milk) to equivalent listing.
2. Prepare Tomato Sauce. Remove from heat. Stir in 1 tablespoon plus 1 teaspoon vegetable oil. Serve at mealtime only. Add 1 serving Fat to equivalent listing.
3. Prepare Tomato Sauce. Stir in 4 oz grated Parmesan cheese. Divide evenly. Makes 4 midday meal servings. Supplement as required. Add 1 oz Hard Cheese to equivalent listing.
4. Prepare Tomato Sauce. Stir in 8 oz cooked minced beef, crumbled, and 4 fl oz water. Divide evenly. Serve each portion topped with 1 oz grated hard cheese. Makes 4 midday meal servings. Add 2 oz 'Beef' Group and 1 oz Hard Cheese to equivalent listing.
5. Add 1 oz diced carrots and 1 oz diced celery when cooking vegetables in Tomato Sauce recipe. Omit basil and oregano and add 1 teaspoon thyme. Add ⅙ serving Vegetables to equivalent listing.

Creamy Yogurt Thousand Island Dressing

5 fl oz natural unsweetened yogurt
1 tablespoon plus 1 teaspoon chili
   sauce
½ oz pickled cucumber, chopped

2 teaspoons dried onion flakes
½ teaspoon lemon juice
½ teaspoon prepared mustard
¼ teaspoon salt

Combine all ingredients in a small bowl. Cover and chill. Divide evenly. Makes 4 servings.

    Each serving is equivalent to: ¼ serving Milk (1¼ fl oz yogurt); ½ serving Something Extra (1 teaspoon chilli sauce)

Tangy Yogurt Dressing

In a bowl combine 5 fl oz natural unsweetened yogurt, 2 teaspoons lemon juice, ¼ teaspoon grated lemon rind and ¼ teaspoon celery seed. Chill. Divide evenly. Makes 4 servings.

    Each serving is equivalent to: ¼ serving Milk 1¼ fl oz yogurt)

Tart Yogurt Dressing

5 fl oz natural unsweetened yogurt
2 fl oz cider vinegar
1 tablespoon vegetable oil

1 teaspoon salt
pinch freshly ground pepper

Place ingredients in jar with tight-fitting cover; shake to combine. Divide evenly. Serve over shredded cabbage, sliced tomatoes, salad greens or cooked vegetables. Makes 3 servings. Serve at mealtime only.

    Each serving is equivalent to: $\frac{1}{3}$ serving Milk ($1\frac{2}{3}$ fl oz yogurt); 1 serving Fat

Yogurt Asparagus Dressing

Combine 6 oz cooked asparagus, 5 fl oz natural unsweetened yogurt, 1 garlic clove, ½ teaspoon lemon juice and ¼ teaspoon lemon rind in blender container. Blend until smooth. Divide evenly. Delicious as a dressing or spread. Makes 4 servings.

Each serving is equivalent to: ½ serving Vegetables; ¼ serving Milk (1¼ fl oz yogurt)

Yogurt Blue Cheese Dressing

In bowl combine 5 fl oz natural unsweetened yogurt, 1 oz crumbled blue cheese, ½ teaspoon cider vinegar and a pinch of salt. Blend; chill. Serve over green salad. Makes 1 midday meal serving. Supplement as required.

Each serving is equivalent to: 1 serving Milk (5 fl oz yogurt); 1 oz Hard Cheese

Yogurt Cinnamon Fruit Dressing

Drain the juice from 1 serving canned fruit, no sugar added, into bowl. Stir in 5 fl oz natural unsweetened yogurt. Add artificial sweetener to equal 1 teaspoon sugar, or to taste, if desired, and cinnamon to taste. Use as dressing for the fruit. Makes 1 serving.

Each serving is equivalent to: 1 serving Fruit; 1 serving Milk (5 fl oz yogurt)

Yogurt Cucumber Sauce

5 fl oz natural unsweetened yogurt
1½ oz cucumber, peeled, seeded
  and diced
1 teaspoon lemon juice or cider
  vinegar
¼ teaspoon dill weed

¼ teaspoon paprika
⅛ teaspoon salt, or to taste
2 tablespoons mayonnaise
  (optional)
½ teaspoon aromatic bitters
  (optional)

In bowl combine yogurt and cucumber. Stir in lemon juice or cider vinegar, dill weed, paprika and salt. Blend in mayonnaise and aromatic bitters if desired. Excellent with salmon or cold poached fish. Divide evenly. Makes 4 servings. If mayonnaise is used, serve at mealtime only.

Each serving is equivalent to: ¼ serving Milk (1¼ fl oz yogurt); ⅛ serving Vegetables; 1½ servings Fat (optional)

Yogurt Dill Sauce for Salmon or Fish Mousse

5 fl oz natural unsweetened yogurt
1 tablespoon plus 1 teaspoon
    mayonnaise
1½ teaspoons chopped fresh dill or
    ½ teaspoon dill weed

½ teaspoon prepared horseradish
pinch each salt, white pepper and
    hot sauce

Combine all ingredients in a bowl. Divide evenly. Makes 4 servings. Serve at mealtime only.

Each serving is equivalent to: ¼ serving Milk (1¼ fl oz yogurt); 1 serving Fat

Yogurt Herb Dressing

In bowl combine 5 fl oz natural unsweetened yogurt with 1 table-spoon chives, 1 tablespoon chopped fresh parsley, ½ crushed garlic clove, if desired, and ⅛ teaspoon grated lemon rind. Chives can be replaced with any other fresh herb. 1 teaspoon chopped capers can be added. Divide evenly. Serve over cooked vegetables. Makes 4 servings.

Each serving is equivalent to: ¼ serving Milk (1¼ fl oz yogurt)

Yogurt Horseradish Sauce

In bowl combine 5 fl oz natural unsweetened yogurt, 1 tablespoon prepared horseradish, ¼ teaspoon prepared mustard, ⅛ teaspoon salt and a dash of hot sauce. Divide evenly. Serve with sliced turkey or tongue. Makes 4 servings.

Each serving is equivalent to: ¼ serving Milk (1¼ fl oz yogurt)

Yogurt Mustard Sauce

In bowl blend 1 tablespoon prepared mustard and 2 teaspoons cider vinegar with 5 fl oz natural unsweetened yogurt. Divide evenly. Serve with cold beef. Makes 4 servings.

Each serving is equivalent to: ¼ serving Milk (1¼ fl oz yogurt)

Yogurt Onion Dressing

In bowl stir 1 teaspoon onion powder plus ½ teaspoon seasoning salt into 5 fl oz natural unsweetened yogurt. Divide evenly. Makes a piquant dip for raw vegetables. Makes 4 servings.

Each serving is equivalent to: ¼ serving Milk (1¼ fl oz yogurt)

Yogurt Tomato Dressing

In bowl combine 5 fl oz natural unsweetened yogurt, 2 oz tomato purée mixed with 2 fl oz water, 1 teaspoon basil and ¼ teaspoon celery seed. Refrigerate for 1 hour before using. Divide evenly. Makes 4 servings.

Each serving is equivalent to: ¼ serving Milk (1¼ fl oz yogurt); ¼ serving Bonus (½ oz tomato purée)

OPTIONAL

*

To provide new taste lifts, we've added a number of speciality foods, seasonings, condiments and 'Something Extra', including hot and cold soups, herb teas and a variety of delicious drinks.

Beverages

Water, Artificially sweetened carbonated beverages, soda water, coffee and tea in reasonable amounts

Bonus

Select up to 1 serving daily, if desired.
    Mixed vegetable juice, *8 fl oz*
    Tomato juice, *8 fl oz*
    Tomato double-concentrated purée or paste, *2 oz*

Seasonings and Condiments

Use reasonable amounts of the following: artificial sweeteners, baking powder, baking soda, browning sauce, dried vegetable flakes, flavourings, herbs, horseradish, hot sauce, lemon juice, lime juice, mustard, pepper, pepper sauce, rennet tablets, salt, seasonings, seaweed, soy sauce, spices, steak sauce, vinegar and Worcester sauce.

1. Any type of vinegar is 'legal' except those with sugar added.
2. Fresh fruit rinds are 'legal' as seasonings.

Something Extra

Select up to 3 servings daily, if desired.
 arrowroot, cornflour, flour, *1 level teaspoon*
 Bouillon and stock:
  stock cube, *1*
  stock powder, *1 level teaspoon*
 cocoa, unsweetened, *1 level teaspoon*
  concentrated yeast extract, *1 level teaspoon*
 gelatine, unflavoured, *1½ level teaspoons*
  tomato ketchup, chilli sauce, *2 level teaspoons*
 Seeds:
  Caraway, poppy, sesame, *1 level teaspoon*

Speciality Foods

Members generally need not be concerned about counting calories (kJ). However, if the following items are used, calories (kJ) MUST be counted. Limit intake to a total of 15 calories (65kJ) per day. Check labels carefully for calorie count. *Do not use if label does not indicate calories (kJ).*

 Beverages, noncarbonated, low-calorie (kJ)
 Jams, low-calorie (kJ)
 Tomato ketchup, salad dressings, low-calorie (kJ)

In addition, one serving of the following item may be substituted once daily, for one milk serving:

 flavoured milk desserts, low-calorie (kJ), 5 oz

Pep Up Your Meals With Spices and Herbs

Allspice—Delicate West Indian spice. Flavour resembles a blend of nutmeg, cinnamon and cloves. Whole, it's a favourite seasoning for pickles, stews and boiled fish.

Basil—Means 'king', and this herb adds the crowning touch to all tomato dishes. Gives zest to eggs, fish, soups, stews and salads.

Bay Leaf—The classic seasoning for stews, soups, pickles, sauces and fish. Remove the leaf before serving.

Bitters—A liquid blend of herbs and spices, often used in drinks. Add a few drops to tomato juice. For unusual flavour, try a few drops in scrambled eggs.

Bouquet Garni or Bouquet of Herbs—A combination of herbs either tied together or wrapped in muslin and tied into bags. Usually added during the last half-hour of cooking and removed before serving.

Capers—Pickled buds of the caper bush. They taste like sharp gherkins. Use in sauces and salads.

Cardamom—Native to India. The seeds are delicious in coffee; the pods are used in pickling. Powdered or ground, it is nice sprinkled on melon and other fruits.

Cayenne—Small hot red pepper, ground and used sparingly to season eggs, meats and fish.

Celery Seed—Pungent seed, used in stews, cole slaw, potato salad and salad dressings.

Chervil—Delicate herb of the carrot family. Combines well with other herbs. Delicious fresh or dry, in salads, soups, egg and cheese dishes.

Chilli Powder—The ancient Aztecs are credited for this blend of chilli, allspice, red peppers, cumin seed, oregano, garlic powder and salt. Use sparingly in cocktail sauces, eggs, stews and meat loaf.

Chive—Has a mild onionlike flavour. Adds colour and flavour to cottage cheese, eggs, potatoes, vegetable dishes and soups.

Cinnamon—Bark of the cinnamon tree. Ground and mixed with artificial sweetener, it's a favourite on French toast, pancakes and puddings.

Cloves—Nail-shaped dried flower bud. Once available only to the rich, today it can be enjoyed by everyone. Whole, it is used in baking ham, in pickling and in drinks. Many desserts call for it in ground form.

Coriander—Use this pungent herb sparingly. Gives character to pickles and stuffing to be served with poultry. It is one of the many spices found in curry powder.

Cumin—Aromatic seeds used whole or ground, in egg and cheese dishes, sauerkraut, meats, rice, pickles and Mexican foods.

Curry Powder—A blend of spices from India. Used in curries of meat, fish, eggs and chicken and to perk up leftover stews.

Dill—The tender fresh or dried leaves, as well as the seeds; add a delightful flavour to eggs, cheeses, salads and potatoes. A favourite in Scandinavian cookery.

Fennel—Has a slight liquorice taste. Gives special flavour to apples and steamed fish.

Garlic—This indispensible seasoning is available fresh, dried, minced, flaked and in salt and powder form.

Ginger—The fresh root is a staple of Oriental cookery. Dried and ground, it is used in soups, stews and desserts.

Italian Seasoning—You can buy this blend of herbs or you can make your own by combining basil, oregano, rosemary, red pepper, garlic, marjoram, thyme and sage. Used over fish, meats, poultry, liver, rice and pasta.

Mace—The lacy covering of the inner shell holding the nutmeg. Delicious in spinach.

Marjoram—One of the best-known herbs. Gives nice flavour to peas and beans.

Mint—Everyone knows this aromatic herb. Delicious with lamb and in cool drinks and hot tea.

Mustard—The whole seed is used in pickling; ground, with a little water added, it's the hot mustard used in Oriental cookery. Prepared mustard is the favourite with all sausages and is delicious in sauces and salad dressings.

Nutmeg—Traditionally used in desserts. Also adds a special flavour to spinach and Brussels sprouts.

Oregano—Wild marjoram, stronger in flavour than its cultivated cousin. Widely used in Mexican and Italian dishes.

Paprika—A member of the pepper family. Available in mild and fiery flavour. Used for colour and flavour.

Parsley—Used in foods for flavour and for garnish. Fresh parsley is available with either a curly or a flat leaf. Save the stems to use when preparing soup stock.

Pepper—Available black or white. Used whole in pickling and soups; ground in most meat, poultry, fish, egg and vegetable dishes.

Poultry Seasoning—A mixture of several spices used to season poultry and meats.

Rosemary—Rosemary is for remembrance, and its sweet fresh flavour makes lamb stews, boiled potatoes, turnips and cauliflower memorable.

Saffron—The world's most expensive spice, so make a little go a long way. Place a pinch in boiling water, before adding rice, to develop golden colour and appetizing flavour. Turmeric may be used as a substitute.

Sage—Used in poultry seasoning, it is the perfect compliment to chicken, pork and fish dishes.

Savory—Lightly aromatic; good with green beans, meats, chicken and scrambled eggs.

Tarragon—Add this anise-flavoured herb to vinegar, salad dressings, and sauces for meat, poultry and seafood.

Thyme—Has a pungent flavour. Use sparingly with onions, aubergine, tomatoes and celery.

Turmeric—This slightly bitter-tasting herb adds a saffronlike natural colouring to rice, chicken and seafood.

Vanilla Beans—For the true vanilla flavour, add a whole vanilla bean to the milk when heating it for custards, puddings and drinks. The beans may be washed, dried and used again and again.

Bouquet Garni

Bouquet Garni No 1
Tie together between 2 celery ribs:

4 parsley or chervil sprigs
1/3 bay leaf
2 thyme sprigs

1 leek, white portion only, stuck with 2 cloves

Bouquet Garni No 2
Wrap the following herbs in a 4-inch square of muslin and tie into
a bag:

½ teaspoon dried parsley flakes	small piece of bay leaf
¼ teaspoon each thyme and	½ teaspoon celery seed
marjoram	

Add Bouquet Garni during last half-hour of cooking. Remove before serving.

Directions for Making a Basic Gelatine Mixture

In saucepan sprinkle 1 tablespoon unflavoured gelatine over 4 fl oz
cold liquid. Place over low heat and stir until gelatine is dissolved.
Remove from heat and add remaining liquid called for. Pour mixture into mould. Chill for 3 to 4 hours or until firm. To turn out,
dip mould in warm water to depth of gelatine. Loosen round edge
with the tip of a small knife. Place serving dish on top of mould
and turn upside down. Shake, holding dish tightly to the mould. If
gelatine does not unmould, repeat process.
    1 tablespoon gelatine is equivalent to: 2 servings Something Extra

Herbal Teas and Soup

For each serving:

Herb—In teapot place 1 or 2 tablespoons chopped fresh herbs.
Add 10 fl oz boiling water. Cover and steep for 5 minutes or more.
Strain and serve. Use as a tea or mix with 1 stock cube and serve
as soup. If stock cube is used, each serving is equivalent to 1 serving
Something Extra.
    Mexican—In saucepan combine a stick of cinnamon and 10 fl oz
water and bring to a boil. Boil several minutes; remove from heat
and add 1 teaspoon tea leaves or 1 tea bag. Steep for 5 minutes.
Strain and serve.

Mint—In teapot place ⅛ teaspoon dried mint or 1 tablespoon fresh mint leaves and 1 teaspoon tea leaves or 1 tea bag. Add 10 fl oz boiling water and steep for 5 minutes. Strain and serve.

Creamy Cold Tomato Soup

8 oz tomato purée
3 oz nonfat dry milk
1 pint water
3 to 4 ice cubes

¼ teaspoon oregano or thyme
5 fl oz natural unsweetened yogurt
1 oz onion or spring onions,
    chopped (optional)

In blender container, combine tomato purée, milk, water, ice cubes and oregano or thyme. Blend until ice is crushed. Divide evenly into 4 soup bowls. Divide yogurt between the bowls and fold in. Sprinkle each with ¼ oz of the onion or spring onion, if desired. Serve immediately. Makes 4 servings.

Each serving is equivalent to: 1 serving Bonus (2 oz tomato purée); 1 serving Milk (7½ fl oz skim milk and 1¼ fl oz yogurt); ¼ oz Limited Vegetable (optional)

Hot Tomato-Beef Drink

8 fl oz tomato juice
6 fl oz beef bouillon (made with 1
    stock cube)

⅛ teaspoon hot sauce
lemon slices to garnish

In medium saucepan combine tomato juice, bouillon and hot sauce. Bring to a boil, Serve, evenly divided, in mugs. Garnish with lemon slices. Makes 2 servings.

Each serving is equivalent to: ½ serving Bonus (4 fl oz tomato juice); ½ serving Something Extra (½ stock cube)

Clear Tomato Soup

1 pint 16 fl oz tomato juice
1 pint 4 fl oz beef bouillon (made
    with 4 stock cubes)

1 tablespoon Worcester sauce
dash hot sauce
6 mint sprigs

Combine all ingredients, except mint, in large saucepan. Bring to a boil. Reduce heat and simmer for 5 minutes. Serve, evenly divided, in bowls or soup mugs. Garnish with mint. Makes 6 servings.

Each serving is equivalent to: ¾ serving Bonus (6 fl oz tomato juice); ⅔ serving Something Extra (⅔ stock cube)

Iceberg Floats

hot sauce to taste	3 pints 4 fl oz tomato or mixed
16 parsley sprigs	vegetable juice

Fill a 16–compartment ice cube tray with water. Add hot sauce and a parsley sprig to each compartment. Freeze until solid. Divide juice equally into 8 tall glasses. Place 2 'icebergs' in each glass. Makes 8 servings.

Each serving is equivalent to: 1 serving Bonus (8 fl oz tomato or mixed vegetable juice)

Red Mary Mix

1 pint 4 fl oz tomato juice	hot sauce to taste
1 tablespoon plus 1 teaspoon	salt and freshly ground pepper to
Worcester sauce	taste
1 teaspoon lime juice	1 lime or lemon, cut into wedges

Combine all ingredients except lime or lemon wedges in cocktail shaker. Shake; divide evenly into 4 glasses, over ice. Garnish each with lime or lemon wedge. Makes 4 servings.

Each serving is equivalent to: ¾ serving Bonus (6 fl oz tomato juice)

Soda Sparkler

Try this at your next party. Pour 4 fl oz soda water over 3 ice cubes in a 6 oz glass. Add 1 teaspoon sherry flavouring and a slice of lemon or lime.

FAVOURITE RECIPES

 *

In this chapter we've collected together some of the most popular recipes from a previous edition of this book—do try them!

Cinnamon Toast

1 slice white bread, lightly toasted
1 teaspoon margarine
artificial sweetener to equal 1
  teaspoon sugar, or to taste

¼ teaspoon cinnamon
pinch nutmeg (optional)

Spread margarine on toast. In small cup combine sweetener, cinnamon and nutmeg, if desired. Sprinkle on toast. Place under the grill for about ½ minute. Makes 1 serving. Serve at mealtime only.
    Each serving is equivalent to: 1 serving Bread; 1 serving Fat

Not-So-Danish Pastry

2½ oz cottage cheese
artificial sweetener to equal 1
  teaspoon sugar, or to taste

½ teaspoon vanilla flavouring
pinch cinnamon
1 slice white bread, toasted

In small bowl combine cottage cheese with sweetener, flavouring and cinnamon. Spread on toast and place under grill until hot and bubbly. Makes 1 morning meal serving.
    Each serving is equivalent to: 2½ oz Soft Cheese; 1 serving Bread

Variations:
1. Omit flavouring; add ¼ teaspoon imitation butter flavouring and ¼ teaspoon grated orange peel to cottage cheese mixture. Proceed as above.
2. Omit sweetener, flavouring and cinnamon; combine cheese with ½ teaspoon caraway seeds and salt to taste. Spread on toast. Proceed as above. Add ½ serving Something Extra (½ teaspoon caraway seeds) to equivalent listing.

Cheese Latkes (Pancakes)

You don't have to be Jewish to enjoy latkes. They're a great treat with or without the blueberry (or blackberry) topping. Other fruits may be substituted, if desired, so try your favourite.

1 standard egg, beaten
2½ oz cottage cheese
2½ fl oz skim milk
¼ teaspoon salt

1 slice white bread, made into crumbs
Blackberry (or Blueberry) Topping (see following recipe)
1 lemon, cut into 6 wedges

In a bowl combine all ingredients except blueberry (or blackberry) Topping. Using a tablespoon, drop mixture by the spoonful onto a preheated nonstick frying pan. Brown lightly; turn with a spatula to brown other side. Serve warm with Blueberry (or Blackberry) Topping. Garnish with lemon wedges. Makes 1 midday meal serving.

Each serving is equivalent to: 1 Egg; 2½ oz Soft Cheese; ¼ serving Milk (2½ fl oz skim milk); 1 serving Bread; Blueberry or Blackberry Topping (recipe follows)

Blackberry (or Blueberry) Topping

5 oz blackberries (or blueberries)
1 tablespoon water

artificial sweetener to equal 1 teaspoon sugar, or to taste

Combine ingredients in saucepan and simmer until berries are soft. Serve with Cheese Latkes. Makes 1 serving.

Each serving is equivalent to: 1 serving Fruit

Coconut Bread Pudding

10 fl oz pint skim milk	1 teaspoon coconut flavouring
1 standard egg	(optional)
artificial sweetener to equal 3	½ teaspoon vanilla flavouring
teaspoons sugar, or to taste	1 slice white bread, cut into cubes
	cinnamon to taste

Combine all ingredients except bread and cinnamon in blender container; blend until frothy. Pour mixture into small baking dish. Press bread cubes into mixture. Sprinkle with cinnamon. Set baking dish in a pan containing approximately ½ inch of hot water. Bake at 350°F, Gas Mark 4, for about 50 minutes or until knife inserted in centre comes out clean. Makes 1 morning or midday meal serving. Supplement as required.

Each serving is equivalent to: 1 serving Milk (10 fl oz skim milk); 1 Egg; 1 serving Bread

Note: For a fluffier pudding, separate egg. Beat white separately until stiff peaks form. Fold into blended mixture and bake as above.

Variation:
Orange Bread Pudding—Instead of 10 fl oz skim milk use 4 fl oz orange juice and 5 fl oz skim milk. Omit coconut flavouring and cinnamon. Add 1½ teaspoons grated orange peel and ¼ teaspoon orange flavouring. Follow above directions.

Each serving is equivalent to: ½ serving Milk (5 fl oz skim milk); 1 serving Fruit; 1 Egg; 1 serving Bread

Matzo Omelette

Here's another recipe to enjoy during the Passover holiday.

1 matzo board	¼ teaspoon salt
2 standard eggs, well beaten	pinch pepper
2 tablespoons water	cinnamon to taste (optional)

Break matzo into 2-inch pieces and place in colander. Pour boiling water over matzo and drain quickly to prevent sogginess. In bowl combine eggs, water, salt, pepper and matzo. Heat a 7-inch non-stick frying pan. Add matzo-egg mixture and cook over low heat until golden brown on one side, then turn carefully and brown the other side. Sprinkle with cinnamon, if desired. Divide evenly. Makes 2 morning or midday meal servings. Supplement as required.

Each serving is equivalent to: 1 serving Bread; 1 Egg

Pizzaiolas

A delicious midday meal! Hide the seasoning under the cheese, where the heat won't scorch it and make it bitter.

1 slice white bread	pinch each of oregano, garlic
1 oz tomato purée, mixed with 2	powder and basil or Italian
tablespoons water	seasoning
	2 oz hard cheese, grated

Toast bread lightly; spread with purée and sprinkle on seasonings. Top with cheese. Grill until cheese is melted. Makes 1 midday meal serving.

Each serving is equivalent to: 1 serving Bread; ½ serving Bonus (1 oz tomato purée); 2 oz Hard Cheese

Variation: Omit tomato purée. Place 3 oz tomato on bread before adding remaining ingredients. Omit Bonus from equivalent listing and add 1 serving Vegetables.

Reuben Sandwich

1 slice rye bread	2 oz pickled cucumber, sliced
2 oz cooked turkey, sliced	watercress to garnish
1 oz drained sauerkraut	radish roses to garnish
1 oz hard cheese, sliced	

Lightly toast bread. Arrange turkey on toast. Spread sauerkraut over turkey and top with cheese. Place on baking sheet; bake at 450°F, Gas Mark 8, or place under preheated grill and heat until cheese is melted. Garnish with pickle slices, watercress and radish roses. Makes 1 midday meal serving.

Each serving is equivalent to: 1 serving Bread; 2 oz Poultry; 1 serving Vegetables; 1 oz Hard Cheese

Soup, Croutons and Meringues

Complete this lunch menu by adding a green salad.

_____

Soup

8 fl oz tomato juice
½ teaspoon beef stock powder
pinch garlic powder (optional)

pinch chopped fresh parsley
1 oz pickled cucumber, sliced
   (optional)

In saucepan combine all ingredients except pickle. Bring to a boil, reduce heat and simmer for 2 minutes. Serve in a mug and garnish with pickle slices if desired. Makes 1 serving.

Each serving is equivalent to: 1 serving Bonus (8 fl oz tomato juice); ½ serving Something Extra (½ teaspoon stock powder); ⅓ serving Vegetables (optional)

_____

Croutons

1 standard egg yolk
1 oz Parmesan cheese, grated
pinch each salt and pepper

pinch dry mustard
2 thin slices white bread (see page
   77)

Beat egg yolk in a bowl, stir in cheese, salt, pepper and mustard to make a paste. Cut bread slices into quarters. Divide egg yolk mixture evenly into 8 portions. Mound onto bread. Place on a baking sheet and bake at 250°F, Gas Mark ½, for 20 minutes or until cheese melts. Croutons must be consumed at the same meal as Meringue Kisses (recipe follows), which contain the remaining egg white.

For serving equivalents, see following recipe.

Meringue Kisses

1 standard egg white
artificial sweetener to equal 2
  teaspoons sugar, or to taste

¼ teaspoon vanilla flavouring
⅛ teaspoon cream of tartar
pinch salt

Line baking sheet with parchment paper or aluminium foil. In bowl beat egg white until foamy; add remaining ingredients and continue beating until stiff. Using a teaspoon, drop mixture onto paper leaving 2 inches between meringues. Bake at 250°F, Gas Mark ½, for 40 minutes or until lightly golden. Turn off oven and let stand for 10 minutes. Using a spatula, remove meringues from paper. Serve in hot soup. Makes 1 midday meal serving. Meringue Kisses must be consumed at the same meal as Croutons (see preceding recipe), which contain the remaining egg yolk.

Each serving is equivalent to: 1 Egg; 1 oz Hard Cheese; 1 serving Bread

Hot and Cold Soups

Beef Broth

In small saucepan heat 6 fl oz beef bouillon (made with 1 stock cube), pinch each of garlic powder and chopped fresh parsley and a dash of Worcester sauce. Makes 1 serving.

Each serving is equivalent to: 1 serving Something Extra (1 stock cube)

Chilled Beef Soup

Freeze 6 fl oz beef bouillon (made with 1 stock cube). Crush frozen bouillon and combine with 8 fl oz soda water. Serve in chilled glass garnished with a lemon wedge. Makes 1 serving.

Each serving is equivalent to: 1 serving Something Extra (1 stock cube)

Chicken Soup

In small saucepan heat 6 fl oz chicken bouillon (made with 1 stock cube) with 1 oz cooked diced carrots, 1 oz cooked diced celery, 1 teaspoon dried onion flakes, ½ teaspoon chopped fresh parsley and salt and pepper to taste. Makes 1 serving.

Each serving is equivalent to: 1 serving Something Extra (1 stock cube); ²/₃ serving Vegetables

'Old Fashioned' Vegetable Soup

In small saucepan heat 6 fl oz liquid from cooked or canned vegetables, *1 oz each cooked diced celery and carrots, 2 tablespoons chopped fresh herbs and 1 chicken stock cube. Makes 1 serving.

Each serving is equivalent to: ²/₃ serving Vegetables; 1 serving Something Extra (1 stock cube)

Note: Do not use liquid from Limited Vegetables for this recipe. See page 238 for list of Limited Vegetables.

'Wonton' Soup

Add ½ oz shredded spinach or lettuce to Chicken Soup or 'Old Fashioned' Vegetable Soup (see preceding recipes) and allow to wilt. Makes 1 serving.

Each serving is equivalent to: ¹/₆ serving Vegetables; for Chicken Soup or 'Old Fashioned' Vegetable Soup see preceding recipe

Tomato Soup

In saucepan combine 16 fl oz tomato juice, 1 oz diced celery, 1 beef stock cube, 1 tablespoon dried onion flakes, 1 teaspoon lemon juice, artificial sweetener to equal ½ teaspoon sugar, or to taste, pinch cayenne pepper and salt to taste. Bring to a boil, reduce heat and simmer for 10 to 12 minutes or until celery is tender. Transfer to blender container and blend. Wet rims of 2 mugs and dip in salt.

Evenly divide soup into mugs. Garnish each with chopped fresh parsley. Makes 2 servings.

Each serving is equivalent to: 1 serving Bonus (8 fl oz tomato juice); $^1/_6$ serving Vegetables; ½ serving Something Extra (½ stock cube)

Madrilene (Jellied Tomato Soup)

In saucepan sprinkle 1 tablespoon of unflavoured gelatine over 2 fl oz of water and allow to soften. Heat, stirring to dissolve gelatine. Add to preceding recipe for Tomato Soup. Refrigerate until chilled. Garnish with chopped fresh parsley or chives. Divide evenly. Makes 2 servings.

Each serving is equivalent to: 1 serving Something Extra (1½ teaspoons gelatine); for Tomato Soup see preceding recipe

Chicken Liver Paté

12 oz chicken livers
juice of 2 lemons
1 tablespoon plus 1 teaspoon
  Worcester sauce
½ teaspoon each salt and nutmeg
¼ teaspoon garlic powder

2 slices white bread, made into
  crumbs
2 medium apples, cored and sliced
lettuce leaves
1 lemon slice
parsley sprigs to garnish

Combine first 5 ingredients in saucepan; simmer for 10 minutes. Stir in breadcrumbs. Transfer to blender container and blend until smooth. Pour into dish and chill. Line a serving platter with lettuce leaves. Transfer paté to centre of platter. Surround with apple slices and garnish with lemon slice and parsley sprigs. Divide evenly. Makes 2 midday meal servings.

Each serving is equivalent to: 4 oz Liver; 1 serving Bread; 1 serving Fruit

Cioppino

16 fl oz tomato juice
3 tablespoons red wine vinegar
2 tablespoons dried onion flakes
2 tablespoons dried pepper flakes
1 tablespoon chopped fresh parsley
1 tablespoon drained capers
2 teaspoons basil

2 teaspoons lemon juice
artificial sweetener to equal 1
   teaspoon sugar, or to taste
1 teaspoon rosemary
¼ teaspoon garlic powder
1 lb assorted boned fish and
   shellfish, cut into 1-inch pieces

In saucepan combine all ingredients except fish. Bring to a boil, reduce heat and simmer until reduced to half. Add fish, cover and simmer until fish is done. Divide evenly. Makes 2 evening meal servings.

Each serving is equivalent to: 1 serving Bonus (8 fl oz tomato juice); 6 oz Fish

Gefilte Fish

12 oz boned white fish, chopped
12 oz boned pike, chopped
4 oz onion, chopped
1 oz celery, chopped
2 teaspoons salt
¼ teaspoon garlic powder

¼ teaspoon pepper
2 fl oz skim milk
1 tablespoon unflavoured gelatine
16 fl oz water
1 teaspoon chicken stock powder
6 oz cooked carrots, sliced

Put fish, onion and celery through the mincer twice. In bowl combine fish mixture with salt, garlic powder and pepper. Gradually add milk and combine. Shape into 4 equal, oval patties. Poach in simmering, salted water for 15 minutes. Remove patties with a slotted spoon and place on serving dish. Allow to cool, cover and refrigerate. In another saucepan, sprinkle gelatine over water and allow to soften. Add stock powder and heat, stirring to dissolve. Chill until slightly firm. Dice and arrange jelly and carrots round poached fish. Divide evenly. Makes 4 midday meal servings.

Each serving is equivalent to: 4 oz Fish; 1 oz Limited Vegetable; ½ serving Vegetables, $\frac{1}{20}$ serving Milk (½ fl oz skim milk); ¾ serving Something Extra (¾ teaspoon gelatine and ¼ teaspoon stock powder)

Chips for Your Fish and . . .

3 oz peeled potato, cut into
  matchstick pieces

onion salt to taste
2 teaspoons margarine (optional)

Place potato sticks in flameproof casserole and sprinkle with onion salt. Bake at 400°F, Gas Mark 6, for 15 minutes or until crisp, turning to brown all sides. Remove from oven and toss with margarine if desired. Place under grill for 1 minute. Makes 1 serving. Serve at mealtime only.

Each serving is equivalent to: 1 serving Choice Group; 2 servings Fat (optional)

Stewed Tomatoes

6 oz tomatoes, peeled and diced
1 slice wholemeal bread, diced
2 teaspoons dried onion flakes,
  reconstituted in 2 teaspoons
  water

½ teaspoon salt
freshly ground pepper to taste
pinch basil

Place tomatoes in small saucepan. Bring to a boil, add bread, onion flakes, salt, pepper and basil. Stir to combine. Makes 1 serving. Serve at mealtime only.

Each serving is equivalent to: 2 servings Vegetables; 1 serving Bread

Stuffed Tomatoes

Cut a thin slice from top of a 4-oz tomato. Use this top slice as a lid for stuffed tomatoes, or dice the removed slice of tomato and use as part of the stuffing. With spoon, scoop out, dice and reserve the pulp of the tomato, leaving a firm shell; invert to drain. Prepare desired stuffing, combine with diced tomato pulp and pack firmly into the tomato shell. This can all be done several hours ahead.

How to Cook Stuffed Tomatoes:

Oven-Baked Tomatoes—Arrange stuffed tomatoes in a shallow baking tin; add a little water and bake at 375°F, Gas Mark 5, for 15 to 20 minutes. Don't overbake. Tomato shells should be firm and the stuffing hot and bubbly.

Top-of-Stove Stuffed Tomatoes—Arrange 2 to 4 stuffed tomatoes in saucepan; add 3 tablespoons water. Cover and cook at medium heat for 8 to 10 minutes. If water evaporates, add a tablespoon or two as necessary.

Fillings for Stuffed Tomatoes:

Rice Filling—For two 4-oz tomatoes, in bowl combine 3 oz cooked rice with scooped-out diced tomato pulp. Season with salt, pepper and basil. If desired, ½ teaspoon margarine, melted, or vegetable oil may be added to each stuffed tomato just before serving. Makes 1 serving. Serve at mealtime only.

Each serving is equivalent to: 2⅔ servings Vegetables; 1 serving Choice Group; 1 serving Fat (optional)

Spinach Filling—For two 4-oz tomatoes, in a bowl combine 4 oz well-drained cooked, chopped spinach, seasoned with salt, lemon juice and poultry seasoning with scooped-out diced tomato pulp, 2½ oz cooked, chopped mushrooms, bean sprouts or green peppers, seasoned to taste, may be substituted for the spinach, alone or in combination. Makes 1 serving.

Each serving is equivalent to: 4 or 3½ servings Vegetables

Meat Filling—For two 4-oz tomatoes, in a bowl combine 4 oz diced, cooked chicken, lamb or liver with scooped-out diced tomato pulp. Season to taste. Makes 1 midday meal serving.

Each serving is equivalent to: 2⅔ servings Vegetables; 4 oz Poultry, 'Beef' Group or Liver

Fish Filling—Remove top slice and pulp from two 4-oz tomatoes, leaving a thin shell. Transfer pulp to bowl and combine with 4 oz drained, canned tuna, 1 tablespoon mayonnaise and salt to taste. Spoon as much as possible into tomato shells; replace top slice. Arrange on bed of watercress. Surround with remaining filling mixture. Sprinkle with finely chopped fresh dill. Makes 1 midday meal serving.

Each serving is equivalent to: 2⅔ servings Vegetables; 4 oz Fish; 3 servings Fat

Pimientos

Pimientos or roasted peppers, packed in vinegar or water, may be purchased in cans or jars. Once opened, they spoil quickly. Place canned peppers in an airtight container. If desired, drain packing liquid and replace with water; add ½ teaspoon vinegar and ⅛ teaspoon oregano for each 8 fl oz water. Cover tightly and refrigerate. They will last for a week.

Sweet-Sour Red Cabbage with Apple

To help retain its bright colour, add vinegar or lemon juice when cooking red cabbage.

1 lb 2 oz red cabbage, shredded	1 teaspoon lemon juice
12 fl oz water	1 teaspoon caraway seeds
3 fl oz cider vinegar	3 medium apples, peeled, cored
artificial sweetener to taste	and sliced

In a saucepan combine all ingredients except apples. Cover and cook over medium heat for 20 minutes. Add apples, cook for 30 minutes longer. Divide evenly. Makes 6 servings.

Each serving is equivalent to: 1 serving Vegetables; $\frac{1}{6}$ serving Something Extra ($\frac{1}{6}$ teaspoon caraway seeds); ½ serving Fruit

Cinnamon Spice Spread

Serve this with Currant French Toast (see page 47) or try it on Baked Fresh Fruit (see page 314)

2 tablespoons margarine	2 teaspoons cinnamon
artificial sweetener to equal 2	pinch each ground cloves, nutmeg
teaspoons sugar, or to taste	and ginger

Combine all ingredients in small bowl or cup. Divide evenly. Makes 2 servings. Serve at mealtime only.

Each serving is equivalent to: 3 servings Fat

Mock Béarnaise Sauce

Delicious over poached eggs, fish, grilled steaks or hamburgers.

2 tablespoons low-fat spread
1 tablespoon mayonnaise
1 tablespoon tarragon vinegar
¼ teaspoon dried onion flakes,
  reconstituted in ¾ teaspoon
  water

⅛ teaspoon chopped fresh parsley
2 to 3 drops butter flavouring

Melt margarine in top of double boiler over boiling water. Stir in remaining ingredients. Cook, stirring constantly, until heated. Divide evenly. Makes 2 servings. Serve at mealtime only.
  Each serving is equivalent to: 3 servings Fat

Pesto (Basil) Sauce

Stir Pesto into 3 oz hot, cooked macaroni, spaghetti or noodles. Also served on sliced tomatoes or over poached fish.

½ oz fresh basil, chopped
1 oz Parmesan cheese, grated
1 tablespoon vegetable oil
1 teaspoon chopped fresh parsley
  (optional)

½ garlic clove, crushed
½ teaspoon salt
freshly ground pepper to taste

Combine all ingredients in small bowl or place in blender container and blend for 30 seconds; let stand for 1 hour before using. Makes 1 midday meal serving. Supplement as required.
  Each serving is equivalent to: 1 oz Hard Cheese; 3 servings Fat

Pimiento Dressing

8 oz canned pimientos
2 tablespoons cider vinegar
2 tablespoons prepared mustard

artificial sweetener to equal 2
  teaspoons sugar, or to taste

Combine all ingredients in blender container and blend until smooth. Divide evenly. Makes 4 servings.

Each serving is equivalent to: $^2/_3$ serving Vegetables

Tangy French Dressing

This is a bonus, as it's made without oil, but you may wish to add some at serving time.

4 fl oz tomato juice	**¾ teaspoon Worcester sauce**
1 tablespoon cider vinegar	**½ teaspoon prepared mustard**
1 teaspoon chicken stock powder	**pinch each garlic powder and**
1 teaspoon dried onion flakes	**cinnamon**

Combine all ingredients in blender container and blend. Divide evenly. Makes 2 servings.

Each serving is equivalent to: ¼ serving Bonus (2 fl oz tomato juice), ½ serving Something Extra (½ teaspoon stock powder)

Baked Fresh Fruit

Baked fruits add variety to your meals. These go well with fish or meat.

8 medium apricots, 4 medium peaches, or 4 small pears	**2 teaspoons lemon juice**
4 fl oz boiling water	**¼ teaspoon ground cloves**
artificial sweetener to taste	**¼ teaspoon nutmeg**
	¼ teaspoon ginger

Cut fruit in half and remove stones or cores. Arrange in shallow baking dish, hollow side up. In small bowl combine remaining ingredients and sprinkle over fruit. Bake uncovered, at 400°F, Gas Mark 6, until fruit is tender—about 20 minutes for apricots, 30 minutes for peaches, 45 minutes for pears. Divide evenly. Makes 4 servings.

Each serving is equivalent to: 1 serving Fruit

Grilled Fresh Fruit

Watch fruit carefully to avoid scorching.

4 medium apples, cored and cut into ¼-inch think slices, or 4 medium peaches, peeled, stoned and sliced or 2 medium bananas, peeled and halved lengthwise	**1 tablespoon lemon juice** **½ teaspoon coconut flavouring (optional)**

In bowl toss fruit with lemon juice. Arrange on grill pan. Grill until tender, turning once. Allow about 5 minutes for apples and bananas, and 6 to 8 minutes for peaches, or until fruit is tender. Sprinkle with flavouring before serving, if desired. Divide evenly. Makes 4 servings.

Each serving is equivalent to: 1 serving Fruit.

Tips on Gelatine

1. One tablespoon of unflavoured gelatine will set 1 pint of liquid and solids combined.
2. For easier unmoulding, rinse mould in cold water before adding gelatine mixture.
3. If gelatine mixture becomes too firm to fold in solid ingredients, place basin containing gelatine mixture in a bowl of hot water 2 inches below rim of bowl. Stir until desired consistency, add ingredients, and place in mould. Chill.
4. Allow 2 to 3 hours for chilling of gelatine (less if gelatine is liquid, more if it contains solids).
5. To turn out—Gently run a knife along the inside edges of the mould. Dip base of mould in a bowl of hot water. Turn serving plate upside-down over mould and invert both mould and plate. Shake mould and plate and, if necessary, cover inverted mould with a warm towel until gelatine loosens. Remove mould.

Jellied Orange Cups

1 tablespoon unflavoured gelatine	2 teaspoons orange flavouring
12 fl oz water	4 medium oranges
artificial sweetener to equal 6	mint sprigs to garnish
teaspoons sugar, or to taste	

In bowl soften gelatine in 2 fl oz water. Heat remaining water; add to gelatine and stir to dissolve. Add sweetener and flavouring. Cut off top of each orange in a zigzag fashion. Carefully remove all flesh. Chop flesh roughly and return an equal amount to each orange shell. Fill each shell with 4 tablespoons of gelatine mixture, and set aside remainder in another dish, to be diced. Chill orange cups and remaining gelatine mixture until set. To serve, place crushed ice in each of 4 dessert dishes. Place 1 orange cup in each dish. Dice remaining orange jelly. Spoon an equal amount into each orange cup. Garnish with mint sprigs. Makes 4 servings

Each serving is equivalent to: ½ serving Something Extra (¾ teaspoon gelatine); 1 serving Fruit

Gelatine Dessert Whips

In small saucepan sprinkle 1 tablespoon unflavoured gelatine over 4 fl oz low-calorie fruit-flavoured carbonated drink. Allow to soften. Heat, stirring to dissolve gelatine. Transfer to blender container and add 12 fl oz of the same-flavoured drink. Blend until frothy, pour into mould and chill until firm. Turn out and garnish with 2 servings fresh fruit, if desired. Divide evenly. Makes 2 servings.

Each serving is equivalent to: 1 serving Something Extra (1½ teaspoons gelatine), 1 serving Fruit (optional)

Gelatine Pick-Me-Up

In saucepan sprinkle 1½ teaspoons unflavoured gelatine over 6 fl oz tomato juice. Heat to dissolve gelatine. Add a dash of aromatic bitters. Serve hot. Makes 1 serving.

Each serving is equivalent to: 1 serving Something Extra (1½ teaspoons gelatine) ¾ serving Bonus (6 fl oz tomato juice)

Mint Jelly

In small saucepan sprinkle 1 tablespoon unflavoured gelatine over 4 fl oz low-calorie lemon-flavoured carbonated drink. Heat, stirring to dissolve gelatine. Stir in 12 fl oz low-calorie lemon-flavoured carbonated drink, artificial sweetener to equal 1 teaspoon sugar, or to taste, 1 teaspoon mint flavouring and a few drops green food colouring. Refrigerate until firm. Serve with roast lamb. Divide evenly. Makes 4 servings.

Each serving is equivalent to: ½ serving Something Extra (¾ teaspoon gelatine)

Best Whipped Topping

1½ teaspoons unflavoured gelatine
2 fl oz water
artificial sweetener to equal 3
   teaspoons sugar, or to taste

¼ teaspoon vanilla flavouring
½ oz nonfat dry milk, mixed with
   2 fl oz water, chilled

In small pan sprinkle gelatine over water; heat slowly, stirring until gelatine dissolves. Pour into small mixing bowl; add sweetener and vanilla. Cool. Add chilled milk. Beat at high speed until very thick. Cover and refrigerate until ready to use. Divide evenly. Makes 4 servings.

Each serving is equivalent to: ¼ serving Something Extra (⅜ teaspoon gelatine); ⅛ serving Milk (1¼ fl oz skim milk)

Easy Whipped Topping

1 oz nonfat dry milk
1 fl oz cold water
artificial sweetener to equal 6
   teaspoons sugar, or to taste

2 teaspoons lemon juice
½ teaspoon vanilla flavouring
pinch nutmeg

In bowl combine all ingredients and, using an electric mixer, whip for 10 minutes or until mixture stands in peaks. Use immediately. Divide evenly. Makes 4 servings.

Each serving is equivalent to: ¼ serving Milk (2½ fl oz skim milk)

Coffee and Tea Breaks

Coffee 'Brandy'

Combine 4 fl oz boiling water, artificial sweetener to equal 1 teaspoon sugar, or to taste, 1 teaspoon instant coffee, ½ teaspoon brandy flavouring and a twist of lemon rind in a small coffee cup. Makes 1 serving.

Iced Coffee

Pour 8 fl oz freshly brewed coffee into ice cube tray; freeze until solid. Divide frozen coffee cubes into 2 tall glasses. Pour 8 fl oz chilled coffee over cubes in each glass. Serve each portion with 2 fl oz skim milk and artificial sweetener to taste if desired. Makes 2 servings.

Each serving is equivalent to: ⅕ serving Milk (2 fl oz skim milk)

Variation: Combine all ingredients in blender container and blend until ice is crushed. Divide evenly into 2 tall glasses.

Chocolate 'Rum' Sorbet

Combine 2 fl oz low-calorie chocolate-flavoured carbonated drink, 2 fl oz freshly brewed coffee, and ½ teaspoon rum flavouring in freezer tray. Freeze until mushy. Serve in a chilled dessert glass. Makes 1 serving.

Hot Mint Tea

Combine 8 fl oz boiling water with 1 teaspoon dried mint leaves or 1 tablespoon fresh mint leaves. Steep for 15 minutes. Strain and add artificial sweetener to taste. Makes 1 serving.

Mint Sorbet

Pour Hot Mint Tea (see preceding recipe) in freezer tray; freeze until mushy. Serve in a chilled glass. Makes 1 serving.

Banana 'Daiquiri'

Pour 12 fl oz low-calorie carbonated lemonade into ice cube tray; freeze until solid. Transfer cubes to blender container. Add 1 medium banana, sliced, ½ teaspoon rum flavouring, dash banana flavouring and artificial sweetener to taste; blend until mushy. Divide evenly. Makes 2 servings.

Each serving is equivalent to: 1 serving Fruit

Caribbean Cocktail

1 chicken stock cube	**8 fl oz tomato juice**
6 fl oz boiling water	**4 fl oz orange juice**

In small jug, stir stock cube in water to dissolve. Add tomato and orange juice. Divide evenly. Serve with ice. Makes 2 servings.

Each serving is equivalent to: ½ serving Something Extra (½ stock cube); ½ serving Bonus (4 fl oz tomato juice); ½ serving Fruit

'Champagne' Fizz

Combine 8 fl oz low-calorie ginger ale, ¼ teaspoon vanilla flavouring and ¼ teaspoon sherry flavouring in ice cube tray; freeze until solid. Transfer cubes to blender container; blend until mushy. Divide evenly into two champagne glasses. Makes 2 servings.

'Crème de Menthe' Frappé

Combine 8 fl oz cold water, ¼ teaspoon peppermint flavouring and a few drops of green food colouring in a tall glass over crushed ice. Makes 1 serving.

Horses' Neck Highball

Combine 8 fl oz soda water, dash aromatic bitters and a dash lemon juice in a tall glass. Add ice cubes and garnish with a twist of lemon or lime rind. Makes 1 serving.

'Margarita'

Pour 8 fl oz low-calorie orange- or lemon-flavoured carbonated drink into ice cube tray; freeze until solid. Dip two glasses in water; place in freezer for about 5 minutes or until frosty. Dip rim of each glass in lime juice, then salt. Set aside in freezer. In blender container combine frozen cubes, 2 fl oz fresh lime or lemon juice and artificial sweetener to equal 2 teaspoons sugar. Blend until mushy. Divide evenly into prepared glasses. Makes 2 servings.

Hawaiian Fruit Cocktail

When you're serving Hawaiian Veal (see page 152) or Polynesian Beef (see page 163), you'll want to sip on this Hawaiian speciality.

4 fl oz grapefruit juice
½ teaspoon rum flavouring
⅛ teaspoon orange flavouring

artificial sweetener to equal 1
teaspoon sugar, or to taste
(optional)
mint sprig to garnish

In measuring cup combine grapefruit juice with flavourings and sweetener, if desired. Pour into a tall glass, half filled with crushed ice. Garnish with mint sprig. Makes 1 serving.

Each serving is equivalent to: 1 serving Fruit

'Piña Colada'

4 fl oz water
1 oz nonfat dry milk
1 slice canned pineapple, with 1
tablespoon juice, no sugar added

artificial sweetener to equal 1
teaspoon sugar, or to taste
¼ teaspoon coconut flavouring
¼ teaspoon rum flavouring

Combine all ingredients in blender container; blend about 30 seconds. Serve over ice cubes. Makes 1 serving.

Each serving is equivalent to: 1 serving Milk (10 fl oz skim milk); ½ serving Fruit

Puerto Rican Punch

4 fl oz orange juice
1 tablespoon lime or lemon juice

½ teaspoon rum flavouring
dash aromatic bitters

Fill a 6-oz glass with crushed ice and add fruit juices, flavourings and bitters. Stir and serve. Makes 1 serving.

Each serving is equivalent to: ½ serving Fruit

'Rum' and Cola

Combine 6 fl oz low-calorie cola with ¾ teaspoon rum flavouring in a tall glass over ice cubes. Makes 1 serving.

Spiked Tomato Juice on the Rocks

Combine 6 fl oz tomato juice, ½ teaspoon lemon juice, dash each celery seed, cayenne pepper and hot sauce. Serve in a tall glass over ice, garnished with a celery stick. Makes 1 serving.

Each serving is equivalent to: ¾ serving Bonus (6 fl oz tomato juice)

Tomato Frappé

1 pint 4 fl oz tomato juice	¼ teaspoon celery salt
10 fl oz buttermilk	¼ teaspoon celery seed
1 chicken stock cube	hot sauce to taste
1 teaspoon dried onion flakes	lime or lemon wedges to garnish

Combine all ingredients except lime wedges in blender container. Blend to combine. Divide evenly and serve, very cold, in chilled glasses over ice cubes. Garnish with lime or lemon wedges. Makes 4 servings.

Each serving is equivalent to: ¾ serving Bonus (6 fl oz tomato juice); ¼ serving Milk (2½ fl oz buttermilk); ¼ serving Something Extra (¼ stock cube)

Tommy Collins

Combine 2 fl oz low-calorie tonic water, 1 teaspoon rum flavouring, 1 teaspoon lemon juice and artificial sweetener to equal ½ teaspoon sugar, or to taste, in a glass over ice cubes. Makes 1 serving.

Lemonade

In a tall glass combine 8 fl oz water, 2 tablespoons lemon juice and artificial sweetener to equal 2 teaspoons sugar, or to taste. Serve over ice. Garnish with mint leaves. Makes 1 serving.

Spinach Cocktail

12 fl oz tomato juice
½ teaspoon salt
generous pinch garlic powder
4 spinach leaves

1 oz spinach, blanched and
  shredded
7 oz cauliflower florets
1 tablespoon lemon juice
1½ teaspoons grated horseradish

In saucepan combine tomato juice, salt and garlic powder. Cook uncovered, over medium heat, until tomato juice is reduced by half. Chill. Place 2 spinach leaves in each of 2 large wine goblets or small bowls. Place ½ of shredded spinach in each and fill each glass with ½ of the cauliflower florets. Combine reduced tomato juice, lemon juice and horseradish and pour ½ of mixture into each goblet. Makes 2 servings.

Each serving is equivalent to: ¾ serving Bonus (6 fl oz tomato juice); 1½ servings Vegetables

Pineapple Coleslaw

½ head green or white cabbage,
  shredded (about 1lb 12oz)
4 oz onion, finely chopped, divided
3 oz celery, chopped
3 oz green pepper, seeded and
  chopped
3 oz carrots, grated

2 oz radishes, sliced
5 fl oz natural unsweetened yogurt
2 tablespoons cider vinegar
2 teaspoons salt
artificial sweetener to taste
4 oz canned pineapple chunks, no
  sugar added
radish rose to garnish

In bowl combine cabbage, 2 oz onion and the celery, pepper, carrots and radishes. In another bowl or measuring jug mix yogurt, remaining onion, vinegar, salt and sweetener. Cover and refrigerate both mixtures. Just before serving, transfer vegetable mixture and dressing to serving dish and mix to combine. Fold in ½ of the pineapple; top with remaining pineapple and garnish with radish rose. Divide evenly. Makes 2 servings.

Each serving is equivalent to: 6½ servings Vegetables; 2 oz Limited Vegetable; ½ serving Milk (2½ fl oz yogurt); ½ serving Fruit

Spiced Beetroot

8 oz cooked beetroot, thinly sliced
2½ fl oz cider vinegar
2 bay leaves

2 teaspoons pickling spice
½ teaspoon salt
pepper to taste

Place beetroot in serving dish and set aside. Combine remaining ingredients in small saucepan; bring to the boil. Strain vinegar mixture over beetroot. Garnish with bay leaves. Serve immediately or chill. Divide evenly. Makes 2 servings.

Each serving is equivalent to: 4 oz Limited Vegetable

Artichokes in Tomato Jelly

½ envelope unflavoured gelatine
8 fl oz tomato juice
1½ teaspoons Worcester sauce
¼ teaspoon onion salt
¼ teaspoon finely grated
  horseradish

salt and pepper to taste
8 oz drained canned artichoke
  hearts, quartered
4 strips lemon rind
parsley sprigs to garnish

In saucepan sprinkle gelatine over 2 tablespoons tomato juice; cook over low heat, stirring constantly, until gelatine dissolves. Stir in remaining tomato juice and seasonings. Chill just until mixture begins to set. Fold in artichoke hearts and divide jelly evenly into 2 wine glasses. Chill until firm. Garnish each with 2 lemon strips and parsley sprigs. Makes 2 servings.

Each serving is equivalent to: ½ serving Something Extra (1 teaspoon gelatine); ½ serving Bonus (4 fl oz tomato juice); 4 oz Limited Vegetable

Coriander Lamb

Serve with salad.

1 large garlic clove
2 tablespoons coriander seeds
salt and pepper to taste

4 slices lamb from top of leg, 10 oz
    each
radish roses and parsley sprigs to
    garnish

Crush garlic with coriander seeds and mix thoroughly with salt and pepper. Press mixture into both sides of lamb slices and set aside, in a cool place, for at least 1 hour. Grill lamb on rack, turning once. Allow approximately 6 minutes each side, or grill until meat is cooked through and both sides are crisp and brown. Transfer to serving platter; garnish with radish rose and parsley. Makes 4 evening meal servings.

Each serving is equivalent to: 6 oz 'Beef' Group

Frankfurters in Tomato Sauce

12 fl oz tomato juice
6 oz green pepper, seeded and cut
    into 1-inch strips
1 tablespoon dehydrated onion
    flakes
½ teaspoon mixed herbs
dash each garlic powder, celery
    salt, parsley flakes and thyme

salt and pepper to taste
8 oz frankfurters, cut into 1-inch
    pieces
2 oz peas
1 oz sliced carrots
parsley sprigs to garnish

Combine all ingredients, except frankfurters, peas, carrots and parsley sprigs in frying pan; simmer for 20 minutes. Grill frankfurters until golden brown. Add frankfurters, peas and carrots to tomato juice mixture; simmer 5 minutes. Garnish with parsley. Divide evenly. Makes 2 evening meal servings.

Each serving is equivalent to: ¾ serving Bonus (6 fl oz tomato juice); $1\frac{1}{6}$ servings Vegetables; 4 oz 'Beef' Group (cured; once-a-week selection); 1 oz Limited Vegetable

Mushroom Stuffed Fish

4 oz button mushrooms, coarsely
  chopped
2 oz tomato, peeled and finely
  chopped
2 oz onion, finely chopped

1 tablespoon chopped fresh parsley
mixed herbs to taste
4 plaice fillets, 4 oz each
parsley sprigs to garnish
4 oz cooked peas

In bowl combine first 5 ingredients. Place an equal amount of vegetable mixture on each fillet; roll. Transfer fillets to foil-lined baking tin and surround with any remaining vegetable mixture. Cover and bake at 400°F, Gas Mark 6, for 20 minutes. Garnish with parsley sprigs. Serve with cooked peas. Divide evenly. Makes 2 evening meal servings.

    Each serving is equivalent to: 1 serving Vegetables; 3 ounces Limited Vegetable; 6 oz Fish

Shrimp Chow Mein

12 fl oz tomato juice
6 oz green pepper, seeded and
  finely sliced
3 oz button mushrooms, finely
  sliced, optional
2 oz celery, diagonally sliced
1 tablespoon soy sauce

2 teaspoons dehydrated onion
  flakes
1 teaspoon lemon juice
salt and pepper to taste
8 oz drained, canned shrimp
7 oz drained, canned bean sprouts

Combine all ingredients, except shrimp and bean sprouts, in saucepan. Bring to a boil; cover, reduce heat and simmer 10 minutes. Add shrimp and bean sprouts; cook for about 3 minutes or until heated through. Divide evenly. Makes 2 midday meal servings.

    Each serving is equivalent to: ¾ serving Bonus (6 fl oz tomato juice); 3 servings Vegetables; 4 oz Fish

Cod Kebabs

Serve with green salad.

1 lb cod fillets, cut into large cubes
4 oz small onions
3 oz green pepper, seeded and cut
  into 1-inch cubes
4 oz tomatoes, cut into quarters
4 button mushrooms

4 small bay leaves
lemon juice to taste
salt and freshly ground pepper to
  taste
¼ teaspoon paprika
chopped fresh parsley to garnish

Cook fish, onions and green pepper in saucepan, with water to cover, for 5 minutes; drain. Divide fish and vegetables into 4 equal portions of each. Thread 1 portion of each and 1 bay leaf onto a skewer, alternating ingredients; repeat with remaining portions and 3 more skewers. Brush with lemon juice and season with salt and pepper. Sprinkle with paprika and grill for about 8 minutes. Turn, brush with lemon juice and season. Sprinkle with parsley. Makes 2 evening meal servings, 2 skewers each.

Each serving is equivalent to: 6 oz Fish; 2 oz Limited Vegetable; $1^1/_3$ servings Vegetables

APPENDIX

*

WEIGHT WATCHERS MAINTENANCE PLAN

Introduction to the Maintenance Plan

The Maintenance Plan is designed for the member who has reached goal weight. Now you are embarking on an adventure; discovering how your body will respond to additional foods. Therefore, the Plan requires *individualisation*.

The Plan consists of eight groups of foods. You will be given a new group each week. The foods *within* each group contain approximately the same energy values. Each food is assigned a *unit* value, with each unit representing approximately 50 calories.

Here's how it works. Each week you may increase the number of units taken daily. The first week, you may take *one* unit per day. The second week, you may take a total of *two* units per day, and so forth. By the eighth week, you may take a total of *eight* daily units. It is possible that your body can tolerate more foods than provided by the eight units, without a weight gain. In that case, you may cautiously add additional units. For example, in the ninth week, you may add nine units; in the tenth week, ten units.

However maintaining weight is a highly individual matter. Additions should be taken with a vigilant eye on the scale. If these additional foods cause a weight gain, cut back to the number of units which enable you to maintain your weight successfully.

These units are interchangeable. For example, in the third week of the Maintenance Plan, you may have either one 3-unit food daily, *or* three 1-unit foods daily, *or* a combination of one 1-unit and one 2-unit food daily.

Each week you will assume the responsibility for a new group of foods, adding them to the basic Maintenance Plan on a daily basis. What you are striving for is a *stable weight*. Therefore, you are trying to determine the number of units required to *maintain* your weight for life. To maintain the same weight, the calories provided by the foods you eat, and the calories used by your body, must *balance*. Reaching this balance is a process of trial and error. Since the final number of daily—or weekly—units will vary for each person, *you* must be the judge for yourself.

Remember: Like all of the food plans, the basic Maintenance Plan is designed for the proper distribution of calorie intake among proteins, carbohydrates and fats; thus allowing for optimum nutrition.

A word of caution. Too often high-calorie foods are highly concentrated sources of fat and refined sugar, with little nutrient content. For this reason concentrated sources of saturated fat and refined sugar have been marked with a symbol (†). Use the foods sparingly, and with caution. *Variety, moderation* and *awareness* continue to be key words.

Menu Plan

Morning Meal

Fruit, 1 serving
Choice of:
  Egg, 1
    or
  Cheese, soft 2½ oz
    or
  Cheese, semisoft or
    hard, 1 oz
    or

Cereal, 1 oz with
  ½ milk serving
  or
Fish, cooked, 2 oz
  or
Poultry or Meat, cooked,
  1 oz
Bread, 1 serving
Beverage, if desired

Midday Meal

Choice of:
  Poultry, Meat or Fish,
    cooked, 3 oz
    or
  Eggs, 2
    or
  Cheese, soft 5 oz
    or
  Cheese, semisoft or
    hard, 2 oz

    or
Dried Peas/Beans,
  cooked, 4 oz
Vegetables
Bread,
  Women, 1 serving,
  if desired
  Men and Teenagers,
  1 serving
Beverage, if desired

Evening Meal

Choice of:
  Poultry, Meat or Fish,
    cooked
    Women and Teenagers,
    4 oz
    Men, 6 oz
  or
  Dried Peas/Beans,
    cooked
    Women and Teenagers,

6 oz
  Men, 8oz
Vegetables
Bread,
  Women, 1 serving
  (if not eaten at
  Midday Meal)
  Men and Teenagers,
  1 serving
Beverage, if desired

Daily

Milk, at any time
  Women and Men,
    2 servings
  Teenagers,
    3 servings
Fats, 3 servings
  at mealtime
Fruits,

Women, 3 servings
Men and Teenagers,
  3 to 4 servings
  (1 serving at Morn-
  ing Meal; other
  servings any time)
Add units as allowed,
  if desired

Note: the midday meal may be interchanged with the evening meal.

In addition to the changes on the menu, make the following adjustments to the Basic Programme.
3. Choice Group
Omit 1 serving of bread and select one item from this list up to 5 times weekly, if desired.
5. 'Beef' Group
Select once a week, if desired, in place of one 'Beef' Group selection: bacola (dried salted codfish), bologna, duck, frankfurters, goose, knockwurst, liver sausage, luncheon meats, offal, salami, salt beef, sausages.

GROUP 1

One (1) Unit Foods
Approximately 50 Calories

Add one of the following daily, if desired:

Appetizers

anchovies, fillets, *4*
caviar,
  1 tablespoon
dip, prepared (cheese,
  onion),
  2 teaspoons

herring, pickled
  1 oz
liver paté,
  1 tablespoon
roe, fish, *1 oz*

Breads

crackers, plain, any type, *2*
crispbread, *2*
water biscuits, *2*

Condiments

chutney,
  2 tablespoons
ketchup,
  3 tablespoons
olives, any type, *8*
pickled cucumber, sweet or

sour,
  1 large
sauce, barbecue,
  2 tablespoons
sauce, chili,
  3 tablespoons

sauce, cranberry,
  2 tablespoons
sauce, seafood cocktail

2 tablespoons
sauce, tartare
  2 teaspoons

Fats

† cream cheese
  1 tablespoon
fat serving,

1 *additional*
salad dressing, any type
  2 teaspoons

Fruits

apricots, halves, dried,
  5 medium or 4 large
coconut, shredded
  1 tablespoon
dates

2 whole or 2 tablespoons,
  chopped
fruit serving
  1 additional
raisins
  2 tablespoons

Milk Products

† cream, double
  1 tablespoon
† cream, single
  2 tablespoons
† cream, sour
  2 tablespoons

† creamer, instant non-dairy
  1 tablespoon
milk, whole
  2 fl oz
† topping, whipped, non-dairy
  3 tablespoons

Snacks

popcorn, plain
  ½ oz popped

Sweets

†honey,
  2 teaspoons
† jams, jellies or preserves
  1 tablespoon
† sauce, chocolate
  1 tablespoon
† sugar, any type

  1 tablespoon
† syrup, golden
  1 tablespoon
† syrup, maple
  1 tablespoon
† treacle, black
  1 tablespoon

Vegetables

'Limited'
  4 oz

Note: Teaspoon and tablespoon measures must be *level*.

Group 2

Two (2) Unit Foods
Approximately 100 Calories

Add one of the following or any combination of foods totalling up to 2 units daily, if desired:

Appetizers

mussels, *4 oz*
scallops, cooked,
  3 oz

Main Course Additions

cheese, semisoft or hard,
  1 oz
cheese, soft,
  4 oz
dried peas/beans, cooked,
  3 oz
egg, cooked, *1*

liver, chopped,
  2 oz
pepperoni,
  1 oz
poultry, fish, meat, liver,
    cooked,
  1 oz

Beverages

brandy or cognac,
  1 fl oz
champagne,
  4 fl oz
gin, rum, vodka, whisky,
  1 fl oz
lemonade,
  8 fl oz

liqueur,
  1 fl oz
sherry,
  2 fl oz
soda, regular, any type,
  8 fl oz
wine, table (red, white or
    rosé),
  3½ fl oz

Breads

bread, any type,
  1 slice (approx. 1 oz)
bread, date and nut,
  1 slice
breadcrumbs,
  1 oz
bread sticks,
  1 oz
cereal, any type,
  1 oz

flour, all purpose,
  1 oz
matzo, any type,
  1 board
pancakes,
  2 (4″ diameter)
roll, hamburger or
    frankfurter, *1*
roll, soft, *1*
scotch pancake, *1*

Choice Group

any item
  1 additional serving

Desserts

biscuits, any type,
2 medium
fruit cake, plain,
1 oz
gingerbread,
1 oz

ice, fruit,
3½ oz
ice lolly, *1*
jelly, fruit flavoured,
4 oz
macaroon, *1*

Fats

† bacon,
2 slices
† bacon fat,
1 tablespoon

† butter,
1 tablespoon
† chicken fat,
1 tablespoon

Fruits

avocado,
¼ medium
fruit in syrup,
4 oz

pomegranate,
1 medium

Milk

1 additional serving

Misc.

borscht,
8 fl oz
gazpacho,
8 fl oz
sauce, cheese,
3 tablespoons
sauce, hollandaise,
2 tablespoons

sauce, spaghetti,
4 fl oz
sauce, tomato,
4 fl oz
sauce, white,
2 fl oz
soup, uncreamed,
8 fl oz

Vegetables

cauliflower au gratin
3 oz
cole slaw
4 oz

ratatouille
6 oz

GROUP 3

Three (3) Unit Foods
Approximately 150 Calories

Add one of the following or any combination of foods totalling up to 3 units daily, if desired.

Appetizers

eggs, devilled,
  2 halves
melon and parma ham,
  1 serving

mushrooms, marinated,
  3 oz
sausage roll, mini, *1*
shrimp balls, *3*

Beverages

apple cider,
  8 fl oz
beer or ale,
  12 fl oz
bloody mary,
  8 fl oz
Cherry B
  3½ fl oz
fruit wine,
  4 fl oz

martini,
  3 fl oz
Pony
  3½ fl oz
sherry (dry),
  3½ fl oz
vermouth, French,
  5 fl oz
vermouth, Italian,
  3 fl oz
wine, dessert (muscatel, port,
    sherry),
  3½ fl oz

Breads

bagel, *1*
bread, garlic,
  2 slices (3″ × 1½″)
croissant, *1*
crumpet,
  1 medium

maltbread,
  1 slice
muffin, English, *1*
roll, hard,
  1 medium

Choice Group

potato, chips,
  10 pieces (2" × ½" × ½")
potato, fried,
  2 oz
potato, mashed,
  7 oz
rice, Spanish,
  4 oz

salad, pasta,
  4 oz
salad, potato,
  4 oz
sweet potato, boiled,
  6 oz

Desserts

apple crumble,
  4 oz
blancmange,
  4 oz
cake, Madeira,
  1 slice (3½" × 3" × ½")
cake, sponge,
  *3" slice from 9" diameter
  cake*
chocolate roll, mini, *1*
crème caramel,
  4 oz
cupcake with icing, *1*

custard, any type,
  4 oz
custard tart, *1*
doughnut, (unfilled), *1*
fruit cake,
  1 slice (3" × 3" × ½")
ice cream,
  3 oz
ice cream bar, chocolate
  covered, *1*
Swiss roll,
  2 oz

Fruits

juice, apple,
  8 fl oz
juice, apricot nectar,
  8 fl oz

juice, grape,
  8 fl oz
juice, pineapple,
  8 fl oz

salad, apple, celery and
  cheese,
  3 heaped tablespoons

salad, carrot and raisin,
  3 heaped tablespoons

Milk

yogurt, natural unsweetened,
  10 fl oz

Snacks

chestnuts, fresh, *10*
corn crisps,
  1 oz
potato crisps, *12* or potato
  sticks, *1 oz*

pretzels, 3 ring, *12*
pretzels, sticks,
  1 oz

Sweets

† boiled sweets,
  1 oz
† caramel, any type, *3*
† chocolate, with or without
  nuts,
  1 oz
† chocolate covered bar,
  1 oz
† chocolate creams, *3*
† chocolate drops,
  1 oz
† chocolate mints, *2*

† fudge, any type,
  1 oz
† halvah, *1 oz*
† jelly beans, *15*
† liquorice, *1½ oz*
† lollipop,
  1 (2¼″ diameter)
† maltesers,
  small packet
† marshmallows,
  5 large
† marzipan, *1 oz*

† peanut brittle, *1 oz*
† peanuts, chocolate covered,
    1 oz
† popcorn, caramel coated
        with peanuts,
    1½ oz

† raisins, chocolate covered,
    1 oz

GROUP 4

Four (4) Unit Foods
Approximately 200 Calories

Add one of the following or any combination of foods totalling up to 4 units daily, if desired.

Appetizers

vol au vent, with filling
    3 small

Beverages

cocoa, hot,
    6 fl oz
coffee, Irish,
    1 serving

gin and tonic, *1*
milk, chocolate,
    8 fl oz
screwdriver, *1*

Breads

scone,
  1 (2 oz)
soda bread,
  2 oz

stuffing, bread,
  3 oz
waffle,
  1 (5" diameter)

Choice Group

potato pancakes, *2*

Desserts

apple, baked, *1*
Charlotte Russe,
  1 serving
chocolate profiteroles,
  2 small

ice cream cornet,
  1 scoop
ice cream wafer, *1*
trifle,
  4 oz

Prepared Foods

These foods may be taken in addition to or in place of Main Course (eggs, cheese, cereal, poultry, meat, fish and dried peas/beans). If the Main Course is omitted, add up to 3 additional units daily, if desired:

beef, pot roast,
  3 oz
blintzes, *2*

chicken or turkey, baked or
  roasted, meat and skin,
  4 oz

croquette, any type,
  3 oz
faggots in gravy,
  2 oz
fish loaf,
  5 oz
fish fingers, cakes or fried
    fish,
  4 oz
French toast,
  1 slice
gefilte fish,
  2 pieces (8 oz)

herring in cream sauce,
  4 oz
pizza,
  ¼ of 9″ pie
salad, lobster, shrimp,
    crabmeat or chicken,
    with dressing,
  3½ oz
sausage, black,
  2 oz
stew, lamb and vegetables,
  8 oz

Snacks

almonds, *22*
Brazil nuts, *7*
cashew nuts, *14*
cob nuts,
  1 oz
peanut butter,
  2 tablespoons

peanuts, *1 oz*
pecan halves, *20*
sunflower seeds,
  1 oz
walnut halves,
  14 (1 oz)

Soups

soup, creamed,
  8 fl oz

Vegetables

salad, Russian,
4 oz

GROUP 5

Five (5) Unit Foods
Approximately 250 Calories

Add one of the following or any combination of foods totalling up to 5 units daily, if desired:

Appetizers

meatballs, *3*
pancake roll, *1*

prawn/shrimp cocktail with
sauce,
1 serving

Desserts

cake, coffee,
*1 piece (2½" × 2½" ×
1½")*
cake, gateaux, (2 layer)
¹⁄₁₆ of 9" cake

doughnut, filled, *1*
fritters, apple,
4 oz
ice cream soda, any flavour,
1

pastry, Danish with icing,
  1 (4½″ diameter)
peach Melba,
  1 serving

roll, sweet, with nuts, raisins
  and frosting, *1*
strudel, any type
  1 piece (3 oz)

Prepared Foods

These foods may be taken in addition to or in place of Main Course (eggs, cheese, cereal, poultry, meat, fish and dried peas/beans). If the Main Course is omitted, add up to 3 additional units daily, if desired:

beef casserole,
  7 oz
bouillabaisse,
  1 serving
chicken cacciatore,
  8 oz
chow mein with noodles,
  7 oz
creole, chicken or shrimp,
  1 serving
goulash, beef,
  8 oz
lasagna,
  1 serving (6 oz)

lobster Newburg,
  5 oz
meat loaf,
  4 oz
ravioli with sauce,
  7 pieces
sandwich, chicken salad
sandwich, liver sausage
sandwich, tuna fish
scampi, fried,
  4 oz
shells, pasta, stuffed,
  3 (4½ oz)
soufflé, spinach,
  6 oz

Vegetables

aubergine, French fried,
  4 oz
courgette, French fried,
  4 oz

onion rings, French fried,
  4 oz

GROUP 6

Six (6) Unit Foods
Approximately 300 Calories

Add one of the following or any combination of foods totalling up to 6 units daily, if desired:

Appetizers

soup, French onion au gratin
1 serving

escargots
1 serving

Choice Group

beans, baked, with tomato
   sauce,
8 oz

potato, stuffed, baked,
   whole,
(6 oz)
rice, fried,
7 oz

Desserts

chocolate mousse,
4 oz
compote, dried fruit,
8 oz
cream puff,
1 medium

éclair,
1 medium
pudding, any type,
3 oz
turnover, fruit, *1*

Milk

yogurt, fruit flavoured,
 10 fl oz

Prepared Foods

These foods may be taken in addition to or in place of Main Course (eggs, cheese, cereal, poultry, meat, fish and dried peas/beans). If the Main Course is omitted, add up to 3 additional units daily, if desired:

chop suey with meat,
 8 oz
coq au vin,
 8 oz
hash, beef,
 8 oz
pepper, stuffed, *1*
pork, sweet and sour,
 1 serving
sandwich, bacon
sandwich, beef

sandwich, cheese
sandwich, egg salad
sandwich, ham
sandwich, ham salad
shish kebab,
 1 serving
soufflé, cheese,
 5 oz
Welsh rarebit on toast,
 4 oz

GROUP 7

Seven (7) Unit Foods
Approximately 350 Calories

Add one of the following or any combination of foods totalling up to 7 units daily, if desired:

Desserts

cheesecake (with or without
fruit topping),
¼ of 6" cake
milk shake, any flavour,

8 fl oz
pie, meringue or custard, any
type,
¼ of 6" pie

Prepared Foods

These foods may be taken in addition to or in place of Main Course
(eggs, cheese, cereal, poultry, meat, fish and dried peas/beans). If
the Main Course is omitted, add up to 3 additional units daily, if
desired:

aubergine with cheese sauce,
6 oz
bagel, smoked salmon and
cream cheese, *1*
chilli con carne,
8 oz
duck, baked or roasted, meat
and skin,
4 oz
egg foo yung,
1 serving
frankfurters and beans,
8 oz

hamburger on roll with
lettuce and ketchup,
moussaka,
1 serving
omelette, any kind,
salad, chef's with dressing
1 serving
sandwich, peanut butter,
sausage roll, *1*
spaghetti with meatballs,
8 oz
veal and ham pie,
3 oz

GROUP 8

Eight (8) Unit Foods
Approximately 400–500 Calories

Add one of the following or any combination of foods totalling up to 8 units daily, if desired:

Desserts

baked Alaska,
 1 serving
baklava,
 1 piece (2″ × 2″)
cake, iced, any flavour,
 1 piece (3″ × 3″ × 2″)
crêpes Suzette,
 2 (7″)

ice cream sundae,
 1 serving
pie, any type,
 ¼ of 6″ pie
strawberry flan with whipped
 topping,
 1 serving (2½″ cube)

Prepared Foods

These foods may be taken in addition to or in place of Main Course (eggs, cheese, cereal, poultry, meat, fish and dried peas/beans). If the Main Course is omitted, add up to 3 additional units daily, if desired:

beefburger on a bap,
 1 serving with 2 burgers
beef Stroganoff over noodles,
 1 serving
brisket,
 3 slices

cannelloni with cheese sauce,
 2 (6″)
chicken, fried,
 *1 large breast or 1 leg and
 thigh*
chicken à la king,
 8 oz

chicken fricassee,
8 oz
coquilles St. Jacques,
1 shell
Cornish pasty,
1 small
cottage pie,
1 small or 1 serving
crab, devilled,
8 oz
curry with rice,
1 serving
duck with orange sauce,
½ duck
eggs, Benedict,
1 serving
fish, baked stuffed,
6 oz
fish and chips,
1 serving
fondue, beef or cheese,
1 serving
haggis,
1 small
hamburger, bacon and
cheese, on bap
macaroni and cheese,
7 oz

paella,
1 serving
pork pie,
1 small
quiche Lorraine,
¼ of 6" pie
salmon mousse,
8 oz
sandwich, double decker
sandwich, fried fish
sandwich, grilled cheese and
bacon
sandwich, salt beef
sandwich, turkey
scampi, 6
spareribs, barbecued,
1 serving (6–8 ribs)
steak and kidney pie,
1 serving
turkey tetrazzini,
8 oz
veal cordon bleu,
1 serving
veal escalope,
1 serving
Wiener schnitzel,
1 serving

Monthly

An ethnic meal at your favourite restaurant. *Bon appetit!*

Goal Weight Charts

The weights have been established from authoritative sources. They are called 'tentative' because they give a variation for sex, age and height. A permanent specific goal for the individual should be selected according to the amount of body fat present when the individual reaches the 'tentative' goal weight.

TENTATIVE GOAL WEIGHTS
GIRLS

Height	10 Years	11 Years	12 Years	13 Years
3' 11"	3.6 –3.13			
4' 0"	3.7 –4.2	3.9 –4.5		
4' 1"	3.8 –4.5	3.10–4.9	3.11–4.13	
4' 2"	3.9 –4.8	3.11–4.11	3.13–5.1	
4' 3"	3.12–4.11	3.13–5.0	4.1 –5.3	
4' 4"	4.2 –5.0	4.3 –5.3	4.4 –5.6	4.4 –5.3
4' 5"	4.3 –5.3	4.6 –5.6	4.7 –5.9	4.6 –5.6
4' 6"	4.6 –5.5	4.9 –5.7	4.10–5.11	4.8 –5.9
4' 7"	4.8 –5.7	4.12–5.8	4.13–6.0	4.10–5.12
4' 8"	4.10–5.9	5.1 –5.10	5.2 –6.3	4.12–6.1
4' 9"	4.12–5.13	5.4 –6.0	5.5 –6.6	5.0 –6.4
4' 10"	5.0 –6.2	5.6 –6.3	5.7 –6.9	5.3 –6.7
4' 11"	5.5 –6.5	5.8 –6.6	5.10–6.12	5.6 –6.10
5' 0"	5.10–6.8	5.11–6.9	5.12–7.0	5.9 –6.13
5' 1"	5.12–6.11	6.0 –6.13	6.2 –7.3	5.12–7.2
5' 2"	6.0 –7.0	6.2 –7.4	6.5 –7.6	6.2 –7.5
5' 3"	6.3 –7.3	6.5 –7.6	6.8 –7.8	6.4 –7.8
5' 4"	6.6 –7.5	6.9 –7.8	6.13–7.11	6.8 –7.11
5' 5"	6.10–7.7	7.0 –7.10	7.4 –7.13	6.12–8.0
5' 6"		7.5 –7.13	7.8 –8.4	7.2 –8.3
5' 7"		7.9 –8.2	7.12–8.8	7.6 –8.6
5' 8"			8.2 –8.12	7.10–8.9
5' 9"			8.6 –9.1	8.0 –8.12
5' 10"				8.5 –9.1
5' 11"				8.10–9.4
				9.1 –9.8
				9.6 –9.12

Height	14 Years	15 Years	16 Years	17 Years
4' 3"	4.7 – 6.0			
4' 4"	4.11– 6.4	5.7 – 6.7		
4' 5"	5.1 – 6.6	5.8 – 6.9	5.9 – 6.10	5.10– 6.12
4' 6"	5.4 – 6.7	5.9 – 6.10	5.10– 6.11	5.12– 7.1
4' 7"	5.6 – 6.8	5.10– 6.11	5.11– 6.12	5.13– 7.1
4' 8"	5.8 – 6.10	5.11– 6.12	5.12– 6.13	6.1 – 7.2
4' 9"	5.11– 6.13	6.0 – 7.1	6.1 – 7.2	6.4 – 7.3
4' 10"	6.0 – 7.2	6.3 – 7.4	6.4 – 7.5	6.6 – 7.6
4' 11"	6.3 – 7.5	6.6 – 7.7	6.7 – 7.8	6.8 – 7.10
5' 0"	6.6 – 7.8	6.9 – 7.10	6.10– 7.12	6.11– 7.13
5' 1"	6.10– 7.11	6.13– 7.13	7.0 – 8.0	7.1 – 8.1
5' 2"	7.0 – 8.0	7.3 – 8.3	7.4 – 8.5	7.5 – 8.6
5' 3"	7.3 – 8.3	7.5 – 8.10	7.6 – 8.11	7.7 – 8.12
5' 4"	7.6 – 8.6	7.8 – 8.12	7.9 – 9.0	7.10– 9.2
5' 5"	7.9 – 8.9	7.11– 9.0	7.12– 9.3	7.13– 9.5
5' 6"	7.13– 8.12	8.1 – 9.5	8.2 – 9.6	8.3 – 9.8
5' 7"	8.4 – 9.1	8.6 – 9.8	8.7 – 9.9	8.8 – 9.11
5' 8"	8.7 – 9.4	8.8 – 9.9	8.9 – 9.12	8.10–10.0
5' 9"	8.12– 9.7	9.0 –10.1	9.2 –10.2	9.3 –10.4
5' 10"	9.2 – 9.11	9.4 –10.3	9.6 –10.6	9.7 –10.8
5' 11"	9.7 –10.1	9.9 –10.6	9.10–10.10	9.11–10.12
6' 0"	9.10–10.5	9.12–10.8	10.0 –10.11	10.1 –11.2
6' 1"	10.0 –10.10	10.2 –11.1	10.4 –11.4	10.5 –11.6

Weight in stones and pounds

TENTATIVE GOAL WEIGHTS
BOYS

Height	10 Years	11 Years	12 Years	13 Years
3'11"	3.6 -3.10			
4'0"	3.8 -3.13	3.9 -4.1		
4'1"	3.10-4.1	3.11-4.2		
4'2"	3.12-4.3	3.13-4.4	4.0 -4.6	
4'3"	4.2 -4.6	4.3 -4.7	4.4 -4.8	
4'4"	4.4 -4.9	4.5 -4.10	4.6 -4.11	
4'5"	4.7 -4.12	4.8 -4.13	4.9 -5.0	4.10 - 5.1
4'6"	4.9 -5.1	4.10-5.2	4.11-5.3	4.12- 5.5
4'7"	5.0 -5.5	5.1 -5.6	5.2 -5.7	5.3 - 5.9
4'8"	5.5 -5.10	5.6 -5.11	5.7 -5.13	5.8 - 6.1
4'9"	5.9 -5.12	5.10-6.0	5.11-6.2	5.13- 6.5
4'10"	5.12-6.2	5.13-6.3	6.0 -6.4	6.4 - 6.9
4'11"	6.2 -6.6	6.3 -6.7	6.4 -6.8	6.9 - 6.13
5'0"	6.6 -6.10	6.7 -6.11	6.8 -6.12	6.12- 7.3
5'1"	6.9 -6.13	6.11-7.1	6.12-7.2	7.2 - 7.7
5'2"	6.13-7.3	7.1 -7.5	7.2 -7.6	7.6 - 7.11
5'3"	7.2 -7.6	7.4 -7.8	7.6 -7.10	7.9 - 8.1
5'4"	7.4 -7.9	7.6 -7.11	7.10-8.0	7.13- 8.5
5'5"	7.7 -7.12	7.9 -8.0	8.0 -8.4	8.3 - 8.9
5'6"		7.13-8.4	8.4 -8.8	8.6 - 8.13
5'7"		8.3 -8.8	8.7 -8.12	8.9 - 9.4
5'8"			8.10-9.2	8.12- 9.7
5'9"			8.13-9.6	9.1 - 9.10
5'10"				9.4 -10.0
5'11"				9.9 -10.4

Height	14 Years	15 Years	16 Years	17 Years
4'7"	5.4 - 5.10			
4'8"	5.9 - 6.3			
4'9"	6.0 - 6.6	6.2 - 6.11		
4'10"	6.5 - 6.10	6.8 - 7.2	6.11- 7.10	
4'11"	6.10- 7.0	6.12- 7.6	7.0 - 7.12	7.3 - 8.2
5'0"	7.0 - 7.5	7.2 - 7.10	7.4 - 8.1	7.7 - 8.5
5'1"	7.3 - 7.10	7.5 - 8.0	7.8 - 8.4	7.10- 8.8
5'2"	7.8 - 8.1	7.10- 8.4	7.12- 8.8	8.0 - 8.11
5'3"	7.13- 8.6	8.1 - 8.8	8.2 - 8.11	8.5 - 9.0
5'4"	8.2 - 8.9	8.4 - 8.11	8.6 - 9.1	8.7 - 9.4
5'5"	8.5 - 8.13	8.7 - 9.1	8.10- 9.4	8.11- 9.7
5'6"	8.9 - 9.3	8.11- 9.5	9.0 - 9.7	9.1 - 9.11
5'7"	8.13- 9.7	9.2 - 9.8	9.4 - 9.10	9.5 -10.1
5'8"	9.3 - 9.11	9.6 - 9.12	9.7 -10.0	9.8 -10.5
5'9"	9.7 -10.0	9.10-10.2	9.12-10.4	9.13-10.9
5'10"	9.11-10.5	10.0 -10.5	10.1 -11.1	10.2 -11.6
5'11"	10.1 -10.9	10.4 -11.1	10.5 -11.6	10.6 -12.0
6'0"	10.6 -10.13	10.8 -11.2	10.9 -11.9	10.10-12.2
6'1"	10.10-11.3	10.10-11.9	10.13-11.12	11.0 -12.7
6'2"		11.3 -11.11	11.4 -12.2	11.5 -13.0
6'3"		11.8 -12.7	11.9 -12.12	11.10-13.8
6'4"		11.13-13.3	12.0 -13.9	12.1 -13.13

Weight in stones and pounds

TENTATIVE GOAL WEIGHTS
WOMEN

Height without shoes	25 Years and over	23-24 Years	21-22 Years	19-20 Years	18 Years
4' 6"	6.4 – 7.8	6.2 – 7.6	6.1 – 7.5	6.0 – 7.3	5.13– 7.1
4' 7"	6.6 – 7.9	6.4 – 7.7	6.2 – 7.6	6.1 – 7.4	6.0 – 7.2
4' 8"	6.8 – 7.10	6.6 – 7.8	6.4 – 7.7	6.3 – 7.5	6.2 – 7.3
4' 9"	6.10– 7.12	6.8 – 7.10	6.7 – 7.8	6.6 – 7.6	6.5 – 7.4
4' 10"	6.12– 8.1	6.10– 7.13	6.9 – 7.11	6.8 – 7.8	6.7 – 7.7
4' 11"	7.1 – 8.4	6.12– 8.2	6.11– 8.1	6.10– 7.13	6.9 – 7.11
5' 0"	7.4 – 8.7	7.2 – 8.5	7.0 – 8.3	6.13– 8.1	6.12– 8.0
5' 1"	7.7 – 8.10	7.5 – 8.9	7.4 – 8.7	7.3 – 8.5	7.2 – 8.4
5' 2"	7.10– 9.0	7.9 – 8.13	7.8 – 8.11	7.7 – 8.9	7.6 – 8.7
5' 3"	7.13– 9.4	7.11– 9.3	7.10– 9.1	7.9 – 9.0	7.8 – 8.13
5' 4"	8.2 – 9.9	8.0 – 9.8	7.13– 9.6	7.12– 9.5	7.11– 9.4
5' 5"	8.6 – 9.13	8.4 – 9.12	8.2 – 9.10	8.1 – 9.8	8.0 – 9.7
5' 6"	8.10–10.3	8.8 –10.2	8.6 –10.0	8.5 – 9.12	8.4 – 9.11
5' 7"	9.0 –10.7	8.12–10.6	8.11–10.4	8.10–10.2	8.9 –10.0
5' 8"	9.4 –10.11	9.2 –10.10	9.0 –10.8	8.12–10.6	8.11–10.4
5' 9"	9.8 –11.1	9.7 –11.0	9.6 –10.12	9.5 –10.10	9.4 –10.8
5' 10"	9.12–11.5	9.11–11.4	9.10–11.2	9.9 –11.0	9.7 –10.11
5' 11"	10.2 –11.9	10.1 –11.8	10.0 –11.6	9.13–11.4	9.12–11.1
6' 0"	10.6 –11.13	10.5 –11.12	10.4 –11.10	10.3 –11.8	10.2 –11.6
6' 1"	10.10–12.3	10.9 –12.2	10.8 –12.0	10.7 –11.12	10.6 –11.10
6' 2"	11.0 –12.7	10.13–12.6	10.12–12.4	10.11–12.2	10.10–12.0

Weight in stones and pounds

TENTATIVE GOAL WEIGHTS
MEN

Height without shoes	25 Years and over	23-24 Years	21-22 Years	19-20 Years	18 Years
5' 0"	8.3 – 9.12	8.2 – 9.11	8.0 – 9.9	7.12– 9.7	7.11– 8.10
5' 1"	8.6 –10.1	8.5 –10.0	8.3 – 9.12	8.1 – 9.10	8.0 – 9.0
5' 2"	8.9 –10.4	8.8 –10.2	8.6 –10.0	8.4 – 9.13	8.3 – 9.4
5' 3"	8.12–10.8	8.11–10.7	8.9 –10.5	8.7 –10.3	8.6 – 9.9
5' 4"	9.1 –10.12	9.0 –10.11	8.12–10.9	8.10–10.7	8.8 –10.5
5' 5"	9.4 –11.2	9.3 –11.1	9.1 –10.13	8.13–10.11	8.12–10.9
5' 6"	9.8 –11.7	9.7 –11.6	9.5 –11.4	9.3 –11.2	9.2 –11.0
5' 7"	9.12–11.12	9.10–11.11	9.8 –11.9	9.7 –11.7	9.6 –11.5
5' 8"	10.2 –12.2	10.0 –12.1	9.12–11.13	9.10–11.11	9.9 –11.9
5' 9"	10.6 –12.6	10.4 –12.5	10.2 –12.3	10.1 –12.1	10.0 –11.11
5' 10"	10.10–12.11	10.8 –12.10	10.6 –12.7	10.4 –12.5	10.3 –12.2
5' 11"	11.0 –13.2	10.12–13.1	10.10–12.13	10.8 –12.11	10.7 –12.9
6' 0"	11.4 –13.7	11.2 –13.6	11.0 –13.4	10.12–13.2	10.11–12.12
6' 1"	11.8 –13.12	11.6 –13.11	11.4 –13.8	11.2 –13.7	11.1 –13.5
6' 2"	11.13–14.3	11.11–14.2	11.9 –14.0	11.7 –13.12	11.6 –13.10
6' 3"	12.4 –14.8	12.2 –14.7	12.0 –14.5	11.12–14.3	11.11–14.2
6' 4"	12.9 –14.13	12.7 –14.12	12.5 –14.10	12.3 –14.8	12.2 –14.6

Weight in stones and pounds

INDEX